To Monica and Kali

Contents

Figures and Tables

Acknowledgments

I would like to thank the candidates, campaign managers, volunteers, and journalists who agreed to be interviewed for this study. In all, over 150 such individuals gave generously of their time. I have not provided a list of everyone I interviewed in order to protect the anonymity of those who requested it.

I am grateful to the University of British Columbia and its Department of Political Science for financial and other support provided during the research phase of this book. As well, the research and publication of the manuscript could not have been completed without two grants from the International Council for Canadian Studies and the assistance of Ms. Paulette Montaigne, Academic and Cultural Relations officer for the Canadian High Commission in Australia.

Special mention should be made of three people who stimulated my initial interest in Canadian politics. David Stewart and Paul Kopas were fellow students who introduced me to things Canadian. Ken Carty encouraged my interest in Canadian political parties and election campaigns. His advice helped direct my research and writing and purged it of many faults. I am deeply grateful for his generous assistance over the years. In addition, Professor John Meisel made a single, cryptic comment that much improved the form of the manuscript.

I would like to thank colleagues at the University of British Columbia, Murdoch University, and the University of Western Australia for their consideration and support during the long gestation period of this book. At UBC, Don Blake and Richard Johnston provided useful intellectual guidance, while Robert Crawford, André Laliberté, and Tim Schouls improved my understanding of Canadian politics. At Murdoch and UWA, David Brown, Ian Cook, Michael Sturma, Campbell Sharman, Jeremy Moon, David Denemark, Alex Coram, Bruce Stone, and Bryce Weber all provided inspiration in one form or another, which helped in the completion of the manuscript.

I owe a special debt of gratitude to Cathryn Gunn, who volunteered for the onerous task of editing and re-editing the manuscript. So too did Ruth Abbey. Their diligence and skill greatly improved the final form of the book. At UBC Press, editors Laura Macleod, Holly Keller-Brohman, and Randy Schmidt worked tirelessly to prepare the manuscript for publication, helping with everything from funding to spell-checking.

Finally, my greatest debt is to Monica Frederica Hess, without whose support of every aspect of my life this book might never have seen the light of day. Thanks M.

Parties, Candidates, and Constituency Campaigns in Canadian Elections

1
Introduction

Watchers of Canadian elections have long noted that the nature of any local campaign is a function of both local conditions and the organizational imperatives of the parties and campaigns of which riding-level political organizations are seminal components (Siegfried 1906; Eagles 1990; Carty 1991a). The link between local and national levels of politics can be stated differently – national elections are the concatenation of individual riding contests (of which there were 295 in 1988 and 1993, and 301 in 1997), and federal party campaigns are similarly entwined with those at the local level.[1] Yet relatively few systematic attempts have been made to explore the interaction of local and nonlocal factors in the riding campaigns that are the basis of national elections.

This book fills this gap by building a detailed picture of the factors that determine both the style and content of local campaigns in Canada. By this I mean the strategies and tactics they adopt, and the organizational and allocational decisions that these imply. This book details the electoral process in eight BC ridings in the 1988 federal election – from nomination to election day – to build a general model of local campaigning in Canada. Two interacting environments shape each stage of the election process, from nomination through to the campaign and election day. First, the world defined by the constituency or riding boundaries, with its peculiar political, geographic, economic, and social character. And second, the partisan world of relations between local associations and their respective national and regional party branches.

This study focuses on the organizational aspects of local campaigns, and corrects the neglect of local constituency organizations of political parties as a spatially delineated element of the Canadian political system (Smiley 1987, 190). It sits between the idiosyncratic portraits of local campaigns found in journalistic accounts of nominations and elections, and the more general survey research by academics that by its very nature focuses on the national campaigns of political parties.[2] Given that the election on which the book focuses is perhaps the most nationalizing of elections in recent decades – that fought over the Free Trade Agreement with the United States – its insights into the place of constituency campaigns should be robust in that any local influences in this election could be expected to have been at their weakest.

In contrast to most studies of constituency campaigning in Canada (see, for example, Meisel 1964), this one does not address directly the link between voters and local campaigns, though it complements much of the work done in this area (see also Meisel 1962). This is because the central role of local party organizations – both before and during an election – is related to high levels of voter volatility and competitiveness at the constituency level (that is, narrow margins of victory in many seats) and the high turnover rate of MPs these produce and which distinguishes Canada from other Anglo-American democracies (Johnston 1996; Blake 1991).

The high turnover of MPs means constituency associations regularly conduct contested nominations, highlighting their central role in this crucial function of political parties and their autonomy in this regard. The competitiveness of local contests suggests to constituency organizers that even if they move only a few percent of the vote their way (Ferejohn and Gaines 1991), this may be enough to win the seat. And voter volatility gives hope to organizers of even poorly placed campaigns that they might convince voters to support their candidate, even when facing an incumbent.

In addition, voter volatility is linked to the federal nature of party identification in Canada (Stewart and Clarke 1998; Bowler 1990). In combination with the distinctive nature of provincial politics, which is sometimes manifest in separate national and provincial party systems, political parties find it difficult to integrate local, regional, and national politics. This is seen in the limited ties between many provincial and national branches of the same party, which prevents provincial organizations from acting as links between national and local party branches. The strength of provincial sources of voter volatility (Leithner 1997, Table 1) suggests that Canadian political parties need to be able to adjust to varying provincial circumstances. But they lack key institutional linkages with provincial organizations that might help in this regard. Only local campaigns are in a position to respond to the exigencies of local and provincial volatility. As such, parties that seek government are beholden to their local affiliates.

Compounding this, the lack of well-integrated provincial organizations means that national parties do not have available a strong, hierarchical management structure to enforce the central party's will at the local level. Their place in the nomination and campaign processes, and the lack of a clear party-focused career path that might make local members subservient to national directives, underpin the independence of local party organizations and the campaigns. While such conditions persist, it is likely that they will continue to enjoy greater autonomy than their counterparts in any other Westminster system, and remain the key means by which national parties can hope to understand and take advantage of the main sources of voter volatility in Canada.

The arrival of the Bloc Québécois and the Reform Party in 1993 signalled the end of the "old" party system and underscored the volatility and provincialization of national elections. For example, in British Columbia, the preeminence of the Tories and New Democrats (and the marginalization of the Liberals who played a spoiler role in 1988) has been replaced by a dominant Reform Party, a small New Democratic Party (NDP), and a somewhat more robust Liberal Party.[3] While the Bloc is much like older, loosely organized Canadian parties, only time will tell whether Reform can retain its distinctive, highly integrated form. To succeed it will have to find a novel way of coming to terms with the tension between powerful local party organizations – which remain central to Canadian politics and Reform's populist appeal – and the party's head office. These tensions are discussed in more detail in Chapter 10.

Associations and Nominations
Parliamentary representation on the basis of geographically defined single member ridings is central to the character of Canadian politics. Despite great variations in the electoral strength of political parties in Canada, "the electoral system, and our contemporary assumptions about what makes a national party, require each party to maintain a local association in each riding" (Carty 1991a, 71). Most of these constituency elections are contested, and the activities of local campaigns have a bearing on electoral outcomes (Heintzman 1991, 43-4). Because of the need to win these constituency battles, a national party's success depends on whatever volunteers it can attract and hold at the local level (Carty 1991a, 72). This underpins the importance of both riding associations and constituency politics in Canada.

Nominations in Canada are, in broad terms, locally controlled and democratic in form. An association announces that it is seeking candidates to run in an election and invites potential candidates to submit their names to a committee established for this purpose. Even sitting members need to be renominated by their associations. Candidates and their nomination organizers then compete to obtain the support of a majority of association members. As well as seeking the support of existing members, candidates sign up new members who are willing to support them. Membership regulations usually allow nomination candidates and their supporters to join the association until quite soon before the date set for the nomination meeting. On occasion, only one candidate comes forward and there is no contest. If there is more than one candidate, local association members cast votes in one or more ballots until a candidate has an absolute majority.

Control over the nomination process gives associations a pivotal role in Canadian parties. They link voters and the political parties that dominate political life. Associations jealously guard local control over the nomination process and tend to select candidates with knowledge of and attachment to the riding. This highlights the importance of local practices and conditions in shaping nominations (Carty 1991a, 25, 178, 181).

Although formally similar across parties and regions, associations vary enormously in size, stability, and level of activity (Carty 1991a, 20-4). The character of an association reflects its competitive position, the nature of the local riding, and the organizational style of the party of which it is a constituent unit. Competitive associations are larger and better funded than are their uncompetitive counterparts.[4] Associations in country ridings have different membership profiles and exist in a very different milieu than those in city and suburban ridings. And mass and cadre-style associations, despite sharing similar organizational rules, have distinctive approaches to their central tasks. These factors shape candidate selection in local nominations and, ultimately, the nature of local campaigns.

Riding conditions, and in particular the competitive positions of the local associations, have implications for the ways in which associations organize nominations. Larger, more competitive associations are better organized to search out candidates and have greater electoral appeal than their less competitive counterparts. Except where the presence of an incumbent restricts competition, the former are more likely to experience contested nominations. Given the volatility of the Canadian electorate (Blake 1991; Heintzman 1991), there is commonly more than one association in most ridings that can claim to be competitive.

The nature of the political community created by riding boundaries will have implications for nominations. Close-knit rural communities may rely much more heavily on personal networks than suburban associations when searching for candidates, while city associations may use their access to the media to broadly advertise their nomination. This creates distinctive modes of organization that favour different sorts of candidates. Often a friend or acquaintance of party members in rural campaigns, a candidate may be more anonymous in a suburban campaign and a well-known public figure in a city constituency.

Duverger's distinction between mass and cadre-style parties (1954, 63) helps explain some of the variation in nominations across Canadian parties. The Liberal and Progressive Conservative Parties have not adopted a mass form, as have most parties in Westminster-style systems (Beer 1967), but rather have retained a cadre-style of organization. Consistent with Duverger's analysis, cadre-style associations in the Liberal and Conservative Parties have a cyclical existence, springing into action in order to send delegates to leadership conventions or to nominate candidates to run in elections. Not only do they vary in strength and membership size, many associations are moribund outside these times. This cyclical existence facilitates the recruitment of new members and reduces the expectation that nomination candidates should come from among those who have demonstrated a long-term commitment to the party.

In contrast, where the NDP has experienced even modest electoral success, its associations have a continuous existence and relatively stable memberships that are largely unaffected by electoral cycles (Carty 1991a, 240). This organizational persistence is characteristic of mass parties as described by Duverger (1954, 70). The presence of a coterie of party members that meets regularly and understands how the association operates discourages outsiders from joining. Moreover, mass parties place substantial long-term demands on their members. By and large, these associations look for candidates from among their own members.

It may be that the continuous, bureaucratic nature of New Democrat associations reflects the "institutionalization of the party as a complex organization" (Morley 1994, 47) as much as its mass nature, or that the party is at best only mass in nature at the local level and even then, not across the whole country (Brodie and Jenson 1988). These observations are largely consistent with the claim made here that the NDP retains many of the forms of a mass party if not always the substance thereof. In comparison to their cadre-style opponents, NDP associations have a bureaucratic, rule-oriented approach to the nomination and campaign process. The mass-cadre distinction is an ideal one that is used to contrast the different approaches to electoral politics adopted by Canadian parties.

This difference in organizational form across Canadian parties coincides with an ideological distinction between left and right. Because the NDP is the only one of the three parties not to have held national government, this division also corresponds to a competitive cleavage. The organizational and ideological divide that coincides with this mass-cadre distinction helps explain differences in the style of associations across parties, the members they attract, their nominations, and the candidates they select, as well as the campaigns they run (Carty and Erickson 1991, 162-9).

While we would expect a local condition such as competitiveness to influence the character of local associations and their nominations, the impact of partisan organizational styles on local riding nominations is less well documented (though see Carty and Erickson 1991). The cyclical existence of cadre-style associations, and their loose organizational arrangements, makes it easy for prospective candidates to gain access to their nominations. The ground rules appear straightforward: a candidate places his or her name before the association committee organizing the contest. Once accepted, he or she then works to attract as many supporters as possible. Many of these are new recruits to the association. The candidate hopes that they will provide him or her with the greatest number of votes at the nomination meeting, and so secure victory.

This process is different in the NDP. As a mass party, the NDP expects its members and candidates to exhibit their commitment to the party and its principles. This underpins the continuity of existence between elections found in many NDP associations. Evidence of solidarity with the party's cause, the defining characteristics of class-based partisan politics, is critical to a candidate's success, usually taking the form of a history of involvement in the party or union movement. The implicit requirement that candidates be party members in good standing reduces the size of the group from which NDP associations can draw candidates. Still, their organizational strength makes them well suited for searching out candidates from among the party faithful.

Because of the relative importance of the existing membership in these associations, nomination candidates focus on convincing current members to support them rather than on recruiting new members. This is reinforced by the difficulty of attracting new members to mass-party associations that appear to demand greater commitment than cadre-style parties. The NDP has also been less successful at the national level than either the Conservatives or Liberals, and has had a more difficult time attracting candidates and members to its associations. The lack of an infusion of recruits just prior to an election, as found in the more permeable Liberal and Conservative Parties (Carty 1991a, 30-9), reinforces the NDP's reliance on existing members as candidates and campaign workers.

The nomination process not only selects the candidate, it is also critical in determining the sort of support a candidate receives during the campaign. The type of candidate that is selected, and his or her relationship with the campaign team, can have a strong bearing on the final shape of the campaign. So too can the resources of the team and its vision of how best to campaign. Campaigns in which the candidate's personality is seen as the key to success are very different from those that focus on the party platform.

Although, generally, competitiveness is associated with well-financed and -staffed campaigns, solidarity among NDP members means that in many uncompetitive associations, some campaigners are experienced party stalwarts. In most NDP associations, party members work for whichever candidate is selected. In fact, the association executive may play an important role in assigning campaign team positions. In looser cadre-style associations, the final form of the campaign team is more likely to depend on who wins the nomination, as many members have allegiances to nomination candidates rather than directly to the party. As a result, the candidate plays a much bigger role in composing the membership of the team.

Variation in the nomination experiences of competitive and uncompetitive associations, and even mass and cadre-style associations, can be seen in the role of nonlocal parties in local nominations. Extremely uncompetitive associations may be unable to attract a candidate and may have to rely on the national party to supply a volunteer from outside the riding. National parties can also become involved in nominations for their own reasons. Ridings that the party is likely to win can attract the attention of national strategists hoping to ensure the party elects a particular mix of MPs. The national party – using the leader's veto – may work to have a particular nominee selected.

There are also some riding contests across Canada that national party strategists believe have an impact on the wider election. This is usually the result of the media attention they have received in previous elections, or some special circumstance that seems certain to attract such attention. Strategists may attempt to ensure that a competent, high-profile candidate wins the nomination in these ridings in order to bolster the party's image. Most such ridings are in metropolitan areas that are serviced by large media outlets.

Such direct strategic intervention is more common in cadre-style parties than in mass parties. This reflects the fact that as well as organizational and ideological divisions between the two cadre-style parties and the NDP, there is also a competitive division. The greater number of competitive Liberal and Conservative associations offer more opportunities for national strategists to advance their own causes by intervening in local affairs. It may also be the case, given the common cause across different levels of the NDP, that local outcomes are more consistent with national party objectives and thus obviate the need for direct national intervention.

The distinctive nomination experiences of competitive associations versus those that are uncompetitive, of those in country, suburban, and city ridings, and of cadre-style associations as opposed to mass-party associations, provides the basic matrix for distinguishing between four types of nominations. Each type of nomination in this typology selects a distinctive type of candidate, around which subsequent campaign teams are built. This then leads us to the election proper.

The Election Contest
During the election, national party intervention – driven by local conditions – can alter the make-up of the campaign team. A party may offer a candidate financial assistance and professional advice on how to run a local campaign. It may even provide workers for key positions. Such intervention

is a double-edged sword, for despite its potential helpfulness, it may introduce incompatible national strategies into the local campaign. Just as
important, the attitude of local campaigners to national party imperatives
can have a profound impact on the strategic direction of the campaign.
Mass-party campaigns are more willing to accept nonlocal strategic direction
than are their cadre-style cousins. Given this, more competitive campaigns
in any party can afford to ignore national advice and the resources that
might come with it, and head off in their own strategic direction.

The local contest itself is critical in shaping the style and content of riding campaigns. The nature of the contest reflects the character of the local
political community, its geography, the media in the riding, and the competitiveness of the local campaigns (Beck 1974; Blake 1978). The character
of the riding shapes the local political agenda to which campaigns must
respond. The amount and type of media that cover the riding are critical
in the formation of this agenda, and to the way in which local campaigns
engage with each other. The lack of media coverage that focuses directly
on the local contest may result in an underdeveloped agenda that can easily be influenced by nonlocal media and campaigns. There is also a
dynamic between the candidate and the local community. Although not
as pronounced as in the United States (Fenno 1978), the ways in which
candidates are presented to the public is shaped by the nature of the local
community.[5]

In addition, the intensity of competition in the riding also influences
the style and content of local campaigns in two ways. Where there is only
one competitive campaign, the election is less intense than those in which
two or more have a chance of success. The final form of any campaign
depends on whether it has a chance of winning the election or whether it
is uncompetitive, and therefore marginalized or excluded from the real
contest.

A campaign's strategic and allocational decisions are shaped by its access
to the media. Campaigners generally believe that the voters' perceptions
of their campaign – its competitiveness and the credibility of the candidate – are greatly affected by media reporting. Campaigns attempt to
attract positive media reporting in influential media by staging news conferences and other events. Most campaigns advertise in local media but
cannot afford to advertise in the major, influential news media. Even if
they could, such media outlets are rarely well targeted to voters within any
one riding. Conversely, those that are well targeted and that campaigns
can afford are often not influential.

The media play another crucial role: they bring the federal election writ
large into the local riding. The reporting of the leaders' tours, their debates,
poll results, and the full panoply of election events can influence the
dynamic of the local contest, including voters' opinions of local campaigns

and the morale of local party volunteers. If nonlocal media dominate reporting in a riding, the view of the election that voters receive is not shaped by or related to the local agenda. The reverse can be true in ridings where there is credible media reporting. Not only does this have implications for the issues that are salient to the local contest; it also may underpin voters' perceptions of the competitiveness of local campaigns.

There is evidence that local and regional conditions play an important role in shaping local political organizations, and that local knowledge can enhance electoral performance (Beck 1974; Huckfeldt and Sprague 1992). Differences in the social composition of ridings and the media available to them have predictable consequences for local campaigning. Also, local geography places distinct demands on constituency campaigns. Variations in the character of country, suburban, and city regions (see Kasarda and Janowitz 1974) help explain the distinctive manner of campaigns in each of these three types of ridings.

The Argument

This book uses the distinctions between contested and uncontested nominations; mass- and cadre-party organizations; and city, suburban, and country ridings to analyze and explain the character of local campaigns and constituency contests in Canada. It commences with the observation, drawn from empirical research, that the two broad types of nominations, contested and uncontested, can be further divided into those to which candidates have ready access and those where restrictions are placed on entry. Such restrictions arise either from partisan organizational mores or from strategic concerns. The result is a four-cell typology which can be used to comprehend the variety of observed nominations. Each category of nomination produces its archetypal local candidate: local notable, party insider, stopgap candidate, and high-profile candidate.

The particular constellation of support and resources needed by each type of candidate to win the nomination produces corresponding differences in the character and structure of their campaigns. The final form any campaign takes also depends on its relations with the national party, the nature of the constituency, the media that cover the riding contest, and the degree of competition between local campaigns. The critical and idiosyncratic role that local associations play in the selection of candidates and construction of campaign teams suggests that they are central to the fabric of Canadian political parties and politics. In building a picture of this important part of the political system, this work provides a clearer understanding of how political parties and elections work, and their impact on Canadian political life. Specifically, it provides insights into the relative importance of local factors over provincial or national concerns, the nature of intraparty relations, and the role of the media in elections.

Knowledge of constituency organizations and politics is relevant to at least two broad areas of study of political parties. One is the debate over the role of parties in Canadian politics, in which they are regularly found wanting (see, for example, Meisel 1991). A related concern is the challenge to their integrative and representative roles by the growth of new interests and modes of political participation (Carty 1991a, 230-1). While parties have both a national and provincial face, and fulfil these tasks in public at these levels, the great bulk of their interaction with voters happens out of sight in local constituencies. How they do this directly shapes the character of Canadian politics.

Second, there is a growing professionalization of political parties in many liberal democracies (Panebianco 1988). This is in response to the centralization of media, and the growing complexities of modern campaigning. Canadian parties have been particularly susceptible to the widespread tendency to focus more heavily on leaders as the personification of party platforms. The implications of this process, which may attenuate links between the national and local parties, can be understood only if we have a clear picture of constituency organizations and politics.

The book is broken into four main sections. Chapters 3 to 5 focus on the nomination process and develop a four-way typology of candidates that provides the basic framework for explaining the nature of campaigns in Canada. Chapter 3 discusses the factors that shape the nomination process and defines four archetypal contests. The following chapter suggests that each of these four nominations selects a particular type of candidate. Chapter 5 extends this discussion, exploring the distinctive character of the campaign teams that surround each of the four candidates.

A second section, Chapter 6, analyzes the relationship between each of the four archetypal local campaign teams and their regional and/or national campaigns. Each type of campaign team has a distinctive relationship with its nonlocal counterparts that reflects the financial and strategic strength of the local campaign, and the importance the party ascribes to the candidate and the local contest.

The third section, Chapter 7, deals with the environment within which the local campaign operates. Some of this has already been taken account of in describing the nomination process. This section allows for the extension of the discussion to factors such as the way in which the national campaign impinges on local affairs and the role competition between campaigns has on their style and content.

The fourth section, Chapters 8 and 9, applies the model of campaigning developed in Chapters 3 to 7 to a number of campaigns during the 1988 federal election. The final chapter compares this model with experiences in some other Western democracies and offers a novel perspective on the nature of Canadian politics and parties.

2
Research Methodology and Choice of Ridings

The lack of academic interest in local aspects of campaigning during Canadian federal elections is not unusual. Agnew (1987) argues that there has been a devaluation of place and local context as explanations in the social sciences.[1] With respect to Canadian elections, there have been only a few attempts to consider the impact of the character of the riding contests on the behaviour of voters, and these have generally used census and survey data (see Blake 1978). A similar pattern is evident in the study of the dynamics of campaigning. There has been a tendency to study them at the national level, leaving local campaigns and contests largely unexplored. This process has also been driven by a growing belief in the importance of national level campaigning and politics, which has been underpinned by the centralization of media (Fletcher 1987, 363-7) and the importance of leaders in Canadian parties (Courtney 1973).

Agnew suggests that if we are to study local political forms successfully, they cannot be understood by simply adding up the factors that cause political behaviour (such as class, ethnicity, and religious affiliation). Rather, it is the manner in which these factors come together in a particular place and time, and in so doing take on meaning for people and determine political outcomes, that provides a basis for coherent political analysis (Agnew 1987, 213; Fenno 1996, 9). Traditional survey data are not well suited to this task. As Barton (1968) notes, "The survey is a meat-grinder, tearing the individual from his social context and guaranteeing that nobody in the study interacts with anyone else in it" (quoted in Blake 1978, 282). In studying elections, contextualization is best accomplished by interviewing candidates, campaigners, party strategists, and journalists.

Selecting the Ridings
Research design is always constrained by available resources and usually involves trade-offs in terms of objectives. To achieve analytical depth, the research on which this book is based could not aim to be representative.

As such, its conclusions are aimed at providing a guide to future, hopefully representative, research. The selection of ridings was guided by the criteria used for an earlier study of local campaigns and their relationship to the media done for the Royal Commission on Electoral Reform and Party Financing. This earlier study distinguished between city and country ridings and was interested in constituency contests that had different media profiles. It focused on constituency contests and campaigns in Vancouver Centre and Kootenay West-Revelstoke (Sayers 1991).

Vancouver Centre, where the Tories were victorious, was selected because it is a high-profile city riding that received inordinate press attention and was very closely contested. In contrast, Kootenay West-Revelstoke is a country riding that was not closely contested and was won by the NDP. In addition, it had its own local media, distinct from the major provincial news organizations based in Vancouver.

To the original study were added ridings and electoral contests that were interesting in their own right, and which a priori exhibited a variety of characteristics that might be expected to impact on the nature of local campaigning. Any critical variables and patterns that could be identified by this study might be tested for representativeness in future studies. Fenno (1978, 3) describes this process with regard to his work on members of Congress in the United States: "I spent a lot of time trying to figure out a priori what types of [constituencies] ... might pose serious tests for, or exceptions to, whatever generalizations seemed to be emerging. Participant observation is not like survey research ... data collection and data analysis ... proceed simultaneously. [It precedes] survey-type questionnaires [and] sacrifices analytical range for analytical depth."

The logistics of personal interviews constrained the number of ridings it was possible to cover. For the same reason, I felt that the study should concentrate on the major parties, though interviews with some Reform Party candidates are included in recognition of the insurgent nature of their campaigns. In order to choose between the ridings in British Columbia, it was necessary to build a profile of constituency elections in the province. Some of this was done using media reports of local contests. Further information on the character of ridings, used extensively throughout the book, was drawn from Eagles et al. (1991) and Canadian Census Data (Canada, Statistics Canada 1987). Campaign funding information and electoral results cited throughout are drawn from two Elections Canada publications (1988a, 1989). Media profiles for ridings are drawn from Canadian Advertising Rates and Data (1988).

As shown in Table 2.1, the closeness of the contest, the winning party, the geography of the riding, the local economy, and the media in the riding were all used to describe and choose among constituency elections in the province. The ridings chosen provide substantial variation across a

Table 2.1

Characteristics of ridings

Riding	BK	FVW	KWR	OC	SN	VC	VIC
Winning party	NDP	PC	NDP	PC	NDP	PC	NDP
Geography	City	Country	Country	Country	Suburban	City	City
Economy	Manufac. Dormitory	Farming Dormitory	Mining Forests Tourism	Farm Tourism Seniors	Service Dormitory	CBD Manufac.	BC Gov't
Marginal	No	No	Yes	No	Yes	Yes	Yes
High profile	Yes	No	No	No	No	Yes	Yes
Media	Local Provincial National	Local	Local	Local Regional	None	Local Provincial National	Local Regional

Note: BK= Burnaby-Kingsway; FVW = Fraser Valley West; KWR = Kootenay West-Revelstoke; OC = Okanagan Centre; SN = Surrey North; VC = Vancouver Centre; VIC = Victoria; CBD = Central Business District.

range of factors that might influence local campaigning and elections, yet were manageable in terms of travel and number of interviews.

Burnaby-Kingsway offered an opportunity to look at a riding with a high-profile incumbent, Svend Robinson, but whose opponents were nowhere near as well known. Although based in the city of Burnaby, the riding includes some suburban areas. The incumbent's personal following and the character of NDP campaigns in one of the party's few strongholds were critical to the shape of the local contest. Robinson was an important player in the NDP and received local, provincial, and national media exposure.

Fraser Valley West is a country riding that was a Tory stronghold. The incumbent had won by the third highest margin of victory of any Tory in Canada in the previous election. The effects of this one-party dominance on local campaigns, media, and the riding contest are of interest. Fraser Valley West is on the perimeter of Vancouver and has its own defined media and local interest. The area is renowned for its conservatism and was important to the governing PCs who were under attack from the right on a number of issues.

Okanagan Centre was a new riding. The growing population of the region surrounding the city of Kelowna required three ridings where there had been but two in the previous election. As such, there was no incumbent. The Tories subsequently won Okanagan Centre. The lack of a clear political history meant that it would be possible to watch local riding associations build themselves from the ground up and try to convince prospective candidates to run. All three parties experienced contested nominations. In addition, the Reform Party had its best result in British Columbia in the riding. Finally, there are sizeable media organizations based in the city of Kelowna, which Okanagan Centre encompasses. This provided a chance to look at a riding that had the undivided attention of influential local media and a distinct local economy and geography.

Surrey North was also a new riding, in the fastest growing suburban area in Canada. It was won by the NDP. It held some of the same attractions as Okanagan Centre but provided a counterbalance to the country and city ridings already selected. The election had been quite close, with both the PC and NDP nominations being strongly contested. In stark contrast to Okanagan Centre, few media organizations were interested in covering this contest. Local campaigns had to communicate with voters by other means. Surrey is in some ways an undistinguished dormitory community lost in the larger Vancouver metropolis.

Victoria, on Vancouver Island, was closely contested, with one of the rare BC Liberal campaigns that did reasonably well against its NDP and Tory opponents. As with Vancouver Centre, an incumbent had retired, leaving three nominations open. Because the riding encompasses the provincial capital, local politics is well covered in the regional media. As a city riding, it offered an opportunity to reconsider some of the findings from the Vancouver Centre study.

In all, there are four ridings that were won by the NDP, and three by Tories. As John Turner was the only successful Liberal candidate in British Columbia, and Vancouver Quadra was not considered to be different enough from Victoria and Vancouver Centre to warrant inclusion, there are no contests that were won by Liberals. While all ridings were contested, four could be considered relatively close contests, while the other three were won by considerable margins. Farming, primary industry, tourism, manufacturing, and services are each represented among the base industries that support local riding populations. There are three country ridings, one suburban, and three city. Three of the twenty-five candidates interviewed were women. Three of the contests could be considered to have had a high profile and good media coverage, while the other four were run-of-the-mill in this regard.

Changes to electoral boundaries alter the politics of a riding. The membership of local associations can change, as can their competitive positions. The disruption to the life of local associations may make their nominations more open to new candidates. New issues may move onto the local political agenda to replace ones that are no longer relevant. As a result, the campaigns run by local associations, and the contests that they produce, reflect boundary changes.

Table 2.2 indicates how each of the seven ridings was constituted following the 1987 redistribution. Victoria, Vancouver Centre, Kootenay West-Revelstoke, and Okanagan Centre (though it was a new riding in name) all contain a high proportion of polls drawn from a single 1984 riding. Burnaby-Kingsway, Fraser Valley West, and Surrey North are less dominated by polls from any single previous riding. The impact of these changes can be adduced from the political history of the constituent parts. If, as in Burnaby-Kingsway, the various polls now grouped together share a similar political history, the change may impact only association membership. The competitive position of the associations, the campaigns they run, and the issues raised may be largely unchanged from previous elections. In the case of Kootenay West-Revelstoke, the proportionally small addition of Revelstoke to Kootenay West had a large impact on the contest, as it added strongly New Democrat polls to a riding with a fine partisan balance.

The transposition of votes from the previous election onto the new boundaries is an indicator of whether there had been a material change in the terms of competition among parties during the intervening period. None of the chosen ridings had experienced such a change (Canada, Elections Canada 1988b). The competitive positions of the local associations were not obviously aberrant.

Table 2.2

Composition of 1988 ridings

Current riding name	Constituent former ridings	Percentages
Fraser Valley West	Fraser Valley East	41.3
	Fraser Valley West	58.7
Surrey North	Fraser Valley West	41.1
	Surrey-White Rock-North Delta	58.9
Okanagan Centre	Okanagan North	78.9
	Okanagan-Similkameen	21.1
Burnaby-Kingsway	Burnaby	41.5
	North Vancouver-Burnaby	33.8
	Vancouver-Kingsway	24.7
Victoria	Esquimalt-Saanich	5.5
	Victoria	94.5
Vancouver Centre	Vancouver Centre	81.3
	Vancouver East	2.8
	Vancouver Quadra	15.9
Kootenay West-Revelstoke	Kootenay East-Revelstoke	13.4
	Kootenay West	86.6

Source: *Almanac of Federal Ridings* (Munroe Eagles et al. 1991).

The Ridings in Detail

Burnaby-Kingsway

An urban riding of 107,948 residents, Burnaby-Kingsway is a constituency that is largely a product of recent redistributions. Almost 60% of the constituency was in two adjacent ridings prior to this election. Redistribution resulted in the elimination of NDP MP Ian Waddell's Vancouver-Kingsway seat. Burnaby-Kingsway is bounded on the west and north by Vancouver ridings, to the south by New Westminster, and to the east by the outer suburban riding of Port Moody-Coquitlam.

At nearly 23%, residents of British extraction make up the largest group in the riding, with Chinese (11.5%), Italian (6.8%), and South Asians (4.5%) being the other major groupings. The riding attracted large numbers of immigrants after the late 1940s, and between 1966 and 1977, 13.1% of the province's immigrants settled here. Simon Fraser University (SFU) and the British Columbia Institute of Technology (BCIT) lie within the boundaries of the constituency.

Light manufacturing industry (including food and beverages, metal fabricating, and paper and allied services) employs 14% of the workforce. Large industrial parks and warehouses, situated to take advantage of Burnaby's central location and proximity to the Port of Vancouver, are also major employers. The average income of $38,528 is above the provincial average, the unemployment rate of 10.7% is 2.7% below the provincial average, and the average value of a private dwelling is $121,330. Low-income families make up 18.2% of the local population, and just over 10% of all income is derived from government transfers, below the provincial average.

The NDP candidate was Svend Robinson, the NDP MP for the seat of Burnaby since 1979. The thirty-six-year-old lawyer had been the NDP's justice critic and had declared his homosexuality during the previous Parliament. His stand on abortion was at odds with the pro-life attitudes of his opponents, and his willingness to defy a court order by participating in the blocking of a logging road on the Queen Charlotte Islands brought condemnation from his opponents. This local race had national exposure – the prime minister made electoral reference to the incumbent – and the NDP worked hard to win the seat, outspending its opponents by more than three to one.

Despite attacks over his stand on abortion and his openness concerning his sexuality, Robinson improved on his 1984 vote share by taking just over 43% of the total vote. His Conservative opponent, Italian-born John Bitonti, who ran a campaign that emphasized traditional values, received 30% of the vote. Bitonti, an urban designer, had run for the Social Credit Party in 1986 but was making his first foray into federal politics. Liberal Sam Stevens, a lawyer and status Algonquin Indian from Quebec, received 22.1% of the vote. These Tory and Liberal vote shares were down marginally from 1984. The Reform Party was the major beneficiary of these losses, garnering 2.7% of the vote.

Burnaby-Kingsway has little media of its own. Two student publications associated with SFU and BCIT, as well as a couple of community newspapers, gave basic coverage to the local contest. However, incumbent Svend Robinson received inordinate media attention from provincial and national news media of all forms commensurate with his role as a national political figure. The nonlocal media by contrast largely ignored his two opponents.

Fraser Valley West
On the eastern fringe of Greater Vancouver, the constituency of Fraser Valley West has the Fraser River as its northern boundary, the US border at its southern extreme, and reaches eastward to Abbotsford. Two-thirds of

the polls are urban and the rest rural, including the small municipalities of Langley, Aldergrove, Matsqui, and Clearbrook. Langley has recently joined the Greater Vancouver Regional District, an indication of the way in which this once-rural riding is changing, with many of its larger agricultural land holdings being converted into small hobby farms.

Most of the 95,014 residents are of British origin, with substantial German and Dutch components, a francophone minority of 2%, and a Native population that accounts for 1% of the riding. The conversion of the Fraser Valley into metropolitan suburbs is seen in the increasing reliance of the population on manufacturing and service sector employment as well as small business. Agriculture accounts for 8.8% of the workforce, and government services 6%. The average family income is $34,564 and unemployment is slightly below the provincial average of 13%. Almost 18% of the population is classified as low income, and just under 14% receive government transfers. Almost 4.5% of the constituency have university degrees.

The recent addition of the Tory strongholds of Clearbrook and Matsqui to this Conservative riding has made it arguably the strongest PC riding in British Columbia. The Conservative candidate was former teacher and businessman Bob Wenman. A Social Credit member of the BC legislature from 1968 to 1972, and a candidate for that party's leadership in 1986, Wenman had been a member of the federal Parliament since 1974. His campaign emphasized the Free Trade Agreement, the environment, and family values. The Liberal candidate was Tony Wattie, a lawyer and first-time candidate. Along with NDP candidate Lynn Fairall, a government Corrections worker, Wattie opposed the Free Trade Agreement. The NDP also campaigned against the Conservatives' proposed tax reforms and attacked their record on the environment.

Support for the Conservatives was 16 percentage points below that of 1984, but with 45.8%, Wenman was 20.2 points ahead of the NDP's Fairall, who captured 25.6% of the vote. Wattie placed third with 19.6%, an increase for the Liberals of 7.6 points over 1984. National leader of the Christian Heritage Party, John Van Woudenberg, received 4.7% of the vote, while the Reform Party's John Russell garnered 3.5% of the vote.

Perched at the periphery of Vancouver, Fraser Valley West has its own small media outlets based in the towns in the riding, including radio, newspapers, and cable television. Local voters also have access to media from Vancouver proper. This creates an interesting media profile. The contest is well reported by local media that is read, watched, and listened to by local voters, while the story of the wider contest is told mainly by the Vancouver media.

Kootenay West-Revelstoke

This constituency is a large sprawling riding approximately 500 kilometres long and running north-south up the Selkirk Mountains and Columbia River of British Columbia. The US border forms its southern boundary, and the Kamloops and Prince George regions its northern boundary. The main provincial transport and communication links run east-west across the riding. There are a number of clearly identifiable towns (Revelstoke in the north; Nelson, Trail, Rossland, and Castlegar in the south) whose economic interests include the large Cominco smelter in Trail, mining, forestry, railway expansion, and tourism. Related manufacturing and service sectors have also been major employers in the region.

In recent times there has been a focus on developing tourism in the area via the skiing industry and the restoration of old towns, some of which have been used by the film industry. This new economy is at odds with the highly unionized industrial sector that remains politically important. The addition of the NDP stronghold of Revelstoke following the narrow Conservative win in the previous election promised a tight race.

Despite an unemployment rate that consistently runs several points above the provincial average, and an average family income that is almost $4,000 below the norm, over 57% of the constituency are homeowners. This constituency also has the lowest percentage of people moving over the past five years of any constituency in British Columbia, and 5% of the population has a university degree. About one-quarter of the 67,317 voters have British ancestry, with large Italian, German, French, and Hungarian communities.

This constituency has proven to be very competitive. The straight NDP-versus-PC battle is typical of the province. Remarkably, the same two men have fought four successive elections, and the seat has swung back and forth. This competition between the PC's Bob Brisco and the NDP's Lyle Kristiansen, the former a local chiropractor and the latter a woodworker and union executive, has meant that in every election for nearly a decade the incumbent faced an experienced campaigner and former MP.

Brisco won the seat in 1979 running against first-time candidate Kristiansen by a margin of 8 percentage points. The latter took the seat in 1980 by 2.8 points, but Brisco won the seat back in 1984, beating Kristiansen by 2.2 points. They were joined by Liberal candidate Garry Jenkins and Green Party candidate Michael Brown, Jenkins a doctor and alderman from Rossland and Brown a self-described hermit. Kristiansen had tried to convince Brown not to run, but in the end, the Greens' 2% vote was not decisive, with Kristiansen winning by more than 10 points over Brisco, who suffered a greater than 10-point drop in support. The Liberals support increased by 8 points.

Most of the larger towns and cities in Kootenay West-Revelstoke have a community newspaper. A few also have larger daily newspapers that have some influence on local events and that report the local contest in some detail. There is a respected radio network with an emphasis on news that broadcasts throughout the riding, which gives the local contest extensive coverage. The local cable station also provides airtime for local campaigns. The fragmentation of the local media and its inability to devote substantial resources to interrogating the local campaigns limit its influence across the riding. The larger provincial and national news outlets available in the riding play an important role in telling the wider election story.

Okanagan Centre

This seat was created after the redistribution in 1987, reflecting the growth in population of this region over recent years. It is made up of more than three-quarters of the old Okanagan North riding. Much of the population growth is associated with the increasing number of retirees moving into the area. The new constituency is half urban and half rural, encompassing the city of Kelowna, home base of the Bennett Social Credit dynasty. The population of 89,730 is made up largely of voters of British ancestry with sizeable German, Ukrainian, French, Dutch, and Italian populations. There is a small Native population.

Though the constituency has some affluence, over 17% of the population is classed as low income. Average family income is $32,289, over $5,000 less than the provincial norm. At about 16%, the rates of unemployment and of those receiving income assistance are above the provincial average, in part as a result of the seasonal nature of employment in tourism and fruit growing. More than one-quarter of all the employment in the riding is accounted for by small business, manufacturing, and service-related industries. Direct agricultural employment is just below 6%, with tourism the fastest-growing industry in the region.

The Conservative bent of the riding is clearly seen in the 1984 Conservative landslide, when the Conservatives won the seat by 34 percentage points from the NDP, capturing 58% of the vote. The local campaign focused on the impact of free trade on local agriculture. Farmers were pulling up vines, and large numbers of orchards were for sale. Conservative Al Horning, a well-known local realtor and alderman, was opposed by NDP's Bryan McIver, an insurance broker and one-time Conservative, and Liberal Murli Pendharkar, former local school superintendent. The Reform Party had a dynamic candidate in Werner Schmidt, a founding member of the party, and the Green Party ran a candidate.

The result was unsettling for the local Conservatives. The Tory vote fell by almost 21 percentage points, but they still managed to win the seat by a 7-point margin. The Reform Party picked up about 14% of the vote, much of which must have come from ex-Tories. The NDP vote increased by 5.4 points to 30.2%, and the Liberals maintained third place by increasing their vote by 2 points to 17.1%.

There are three major local newspapers, two television stations, half a dozen radio stations, as well as community newspapers in this riding encompassing Kelowna. While major provincial and national news sources are available in the riding, its own media is influential, and local campaigns can afford its advertising rates. This self-contained aspect of the riding gives a particular local flavour to politics in Okanagan Centre.

Surrey North

As this largely residential riding of 107,052 was formed after the 1984 election, there was no incumbent. 41.1% of the riding came from the Fraser Valley West riding and 58.9% from the Surrey-White Rock-North Delta riding. Its northern boundary is the Fraser River, while the suburb of Delta is on its western boundary, and Langley is to the east.

Its population is of predominantly British extraction, with a very large East Indian community and smaller German, Dutch, and French communities. Immigrants make up 22.7% of the riding. The average family income is $4,000 below the provincial norm, and 22% of the riding's families are classed as low income. The moderate price of housing has attracted young homebuyers, and 47% of the constituency own their own home. Unemployment runs 2% above the provincial average, and only 3.4% of the population has a university degree, the lowest rate in the province.

The economy of the riding is based on shipping and related industries along the Fraser River. About 16.5% of the local workforce is in manufacturing, 13.2% in service-related work, and there remains an important agricultural sector, now predominantly in market gardening. Because Surrey is a dormitory community for Greater Vancouver, most of its workforce is employed outside the riding.

The Conservatives nominated first-time candidate and local realtor Cliff Blair. The NDP chose Jim Karpoff, a social services consultant and former local alderman. Former Surrey alderman and mayor Don Ross was nominated by the Liberals. Ross, who had been a football player and teacher, had tried unsuccessfully for the Liberals provincially and was, by far, the best-known candidate. The Reform Party and the Christian Heritage Party both ran candidates.

The NDP beat the Conservatives with 37% of the vote to 32.8%. The Liberal vote increased by over 10 points to 24.9%, while the Reform Party and Christian Heritage Party shared most of the remaining vote.

There are nearly no media in Surrey North. A local radio station and two community papers, none of which are strongly identified with Surrey North, gave sporadic coverage to the contest. It is the absence of media that helps make this riding interesting to study.

Vancouver Centre

Vancouver Centre is a densely populated downtown residential riding covering an area of thirty-five square kilometres. It is a cosmopolitan, urban constituency with a population of 104,346 persons and includes the Central Business District (CBD), the Port of Vancouver, and Stanley Park. Long associated with the interests of the business community as well as the ethnically and socially heterogeneous communities within its boundaries, the riding includes sizeable Greek, Chinese, Japanese, French, Spanish, German, Ukrainian, and Italian neighbourhoods. Thirty percent of the riding is of British ancestry, and there is also a significant Jewish population.

The major source of employment is the service sector that provides 15.8% of jobs; manufacturing accounts for 6.4%, and managerial and administrative employees make up 14.3% of the labour force. There is a wide gap between the average family income of $42,309 and the median of $34,605, indicative of the fact that Vancouver Centre has the second-highest percentage of low-income families in British Columbia with 24.4% in this category. Furthermore, home values are high, costing an average of $160,999, and the proportion of home ownership is the lowest in the province. The riding population is transient, with 64% having moved within the previous five years. Three of every ten people are classed as immigrants, while the percentage of the population with university degrees is well above the provincial average.

The boundaries of Vancouver Centre have remained fairly consistent over the last five elections, all of which have been highly competitive. The Liberals won the riding in 1974 and 1979, the Tories have been successful since then, and the NDP has had a strong showing, for it controls much of the area provincially. The high voter turnover and a redistribution that added NDP polls appeared to give all three parties some chance of success, though the NDP and PC candidates were better placed than the Liberals. In 1984, the NDP had placed second to the Tories.

The constituency is of some special interest given the high profile of the local campaign. The retiring member, Pat Carney, had been a government minister and a central figure in negotiations surrounding the Canada-US Free Trade Agreement. The three principal candidates were all high-profile figures: Kim Campbell, an ex-provincial politician who had sought the Social Credit leadership (and premiership) and was widely touted as a rising star in the Conservative firmament (she subsequently was appointed Minister of Justice and later became Canada's first female prime minister); Johanna den Hertog, federal president of the NDP; and Tex Enemark, one-time assistant to local Vancouver Centre MP Ron Basford who was Minister of Justice in the Trudeau government. They were joined by

Reform Party, Green, and Rhino candidates, as well as a number of independent candidates.

The PCs won the election, beating the NDP by 269 votes (0.4 percentage points). This represented a loss of 4.5 points for the Conservatives and a gain of 6.1 points for the NDP. The Liberals performed less well than many pundits had expected, gaining 22.8% of the vote, a drop on the previous election, but still important given the closeness of the contest. Although large enough in absolute terms to alter the outcome, the spoiling effect of the minor parties vote share is hard to judge, with the Reform Party picking up 1.4% of the vote, the Greens 0.8%, and the Rhinos 0.4%.

The local contest in Vancouver Centre was covered extensively by local, provincial, and even national media. This media included the national television networks, two provincially distributed newspapers, several community newspapers, as well as Vancouver radio and television stations. In addition, a number of foreign networks focused on Centre when reporting the wider federal election. Given this, it was one of the best-reported local contests of the election.

Victoria

The capital of British Columbia, Victoria is notable for its large senior population, four times the Canadian average. With 42% of the riding claiming British ancestry, it is the most British riding in British Columbia. The population of 94,597 is spread through the City of Victoria, wealthy Oak Bay, and that part of the District of Saanich that includes the University of Victoria.

The local economy is primarily service oriented, with the service sector supplying 18% of employment. Government employment accounts for 15.3% of local employment; tourism is the other large industry. There is less manufacturing in the riding than in any other in British Columbia. Nearly 14% of the riding has university degrees, well above the provincial average. While it includes some wealthy areas, the riding has a high proportion of low-income families, at 22.7%; state transfers support 15.7% of the population, and average family income is $1,000 below the provincial average.

The NDP has had increased success at both a provincial and municipal level since 1975, including the election of NDP Mayor Gretchen Brewin, spouse of the NDP's federal candidate. This and the fact that the incumbent Conservative Allan McKinnon decided not to run gave the NDP cause for optimism. McKinnon's personal following may have helped protect him from the changing nature of the riding, which increasingly favoured the NDP. From 25 percentage points in 1979, McKinnon's lead over the NDP had been cut to 8 points in 1984 when he defeated former provincial

NDP president John Brewin. Brewin's father had represented a Toronto area in the House of Commons.

The election saw local businessman and alderman Geoff Young selected to run for the Conservatives, and lawyer and former rugby star Michael O'Connor for the Liberals. The NDP gave Brewin his second shot at the seat. Free trade and the NDP defence policy proved to be important issues (the Esquimalt Naval Base is adjacent to the riding). The election saw the Tory vote cut by 16.5 points to 29.9%, 8 points ahead of the Liberals vote, which increased by 8.3 points. The NDP won the seat with a static vote of 38%. The Reform Party's Terry Volb picked 8.2% of the vote, suggesting that the Tories' chances of success may have been hurt by the presence of a Reform candidate.

Like its Vancouver counterpart, the contest in Victoria was well covered by local and regional news media. Much of the media for Vancouver Island is situated in Victoria, and the local contest was widely reported in the Victoria newspapers, as well as on regional radio and television. It did not receive the same level of provincial, national, and even international attention as did Vancouver Centre, but it was still a well-reported contest.

The Interviews

To ascertain the role played by various local campaigners during national elections, a standardized personal interview was conducted with candidates, campaign managers, official agents, communications officers, and party organizers who worked on the election. A similar interview was conducted with various members of the print and electronic media in the seven ridings. The questions were developed from those used for the earlier Lortie Commission study. These interviews attempted to assess the objectives, strategies, and resources each participant brings to a local constituency contest. As well as looking at the relationship between campaigns and the media, the interviews also addressed relations between media organizations and the various branches of political parties.

In the seven ridings, the study covers twenty-five campaigns, more than fifty media outlets, and is made up of 150 personal interviews. Analysis of information from the National Election Survey and surveys of official agents and campaign financing done for the Lortie Commission are used to supplement these interviews.

The next chapter uses the information gleaned from the interviews to build a picture of how local associations organize candidate nominations. It suggests that there are regularities in the nomination contests run by local associations, and that these patterns can be traced to both local conditions and the organizational styles of political parties.

3
Candidate Nomination

The local associations that organize nominations to select national election candidates in Canada lie at the intersection of two political worlds: the first is that of the local riding, the second is that of their own political parties. Although the rules governing nominations are relatively consistent across parties and ridings, the form these contests take can vary in response to the idiosyncratic mix of riding and partisan forces at work in each association (Carty and Erickson 1991). Viewed from the perspective of the national party, riding-centred forces tend to produce variation in the style of nominations within the same party. Conversely, from the perspective of any one riding, local circumstances appear to generate homogeneity, while it is partisan forces that seem to be the source of variation in the nomination experiences of the several local associations.

This chapter explores how competitiveness, party organizational style (whether cadre or mass), and local conditions shape nominations in Canada. Although there are variations in the form nominations take, there are consistencies in the way they function that reflect the nature of the riding as well as the partisanship and competitive position of the local association. As the candidate and the team of supporters he or she can muster are paramount in deciding the style and content of any local election campaign, these forces play a critical role in shaping the nature of that campaign.

Nominations can be classified according to whether or not they are contested, and by the type of candidate that is successful. The intensity of competition for the nomination is important in shaping the resources brought to bear by candidates and determining the criteria for success. It reflects the attraction the nomination holds for candidates and the ease with which candidates can gain access to the nomination. As the product of this process, the successful candidate (nominee) embodies the particular constellation of forces that shape the nomination contest. The appeal a nomination holds for candidates, and the access they have to the nomination, determine both how contested a nomination is and the type of candidate that is successful.

Appeal and access can be thought of as filters that define the terms of the local nomination contest. Association competitiveness is a large component of the appeal a nomination holds for prospective candidates. But competitiveness does not always have a predictable impact on the nature of nominations. While competitive associations often experience contested nominations, some have uncontested nominations while some apparently uncompetitive associations have contested nominations. Moreover, perceptions of competitiveness may be influenced by a number of factors – for example, the organizational structures of individual associations and the strength of the national parties – and can be manipulated by party members and officials.

Access can be thought of as having two components: the first is the organizational permeability of the association; the second is the type of candidate search conducted by the association. Permeability refers to the ease with which members can enter and leave the association. This is related to the organizational coherence of the association, which is determined both by competitiveness and partisan ethos. The criteria an association adopts in searching out potential candidates bear directly on who gains access to the nomination. Both appeal and access have a qualitative and quantitative dimension; they determine how many and what types of candidates contest the nomination, and through this, the criteria for success. It should be noted that the qualitative and quantitative dimensions of these filters are inextricably linked. For example, there may be only one candidate who meets the criteria set by the search committee.

In most cases, these filters remove all but one candidate, who is then acclaimed the nominee. In such cases, appeal and access are quite emphatic in deciding the form of the local contest. Less often, a number of candidates reach the nomination meeting, and one wins on the first ballot. In even fewer instances, the winner will have had to negotiate several ballots.[1] Depending on the nature and intensity of each of these filters, they produce four general types of nominations, each of which can be distinguished by the appeal they hold for potential candidates and the access such candidates have to the contest. Put differently, nominations can be classified by the degree to which they are open or closed to potential candidates (are candidates attracted to the nomination and can they gain access?), and whether or not they are contested (is there more than one candidate at the nomination meeting?). In a few cases, some apparently contested nominations are in fact not true contests, as one candidate has managed somehow to secure victory prior to the vote. The rest of this chapter elaborates the logic of these nomination filters and outlines the four archetypal nominations that they produce.

Association Appeal

The competitiveness of an association is the main quantitative dimension of appeal. The chance to win a seat is a strong attraction for most potential candidates. As well, the support a competitive nonlocal party can offer, or the chance to be on a winning team, can add to a nomination's appeal. A competitive party is in a better position to offer rewards to losing candidates and is a vehicle for a candidate who wishes to sit on the government benches. Of course, perceptions of the appeal of a local association may not be well founded and are sometimes manipulated by party members in order to attract candidates. This may include making exaggerated claims about the competitive position of the association (perhaps citing internal party polling), the strength of the association, or the help that a candidate can expect to receive from the party. Moreover, anything that creates uncertainty about the electoral outcome in a riding – such as new boundaries – may in fact or appearance alter the competitive position of local associations, thus altering their appeal.

The qualitative dimension of appeal also has a number of aspects. A party's ideological complexion influences the sort of candidate that is attracted to its nominations. Even within a single party, the ideological character of riding associations varies and may work to shape the sorts of candidates that are attracted to a particular nomination. Finally, high-profile ridings have a special appeal that has a strong qualitative dimension. Aspiring candidates who see themselves as important public figures, or those who wish to take advantage of the notoriety of contesting a high-profile riding, can be attracted to such contests. Moreover, parties are inclined to try to find well-qualified candidates to run in these ridings. Most such ridings are in metropolitan centres.[2]

Competitiveness

As Carty and Erickson note, competitiveness has an objective and perceptual component (1991, 133). In forming an opinion about the competitive position of an association, and hence its appeal, a potential candidate considers both elements. The main objective component of the competitive position of a local party association is its recent electoral performance. Associations that have won or come close to winning a riding are considered to be competitive. Not only does the chance of winning attract potential candidates, so too does the sheer vibrancy of competitive associations attract them. A history of strongly contested nominations may help attract candidates simply on the grounds that local activists interested in partisan politics are traditionally involved in active associations. The New Democrat association in the strong union riding of Kootenay West-Revelstoke, which has been successful in the past but faced a Conservative incumbent, attracted three times as many candidates as its NDP counterpart in Fraser Valley West, where the party has never come close to winning.

What is true for associations is also true for parties. Parties with a history of forming the government and/or the official opposition have an advantage in that they have access to greater resources than do other parties, and can offer a candidate the chance of being a member of the governing party. They may also be in a position to distribute favours to the party faithful regardless of local success or failure. These parties also have access to extensive polling and other technical information, and are able to use this information as evidence of organizational competence in order to convince potential candidates of the wisdom of running for them. The associations of parties that have had little regional success – whether at the provincial or federal level – are usually weaker. These parties are less able to assist local associations, and their nominations are thus less appealing.

In deciding whether to enter a nomination contest, potential candidates take account of factors that may have altered an association's competitiveness since the last election. Changes in local and national circumstances may alter the actual or perceived competitive position of an association. At the very least, anything that makes local electoral fortunes less certain provides an opportunity for speculation about future electoral performance, and can thus affect the appeal of nominations in a riding. The retirement of an incumbent, new electoral boundaries, or shifts in support for the national parties can alter either or both the objective or perceived competitive position of local associations. Moreover, the relatively low incumbency return rates in Canada have created an environment in which potential candidates have many good reasons to be generous in assessing the direction and intensity of changes in association competitiveness (Blake 1991).

The retirement of an incumbent may disrupt local political traditions and may alter the calculations of candidates about the competitiveness of local associations. Typically, the member has built up some personal following over his or her tenure that now becomes available to opposing parties. Such political opportunities invigorate associations, bolstering their appeal and their capacity to search out good candidates. Despite the potential loss of a retiring incumbent's personal vote, the nomination following a retirement can be especially appealing to prospective candidates. With a history of competitiveness, and having built up considerable financial and human resources during the tenure of the incumbent, the association is in a position to pursue a thorough candidate search and run a strong campaign. Its strength will appeal to prospective candidates. Given that associations with incumbents discourage contested nominations, there may also be party members whose ambitions have been thwarted and who will now seize the opportunity to contest the nomination. The retirements of Tory members in Victoria and Vancouver prior to the election managed to boost the competitiveness of all the major party nominations in these ridings.

On occasion, party officials attempt to manipulate perceptions of competitiveness to attract candidates. Periods of uncertainty encourage such manipulation. The promise of substantial assistance from either the provincial or federal party can play an important role in persuading some candidates to run. Of course, the credibility of these promises depends on evidence that the party can deliver the aid. The general condition of a party – its strength and organizational skills – affects the help it can give, and the perception that it can fulfil its promises of help. Thus, for long periods in recent decades, the endemic weakness of the Liberal Party in western Canada and the Conservative's long exclusion from Quebec made it much harder for them to attract good candidates in those regions.

Changed electoral boundaries alter the objective competitiveness of an association and allow activists and candidates to think their association will be more competitive in an upcoming election. For example, the addition of polls from Revelstoke to the old riding of Kootenay West prior to the election favoured the NDP. Revelstoke has voted strongly NDP over many elections. This gave a boost to the NDP association, which attracted six candidates to its nomination, and deflated the incumbent Conservative, who had barely won the seat in 1984.

This effect can be most pronounced when a new riding is created. Liberals in the new ridings of Surrey North and Okanagan Centre were optimistic about their electoral chances even though the party had a poor record in both areas. This helped motivate association members to seek out potential candidates and improved the appeal of Liberal nominations. Association members can claim that any negative voting history attached to the polls brought into the new riding can be ignored, and that the change provides an opportunity to recreate the local political landscape. On occasion, a lack of previous success can be an advantage for an association if voters are perceived as being willing to vote against incumbent politicians.

New boundaries can also dash the hopes of local associations. The growth of Vancouver has meant that new suburbs regularly encroach into ridings on the periphery of the greater metropolitan area. In BC ridings that are usually NDP-versus-PC contests, this is generally believed to favour the NDP. However, the 1987 redistribution moved the boundaries of Fraser Valley West eastward, away from Vancouver, to include more of the less densely populated and conservative Fraser Valley. This helped protect the incumbent Tory and robbed the New Democrats of a potential advantage.

As for the impact of changes in the competitive position of the national parties on their appeal, NDP associations in British Columbia reported strong interest in their nominations, driven by the belief that Brian Mulroney and the Tories were unpopular and that this would help the New Democrats win seats in British Columbia. Similar perceptions underpinned the heightened appeal of both Liberal and Reform nominations in 1993.

The actual and perceived competitive positions of an association are crucial to the appeal a nomination holds for potential candidates. In fact, as measurement of this objective element becomes more difficult – such as with changing boundaries – it is reasonable to assume that other factors play an increasingly important role in shaping these perceptions. This in part accounts for candidates entering races in associations that with hindsight appear to have been uncompetitive.

Nomination Profile

The public profile of nominations can vary. Some barely attract attention within their own community, while others have a regional or national profile. In particular, nominations in a few ridings seem to have high profiles from one election to the next. Media attention focused on a riding or its nominations is the main mechanism by which this public profile is established. This is the result of media outlets reproducing patterns of reporting built up over a number of elections, the original impulses for which are many and varied. These include a tradition of closely contested elections, a history of sending high-profile members to Ottawa, and the propinquity of the riding to major media outlets. In some cases, factors related to a current nomination battle – such as a challenge to an incumbent – can raise the profile of one or more nominations in a riding.[3]

The profile of a riding has a mainly qualitative impact on the appeal of a nomination. Candidates with a public profile seem to be attracted to nominations in ridings that have a history of sending high-profile candidates to Ottawa and that have been regularly represented by cabinet ministers. As party strategists believe that reports of a strong performance in these ridings – in terms of finding good candidates and running a competitive campaign – can help the party elsewhere, they often encourage this trend.

In general, city ridings tend to have a higher profile than either suburban or country ridings. This is so for a number of reasons. Many of the institutions and infrastructures of social life and communications are located in city ridings. Important political, business, cultural, and sporting events have their focus in such centres. For example, influential news media are based in large metropolitan centres and find it easy to elicit comments from local candidates. Because of the centrality and cosmopolitan nature of these ridings, local candidates are drawn into wider debates, and they and their politics are projected well outside the riding via the major news media that report their comments. They may become either the informal or formal spokespeople for their parties, as did the major party candidates John Brewin, Geoff Young, and Michael O'Connor in Victoria.

Some individuals – notably those with a public profile – are attracted by the opportunity to play such a leading role in the media and their own party. Because parties can be expected to want high-profile candidates in these ridings, they may try to ensure this type of candidate wins by limiting competition for the nomination. So although high-profile ridings may be more appealing to candidates, nominations in these ridings are often uncontested because of efforts by party strategists to ensure a particular candidate wins their party's nomination. Good examples are the nomination of NDP president Johanna den Hertog and ex-provincial MLA Kim Campbell in Vancouver Centre.

Unlike their city counterparts, country and suburban nominations rarely have a profile outside of the local riding. Of the two, rural nominations seem to have a greater notoriety within local communities. Self-contained rural ridings have a basic level of local media and often have a more coherent sense of themselves. Local nomination contests and campaigns have a public profile and attract candidates well known in the local community. Thus, nominations in country ridings such as Kootenay West-Revelstoke and Okanagan Centre are very prominent in the local media.

Suburban ridings on the other hand often have very few local media organizations, and associations find it difficult to gain the attention of city-based outlets. This lack of a mechanism for generating publicity combined with a self-image based on the nebulous set of characteristics associated with suburbia can mean these nominations are lost in the preelection hubbub of a big city. In Surrey North, local newspaper editors could not always name the major party candidates two years after the election. On occasion, the intensity of previous electoral contests, a high-profile candidate, or a controversial nomination attracts the attention of the city media. As a result, some suburban contests are plucked from obscurity. Liberal and Conservative nominations in Svend Robinson's riding of Burnaby-Kingsway fell into this category, in part as a result of his high public profile. So too did those 1993 Liberal nominations in which Jean Chrétien intervened in favour of his preferred candidate.

Ideology
Party ideology also has a largely qualitative impact on the appeal of a nomination. Nominations in any one party are appealing to some people but repel others. Such limits on who is likely to run in a nomination obviously have profound implications for the type of candidates that are likely to be successful in nominations in a particular party. The main divide in Canada is between mass and cadre-style parties. Unionists are more likely to run

for the mass-party New Democrats than are business managers; the reverse is true for the cadre-style Conservatives and Liberals.

As well as this general effect, there is also a more localized or riding effect, which shapes the sorts of candidates that contest nominations. It is noticeable that candidates in city ridings speak to a wider range of often national issues and appear to be more liberal about social policy than their country counterparts. Candidates in country ridings often focus primarily on local economic issues. To some degree then, local concerns may cut across party lines, foreshortening the ideological distance between the associations and candidates of different parties in that riding. Tory Kim Campbell was closer to her New Democrat opponent Johanna den Hertog in Vancouver Centre on the question of abortion than she was with many other candidates from her own party. The NDP candidate in Kootenay West-Revelstoke, Lyle Kristiansen, shared the concerns of his Conservative opponent Bob Brisco about local economic development, and had relatively little interest in the social policy issues that fascinated den Hertog. These differences have their roots in local economic and social circumstances that shape riding agendas, and influence the types of candidates that are attracted to nominations or sought out by associations. City ridings might attract candidates interested in social policy and with a liberal predisposition, while country nominations attract those interested in local economic development with a somewhat more conservative bent.

A special case of the role of ideology are the insurgent campaigns run by interest groups. If a party – notably the governing party, for it can be held responsible for public policy outcomes – has failed to live up to its promises, interest groups may target its nominations with their own candidates. All the contested Conservative nominations in this study experienced insurgent nomination campaigns by pro-life candidates backed by organized interest groups. In fact, pro-life candidates won nominations in both Burnaby-Kingsway and Surrey North. In NDP associations, battles between candidates supported by groupings of unionists, feminists, or environmentalists were common.

Competitiveness, riding profile, and ideology determine nomination appeal directly and indirectly. This appeal is important in flushing out candidates. But wanting to be a candidate is not always enough to ensure an individual will gain access to a nomination. Heightened association competitiveness and greater appeal do not always produce nominations that have large numbers of candidates. Sometimes access to a nomination is restricted because the organizational structure of the association repels potential candidates, or party members make an effort to limit the number of candidates.

Association Permeability

Permeability refers to the ease with which potential candidates and new members can gain access to an association and positions of influence within it. The less permeable an association, the less likely it is that potential candidates will see a means by which they can gain access to the nomination or the critical resources needed to win it. All things being equal, the more permeable an association, the greater the number of candidates that contest the nomination.

Prospective candidates thinking of entering a nomination will attempt to assess their chances of winning. If there are few existing members, it may seem possible to sign up enough new recruits to ensure a majority at the nomination meeting. If there is a sizeable coterie of members, the potential candidate must consider his or her chances of garnering the support of existing members, or overcoming them with new recruits. Anything that makes existing members suspicious of outsiders, or makes it difficult for candidates to recruit new members in order to win the nomination, has a negative impact on entry into the contest, meaning fewer candidates are likely to enter the nomination.

Given that the formal rules governing membership are usually promiscuous (Carty and Erickson 1991, 112), the organizational style of a local association is critical in determining its permeability. The main determinant of this is the organizational ethos of the party. As well, factors that affect the strength and continuity of an association and its capacity to develop rules of behaviour – such as its electoral performance and changing riding boundaries – can also influence its permeability. The restructuring of associations following changes to riding boundaries is likely to weaken them and alter their permeability. This can be offset if the new boundaries strengthen the electoral position and membership of an association.

Mass versus Cadre-Style Parties

Mass parties such as the NDP expect candidates and members in general to display a relatively high level of commitment to the party (Ward 1964, 191; Young 1983, 92; Morley 1984). This expectation raises barriers to potential candidates, increasing the impermeability of NDP associations. On the other hand, cadre-style parties such as the Liberals and Conservatives expect less of potential candidates and new recruits, which eases access to their nominations.

The impermeability of NDP associations is a corollary of the party's commitment to organizational solidarity that is rooted in the very nature of mass parties. The party's links with the union movement serve to highlight the importance of solidarity, the central principle of unionism. This commitment finds expression in the continuous existence of many New

Democrat associations. Members share a sense of comradeship, and as with any community, the rules of behaviour that develop help them distinguish themselves from outsiders. Local New Democrat associations often share members and organizational arrangements with their provincial and municipal counterparts in the party, and members may work on provincial and municipal elections interposed between federal elections. Because of this continuity, NDP associations make longer term demands of their members.[4] These demands can be very intense, particularly when, as was true for this study, there is a coincidence of elections at two different levels of government, in this case, municipal and federal.

Members of associations that exhibit a high degree of solidarity are likely to have a well-defined and shared definition of politics. They look for nomination candidates among existing members and consider service to the association or the union movement to be a prerequisite for both entering and winning the nomination. Because it is expected that candidates be members in good standing, NDP nominations are more often contested among existing party members than either Liberal or Conservative nominations. In fact, all the New Democrat election candidates in this study had worked for the party and/or the union movement, whereas eight of the fourteen successful Tory and Liberal candidates had only recently become party members.

Candidates contemplating contesting such a nomination face a membership that often has its own, exclusionary, definition of a preferred candidate. If they fall outside this definition, they can expect to gain little support from existing members. In this case, the only route available to the would-be candidate is to recruit enough new members to overcome the existing membership. They may find signing new recruits to an NDP association that has a history of demanding high levels of commitment from its members quite difficult in comparison to signing members to cadre-style associations that regularly expand and contract in size, and expect only a small fraction of new members to be actively involved in running the association. Such nominations are unlikely to appeal to insurgent candidates.[5] Even marginally competitive NDP associations can be less permeable than their Liberal and Conservative counterparts, particularly in provinces where the NDP is strong.

Even strong Tory associations seem organizationally loose in comparison with NDP associations. In Surrey North, despite a history of success before the riding boundaries were changed in 1987, there was no formal effort to construct a Tory association until the time came to organize the nomination. In contrast, the local NDP association had been organizing for nearly a year. This pattern was repeated in other ridings.

Although not linked via a permanent association, members of cadre-style parties are often interconnected through a range of other social institutions. This allows members to stay in touch between elections when there is no effective association. In British Columbia, the membership of the Socreds provides such a forum for some Liberal and Tory activists. In Victoria, both the Liberal and Conservative candidates relied on acquaintances from the Socred party to help run their campaigns. In the Okanagan, where there are many active Conservative supporters, the local association was a collection of individuals who interacted in many other forums, such as the local chamber of commerce and even local sporting clubs. The Tory association is simply the particular form these relations take at election time. When Tex Enemark decided to run for the Liberals in Vancouver Centre, he called on a group of friends in the local business community who knew each other and had been Liberal members in the past, rather than rely on the weak Vancouver Centre Liberal association.

Association Continuity

Whether because of electoral success or organizational commitment, association continuity plays a key role in the development of the informal norms of behaviour that can repel outside candidates, increasing the impermeability of an association. Conversely, anything that disrupts the organizational life of an association, such as changes to constituency boundaries, may well increase its permeability.

The persistence of NDP associations between elections rests on the belief in the value of organization commonly found in mass parties. This gives members time to build up a repertoire of organizational norms of behaviour, such as expectations as to what constitutes a good candidate. Given the importance of organization in mass parties, evidence of a long-term commitment to party work is likely to be a prerequisite for success, thus increasing the impermeability of the association. In general, cadre-style associations are less likely to build such strong organizational mores and to expect potential candidates to have exhibited long-term commitment to the party, and are thus more permeable.

Competitive associations are often larger and stronger than their uncompetitive counterparts and more likely to persist between elections, providing an opportunity for members to influence the form of the nomination process. This is true for both cadre-style and mass-party associations (Carty 1991a, 30-9, 110-7; Carty and Erickson 1991, 116-29). But while competitiveness heightens the existing impermeability of mass-party associations, it is often the main cause of impermeability in cadre-style associations. Such associations regularly have a small coterie of long-term members with shared beliefs and idiosyncratic modes of organizational behaviour. The association revives quickly from the relative dormancy of the interelection period to place its imprimatur on the nomination process. Thus, experienced members in strong Liberal and Conservative associations act as gatekeepers for the nomination process. They decide on the formal and informal rules that govern the nomination, such as whether there will be a search committee and how it will be organized. As cadre-style party members are often uncertain of the rules of the game, since they are not exposed to them on a regular basis (compared with members in the NDP), they defer to more experienced members. This is consistent with the greater use of informal search committees in Liberal and Tory associations.

The greater impermeability of competitive associations may be balanced by their heightened appeal, which encourages potential candidates to make great efforts to gain access to these nominations. Competitiveness can offset the impact of even high levels of impermeability, making nominations in different parties appear more similar. But being larger, they present a greater challenge to a candidate who may have to recruit new members in order to overcome the existing membership at a nomination meeting.

Associations with incumbents are special instances of strong local organizations (Carty 1991a, 39-42). While formally separate, the MP's constituency office and the local party organization are often closely connected. Membership lists and other resources important to the local association can be held at the MP's office. This brings some interelection continuity to the life of the association. In contrast to loosely organized associations, these resources are readily mobilized when an election is announced. As well, incumbents have a vested interest in making the association less permeable in order to restrict access to the nomination, and may try to ensure that supporters hold important positions in the association. This combination makes for relatively impermeable associations, even in cadre-style parties. Nevertheless, the formal independence of associations means that local party members are not beholden to an incumbent. Although not common, incumbents are regularly challenged for the party nomination, as was Bob Wenman in Fraser Valley West.

Uncompetitive associations always struggle to maintain some formal structures. Through most of the 1980s, the Liberal association in Kootenay West-Revelstoke did not exist. The NDP and Conservatives divided the political spectrum in two. Local doctor Garry Jenkins managed to sign up enough new members to create an association. But there were few formal structures, and the association was an extension of Jenkins's personality. He went on to run as its candidate.

Changes in local electoral boundaries disrupt the life of local associations. This can seriously weaken associations, breaking up teams of members who have worked on a number of elections and putting together members who are unfamiliar to each other. Moreover, rearranging members and financial resources can lead to bitter disputes and may distract members from the task of organizing a nomination. The patterns of behaviour that directed the organization of the nomination and helped dictate access to the contest are lost, making it more permeable. Liberals in the Fraser Valley complained about the way in which assets were divided among the new associations in the area following the redrawing of boundaries. They felt this division had increased the association's vulnerability to insurgent candidates.

The retirement of an incumbent can likewise upset local associations and alter their permeability. Local Tory organizer Bea Holland notes this effect in Victoria: "In part, the ability of the pro-life candidate to recruit new members and nearly win the nomination was due to the uncertainty created by the retirement of our incumbent Allan McKinnon." The direction once provided by the incumbent and his office was lost, leaving a competitive association vulnerable to insurgent candidates. The disruption caused by candidates recruiting many new members not only caught the association off guard, reducing its ability to direct events, but it also meant that the dynamics of the nomination meeting favoured those candidates who could rely on well-organized support during the early ballots. Insurgent candidates backed by interest groups have just this sort of support.

Any strengthening or weakening of the organizational structures of local associations alters their permeability. Events that affect the persistence of associations between elections are particularly important, for continuity permits the development of the patterns of behaviour that determine permeability. Given that the continuity of mass-party associations such as those of the NDP is rooted in their organizational style, it is not surprising that variations in permeability due to other factors such as competitiveness are more apparent in the more loosely organized cadre-style Liberal and Conservative associations.

The permeability of a nomination directly affects both the type and number of candidates who seek nomination. The candidates who contest impermeable nominations usually have some standing within the association and have demonstrated their commitment to the party. They are likely to be experienced political activists. Nominations in permeable cadre-style associations are much more attractive to insurgent candidates. Moreover, these organizations are less inclined to demand proof of commitment to the party. As a result, permeable associations are much more likely to select nominees who have had little contact with the party.

Candidate Search

A formal candidate search process allows an association to exercise some control over which aspiring candidates gain access to their nomination. But for a variety of reasons, not every association conducts a candidate search, and those that do may approach the task in different ways. The criteria for selecting candidates may focus on their electability – taking account of factors such as personal charisma, ability, and capacity to finance and operate a good campaign – and their suitability in terms of their attitudes, beliefs, and, on occasion, other personal characteristics. These criteria are usually unrestrictive, but there are times when associations are highly selective and attempt to attract a certain type of candidate. This is true of the NDP's recent efforts to encourage women to run as candidates (Carty and Erickson 1991, 149), and where leaders or party elites intervene to ensure that a certain candidate is successful. The use of a search, the style it takes, and the criteria it uses to select candidates depend on the competitiveness of the association, its commitment to structures that demonstrate internal party democracy (which varies from mass to cadre-style parties), and the role of nonlocal party strategists in the process.

Competitive Associations
Competitive, strong associations have greater resources with which to mount a candidate search than do uncompetitive associations, and their wide contacts in the local community help them identify potential candidates. Associations with a long history of running second may also be able to make a credible claim that their candidate will win the election, and use this to attract candidates. Uncompetitive associations, which are usually organizationally weak, may lack the members and resources to mount a search. The task is often left to one or two members of the executive, who call around in an attempt to find someone to run for the nomination. And because this weakness is usually a direct result of electoral failure, these associations have limited access to the local community and little appeal to potential candidates.

Given that competitive associations are larger and better organized, their candidate searches tend to be more thorough than those of their uncompetitive cousins. Competitive associations usually have good access to the sources of power and influence in a riding and the social circles from which candidates are often drawn. This improves their chances of identifying candidates and convincing them to run. As well, they can afford to be more demanding in their definition of what constitutes a suitable candidate. In some cases, particularly in competitive, permeable associations such as the Surrey North and Okanagan Centre Tories, a search is a formality, as large numbers of candidates are attracted to the nomination.

Sometimes a competitive association defers to an influential party member or local notable and refrains from conducting a search. In Victoria and Vancouver Centre, it was well known that two NDP stalwarts who had contested the seats in 1984 would run again, and this all but eliminated the need for a real candidate search. Similarly, where there is an incumbent, it is uncommon for even a competitive association to organize a candidate search, though some do.

In the case of a retiring incumbent, he or she may prefer to be seen handing the reins to a well-qualified successor. Often, the MP – or representatives of the party or local constituency office – coordinate the search for such a candidate. Given that incumbents tend to have developed strong connections to the national party and party strategists, it is not uncommon for nonlocal officials to be involved in such a search and to bring national party objectives to bear on it. On the other hand, they usually have good contacts among the local political elite. This may result in a search for a high-profile candidate who is promised easy access to the nomination, the resources of the retiring incumbent, and perhaps the party at large with which to conduct a campaign. This severely restricts access to the nomination. In Victoria, retiring Tory Allan McKinnon tried hard to find a candidate, but the Tories' uncertain electoral prospects made his job difficult, and he eventually let the association search for candidates.

Uncompetitive associations often struggle to find candidates. Weak NDP associations do better at organizing nominations than their cadre-style counterparts. In Kootenay West-Revelstoke and Burnaby-Kingsway, the uncompetitive Liberals did not conduct a search, yet the weak NDP association in Fraser Valley West did. Where they do take place, searches in noncompetitive cadre-style associations are modest. In the Okanagan, Murli Pendharkar – not a member of any party – was one of a few candidates asked to run by the handful of local Liberals. Where weak associations are unable to find a candidate, the party organization may have to provide one.

While competitive associations are usually better organized than their uncompetitive counterparts and should be more capable of instituting a candidate search, overall, this is not the case. Partisan organizational styles affect the propensity of associations to search out candidates.

Mass versus Cadre-Style Associations

Competitive cadre Liberal and Conservative associations tend to organize fewer searches than might be expected, while even uncompetitive NDP associations often organize candidate searches (Carty and Erickson 1991, Tables 3.17 and 3.42). This is the result of the tendency among cadre-style associations to rely on informal searches, and the NDP's greater commitment to the formal institutions of association democracy.

Because of their commitment to local democracy and institutional modes of behaviour, New Democrat associations make greater use of formal search committees than do Liberal and Conservative associations, even in uncompetitive associations. As well, the manner in which these committees operate differs as a result of the distinctive organizational styles of mass and cadre parties. NDP search committees are more formalized, their work is supervised by the local executive, and they often use selection criteria that favour existing members over insurgents.

Not surprisingly, all the NDP candidates in the ridings in this study were party members in good standing. This is less true in cadre-style associations, where there is often no overview of the process by the local executive or clear guidelines as to how it should be conducted. Being less formal, well-organized Liberal and Conservative associations may find it easier to adopt very strict criteria simply by agreement among the few executive members who are conducting a relatively informal candidate search not subject to any form of public scrutiny.

The strength of the NDP's commitment to forming search committees somewhat independently of their competitive positions is seen in the fact that 44 percent of its associations report having a regular candidate search committee, while 25 percent of Liberal and 17 percent of Tory associations did likewise (Carty 1991a, Table 5.2). When associations with incumbents are removed, the percentage of associations reporting having used search committees is 70, 54, and 51 respectively (Carty and Erickson 1991, Table 3.42). This pattern was evident in all seven ridings in this study. The use of search committees in even uncompetitive NDP associations inflates the number of total contested nominations found in uncompetitive associations.

Given that they tend to have stable memberships, New Democrat associations are usually successful in identifying potential candidates within their own ranks. Even in ridings such as Okanagan Centre, where they had little chance of success, the party was able to identify several good candidates. This reinforces the impermeability of NDP nominations. It also increases the number of NDP associations that produce contested nominations. Only occasionally do New Democrat associations look outside their membership for candidates, and then only if an association wishes to select a high-profile candidate or to meet some wider objective set by the party. Even then, New Democrat associations in British Columbia are connected to a network of party faithful and fellow travellers interested in political office from which candidates can be drawn. Despite their ideological commitment to inclusive politics, this impermeability explains why NDP associations often have fewer links to groups in the local community than do their cadre-style counterparts.[6]

For their part, associations in the cadre-style Liberal and Conservative Parties are more inclined to use a loose collection of experienced local members to pursue an informal search. Because these parties account for most of the competitive associations in Canada, this tendency deflates the number of competitive associations that make use of formal search committees. Competitive cadre-style associations are also almost always permeable. Given that they appeal to many prospective candidates and do not obstruct the candidates' entry into the contest, these associations may not need to make much of an effort to search out candidates. As well, associations in the more successful Liberal and Conservative Parties account for most cases of retiring incumbents who may try to install a successor by suppressing competition for the nomination. This is seen in the weak correlation between electoral competitiveness and the use of formal search committees (Carty and Erickson 1991).

Cadre-style associations often reach beyond their local membership in search of suitable candidates. On occasion, nonlocal party officials encourage this to fulfil a wider strategic objective. Local organizers may believe that the right candidate can win the riding and that no current association member fits this bill. Given the cyclical nature of membership, and the relative lack of solidarity among members of these associations, associations are less likely to define the suitability of candidates in terms of demonstrated commitment to the party. Insurgent candidates influence the character of open searches for candidates in cadre-style parties. They can recruit new members and in so doing overcome any resistance from existing members. It is not surprising that over half of the Liberal and Conservative candidates in this study were new party members.

But there are drawbacks to the loose organizational style of cadre associations. An insurgent candidate who is hostile to the members of a permeable association may hijack the nomination. Informal searches organized by a group of powerful association members may use narrow criteria for selecting candidates and act to limit competition for the nomination. And the lack of an imperative to conduct a formal and accountable search allows cadre-style associations to adopt just such a search regime. Carty notes that 40 percent of association presidents nationwide report that an insider group decided who the candidate would be and worked to get that individual nominated. In 61 percent of these cases, the candidate was acclaimed, compared with just 44 percent in nominations where no such elite manipulation occurred (1991a, 110-1). Finally, uncompetitive cadre-style associations often experience uncontested nominations because they lack the imperative to organize a search, and, unlike NDP associations, they cannot always rely on members to run as candidates.

Competitiveness and partisan organizational style help determine the likelihood that an association will conduct a search and the style that search takes. A minimal level of competitiveness allows associations to organize a search, but it is no guarantee that there will be one. Because of their organizational style, competitive, permeable associations in cadre-style parties tend to adopt informal search processes, or eschew them altogether. This is not true for NDP associations, which have a greater propensity to organize formal searches irrespective of their competitiveness.

In all parties, the presence of an incumbent or preferred candidate stifles candidate searches.

Nonlocal Interference

The intervention of regional and national strategists may also shape the search process. The rare instances of direct interference in riding affairs by nonlocal party officials occur mainly where a local association has little appeal for potential candidates and is too weak to organize an effective candidate search (Carty and Erickson 1991, Table 3.17).[7] In fewer cases, it is the result of some strategic calculation by the party in ridings where it believes a local campaign, or perhaps its wider national campaign, would benefit from having a particular type of candidate. Party strategists believe that running a good candidate in a high-profile riding helps the local and national campaigns. A party may wish to have a certain number of women as a matter of principle, or a number of high-profile candidates for its cabinet if it wins office. Or it may move to protect an incumbent from losing a nomination (or even being challenged) or attempt to ensure an insurgent candidate supported by an interest group does not win a nomination.

In most cases of nonlocal involvement, party officials work with local associations to find candidates. Very occasionally, a party leader vetoes a candidacy by refusing to allow the party label to be used to identify a candidate on the voting ballot. This prevents unwanted but successful candidates from running for the party and may force associations to adopt preferred candidates. The manner in which parties make their wishes known or enforce their preferences, and the experience of local associations in dealing with these demands, vary as a function of the competitive position and organizational style of associations.

There are distinct regional differences in the level of intervention practised by the major parties. Regions where parties have been weak, such as the Atlantic provinces for the NDP and the West for the Liberals, tend to experience high levels of nonlocal interference. NDP headquarters played little role in the selection of candidates in this study. This reflects the strength of NDP associations in British Columbia and their ability to organize formal searches. On the other hand, the Liberal Party had to appoint a young party worker from Quebec, Sam Stevens, as its candidate in Burnaby-Kingsway. The more common form of nonlocal intervention is cooperation between party strategists at various levels in the search for a candidate. In cases where an incumbent is retiring, his or her relationship with the national party facilitates cooperation in the search for a replacement.

Liberal and Conservative nominations in high-profile ridings (in which these parties are usually competitive) often attract the interest of nonlocal party strategists. These ridings usually receive inordinate press attention and may be seen as indicators of a party's general performance. As such, the campaigns that are run in these ridings are often integral components of the national campaign (Sayers 1991, 45). Candidates in these ridings are expected to be adept at dealing with the media and capable of developing a positive image for themselves and the party. National party strategists have an interest in finding good candidates who are offered uncontested rides through their nominations. This requires restricting access to the nomination, which can be done either by fiat – the national party leader can refuse to sign the nomination papers for any other candidate – or through cooperation with the local association.[8] The latter is more common and requires local and nonlocal party members to agree on the preferred type of candidate. This is made easier by the fact that cadre-style Tory and Grit associations regularly pursue informal candidate searches that can be managed in this way. But even the NDP with its commitment to formal internal party processes may use this approach in high-profile ridings, in the hope that the right sort of candidate will assist its cause.

Conservative Kim Campbell and New Democrat Johanna den Hertog in Vancouver Centre benefited from the support of their respective party hierarchies. The parties brought direct and indirect pressure to bear to limit competition for these nominations. Once Campbell agreed to run, the Tory search committee in Centre, made up of local and nonlocal party members, refused to allow other candidates access to the nomination. In den Hertog's case, the difficulty of competing against the party president was compounded by clear signals from leader Ed Broadbent's office that he would prefer den Hertog as a candidate.

The NDP has fewer competitive associations across the country than either the Liberals or Conservatives, and there is less outside interference in the choice of candidates. What interference there is may be driven by principle rather than strategic calculations, such as attempting to have a certain proportion of women and minority candidates (Carty and Erickson 1991, Tables 3.28 and 3.29; Carty 1991a, Table 3.21). Cadre-style parties tend to eschew principled intervention. When they do intervene it is for strategic reasons. Perhaps because of this and a lack of commitment to formal internal party procedures, they appear more willing than the NDP to invoke the leader's veto to impose a preferred candidate. None of the associations in this study had their first choice for nominee vetoed by the party. But in 1993 and 1997, Liberal leader Jean Chrétien used this power (or the threat of veto) to install a number of high-profile candidates across the country. The usual defence offered for this move was that the party needed talented MPs to fill cabinet positions. Less frequent mention was made of any increased chance of winning the ridings into which these candidates were parachuted.

Depending on the objective of the nonlocal interference, it may increase or decrease competition for a nomination. In general, nonlocal involvement occurs more frequently in nominations where there is no contest, but cause and effect are unclear (Carty 1991b, Table 3.49). Weak associations that cannot find a candidate, and which rely on the party to provide one, are included with those where the nonlocal party helps to limit competition for a sought-after nomination to a single candidate. The strategic intervention found most commonly in Liberal and Progressive Conservative associations limits competition. This is because the party elites that intervene in these associations search out specific candidates whom they believe will help their cause in a particular riding. In Victoria, Michael O'Connor, the association president, agreed to a request by his friend Liberal leader John Turner to run for the party.

The NDP's desire to bring underrepresented groups into politics may increase competition for a nomination because those candidates are generally brought into the process without being promised a clear run through the nomination. The relatively formalized relationship between various levels of the party encourages shared definitions of politics and makes local party members more likely to accept the dictates of the party hierarchy. As such, the objectives of the local search usually reflect the preferences of the national executive of the party.

The use of a formal candidate search process depends on the organizational strength of an association and its commitment to guaranteeing access to all association members who wish to enter the race. The manner of the search committee and the criteria it uses determine who has access to the nomination. Formal search committees in NDP associations focus on attracting existing members, while those in Liberal and Conservative associations are more willing to look outside the association for candidates. The presence of an incumbent, or the desire to find a particular type of candidate – whether local or otherwise – reduces the chances of a formal search and restricts access to the nomination. Weak associations that are poorly organized also struggle to arrange a search and may have to rely on the party to provide a candidate.

Classifying Nominations

The style of a nomination meeting is a function of a set of filters on the nomination process that define the terms of the local contest. By setting the criteria for entry to and success at the nomination, these filters determine whether there is a contest and the type of candidate that wins the nomination. The filters can be grouped into those that influence the appeal a nomination holds for potential candidates and those that determine which candidates have access to the nomination. The particular form these filters take, and the combination in which they are found in any nomination, is largely a function of the competitiveness of the association and its organizational style. Local riding and broader partisan forces shape these factors.

Different types and mixes of these filters result in distinctive types of nominations. Figure 3.1 illustrates four distinct nominations and how the appeal they hold for aspiring candidates and the access these candidates have to the race shape each contest.

The first type of nomination is open and contested. The association is permeable, with few if any restrictions placed on entrance to the nomination. It appeals to prospective candidates and attracts at least two, but usually more, who participate in a true contest. Such nominations are most commonly found in competitive, cadre-style associations.

Figure 3.1

Nomination filters

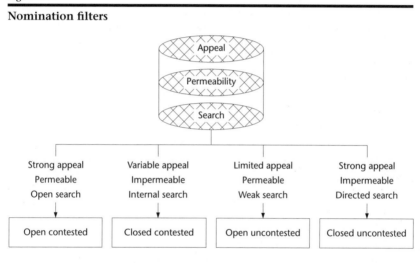

The second type of nomination is closed and contested. Candidates from outside the association are rare or nonexistent in these contests. Those candidates who do enter the race are mostly long-time association members and may be representatives of factions within the local association. Because the nomination has some appeal and attracts several candidates, it is also a real contest. Most of these nominations are found in impermeable NDP associations. But even here, the more competitive the association, the more contested the nomination.

A third type of nomination is open but uncontested or nominally contested. These nominations have difficulty attracting candidates but are open to anyone willing to run. Where more than one candidate enters the race, one-sided nominations often occur in which only one candidate has a real chance of winning. In some cases, this third type of nomination attracts no candidates, and the party must appoint a party worker to run in the riding. In general, uncompetitive cadre-style associations are more prone to these sorts of nominations because they do not have the organizational cohesiveness found in even weak NDP associations.

And the fourth type is a closed and uncontested nomination. Despite being very attractive to potential candidates, only one candidate is allowed access to the contest by nomination organizers. Nonlocal party strategists are often involved in helping to find such candidates. On very rare occasions, more than one candidate gains access to the nomination, but the result is one-sided. The winner is usually a high-profile candidate who benefits from the support of the local and often nonlocal party elite. These nominations occur in competitive associations in high-profile ridings. While it is true that they take place in all parties, cadre-style associations tend to be more susceptible because of their proclivity to conduct informal searches that are better suited to ensuring that a single candidate gains access to the nomination process.

Summary: Four Archetypal Nominations

Candidate nominations in Canadian politics reflect the idiosyncratic confluence of local riding factors and broader partisan influences. Nominations are distinctive but can be understood by taking account of the impact of these factors on the appeal of a nomination and the access candidates have to it. In this way, a single nomination acts as a lens with which to view local and nonlocal party organizational and electoral conditions.

Appeal reflects the competitive position of an association and its ideological complexion. Judgments about the competitive position of an association are not unproblematic; changing boundaries, the fortunes of the wider party, the unrealistic expectations of party members, and the volatility of the Canadian electorate must all be taken into account. Ideological judgments may be more certain, but it is still the case that there is variation within any one party, and associations may be idiosyncratic in the emphasis they give to party beliefs. This may affect the sorts of candidates that are attracted to a particular nomination. On the whole, however, unionists will be disproportionately attracted to the NDP while managers to the Tories.

Access to the nomination process is a function of the permeability of the association and the manner in which the candidate search is conducted. The permeability of an association is related to its competitiveness and organizational ethos. Competitive associations tend to be better organized, and therefore less permeable than uncompetitive ones. Factors that alter competitiveness also alter permeability. Mass-party associations have a greater commitment to organizational solidarity and continuity than their cadre-style cousins, and thus tend to be less permeable than the latter. This is reflected in candidate searches as well. While any competitive association is more able to organize a search, mass parties have a greater commitment to ensuring such internal party organizational processes are followed than do cadre-style parties. The latter may adopt informal means for finding candidates. Furthermore, mass parties are much more likely to look for candidates from among party members who have proven their commitment to the cause than are cadre-style parties.

Understanding the functioning of appeal and access in nominating candidates places factors such as the fortunes of the major parties, changing electoral boundaries, and voter volatility in a new light, and offers a means for explaining the persistence of a Canadian political tradition – the importance of local factors in a relatively stable party system (the election of 1993 notwithstanding); that is, the capacity for parties and the party system to absorb and respond to local politics. Associations and nominations are well adapted to the task of balancing the imperatives of local and partisan politics.

The four archetypal nominations – open and contested, closed and contested, open but uncontested, and closed and uncontested – produce distinctive types of candidates that each attract a particular constellation of supporters. Together they form the basis of the local campaign team that is a key element of any local campaign. In balancing local and national political forces and selecting candidates, associations and nominations play a central role in Canadian electoral politics. The next chapter looks more closely at how nominations shape local campaigns in this way.

4
Nominations and Democracy

Each of the four types of nominations discussed in the previous chapter produces a distinctive form of association democracy as shown in Table 4.1. Open and contested nominations are found in associations that are competitive, permeable, with a permissive candidate search. With few if any constraints on entry, the competitiveness of the association is a main determinant of the contestedness of the nomination. Most such contests occur in cadre-style Liberal and Conservative associations. The recruitment drives of aspiring candidates produce explosive growth in the size of Liberal and Progressive Conservative associations around election time (Carty 1991a, Table 5.3) and large, rambunctious nomination meetings. Their large size in combination with the organizational style of cadre parties limits the opportunities for an insider clique to control the nomination. This results in a robust form of local democracy.

Table 4.1

Nominations and constituency-association democracy

	Competition	
Access	Contested	Uncontested
Open	Local democracy	Latent democracy
Closed	Party democracy	Limited democracy

The second form of contested nomination is closed. This occurs in associations that are usually competitive but that are organizationally impermeable. The candidate search process is formalized, and access to these nominations is restricted to association members who have demonstrated their commitment to the party. These nominations are found mainly in the associations of mass parties such as the NDP. Being well organized, even marginally competitive mass-party associations may manage to find a number of candidates and experience contested nominations. Because the nomination is very much an internal process, recruitment of members during these nominations tends to be muted. While on occasion several factions within the association put forward their own candidates – which can produce sharp contests – nomination meetings are more restrained than in open associations. These nominations thus exhibit a form of party democracy.

Open but uncontested nominations occur in weak associations that are very permeable and, being weak, cannot organize a formal search process. There may be an informal search by a few association executive members. While access to the nomination is straightforward, the association is uncompetitive and thus unappealing to most candidates. There is little or no membership recruitment by candidates, and the nomination meeting is usually low-key. In cases where no candidate can be enticed to run, the party may have to provide a candidate from outside the association. Of the ridings studied, Liberal associations account for most of the nominations in this category. This reflects the difficulties faced by the party in British Columbia. As the reduced competition for these nominations is not manufactured for some strategic purpose but is a function of the circumstances of the association, these nominations are a form of evanescent or latent democracy. That is, they might well be contested if the association were more competitive.

Finally, closed and uncontested nominations occur only in associations that have the desire and ability to restrict their nomination to one candidate. The association is likely to be competitive and appeal to potential candidates. This category includes associations that renominate an incumbent. The candidate search restricts access to just one candidate, though there may be a list of potential candidates who are approached before one is chosen. This intensive, often informal, procedure is conducted by local executive members and may involve nonlocal party strategists who believe their party benefits from running a particular type of candidate in the riding. Associations in this group that do not have incumbents are usually in high-profile ridings, many of which are in urban centres. Because of the lack of a real contest, the nomination does not drive recruitment to the association. The nomination meeting is a staged affair designed to avoid conflict and show off the candidate to the media. It is an exercise in limited democracy.

In choosing a nominee, nomination meetings are also harbingers of the type of election campaign a party will run in a riding. The type of candidate that is successful and the support he or she receives profoundly affects local campaigns. The personal attributes of the candidate are the pillar around which a campaign often constructs its fund-raising and strategic plan. Its ability to implement this plan is a function of the human and financial resources at its command. These are determined largely by the kinds of support a candidate receives in winning a nomination. The rest of this chapter explores the forms of democracy found in nominations and the implications they have for local campaigns. It suggests that to understand how local campaigns are run, it is necessary to understand how nominations bring candidates and teams of volunteers together.

Local Democracy

Local democracy exists where there are open, contested nominations. Such was the case in the Tory association in Okanagan Centre. Its competitiveness was never in doubt in a region that has consistently sent Conservatives to Ottawa. The nomination process was locally organized and controlled. As a cadre-style association in a newly created riding, the association was very permeable, and it had not settled on a preferred candidate prior to the contest. The changed riding boundaries had disrupted long-standing organizational patterns of membership and resources in local associations, making them more permeable and susceptible to insurgent challengers such as pro-life candidate David Richter.

Richter hoped to sign up enough members to swamp the other candidates at the nomination meeting. This recruitment effort forced the other candidates to follow suit in an effort to stay in the contest. As a result, about 4,000 members were recruited. But Richter's main rival, Al Horning, was nearly as successful at recruiting members as Richter, and was much better known among local Conservatives, the result of a long record of community service. He was widely known as a political moderate with an interest in a range of issues. This not only allowed him to recruit many members but was also critical to his success in lobbying other candidates for support on the second ballot.

Typical of open, contested nominations, the Okanagan meeting was a rambunctious affair. Large numbers of new members, as well as the stress of signing them up, created a highly fluid environment. Members' credentials were challenged and incentives were offered to get new members to attend the meeting. Just over 2,100 members voted at the meeting. Of these voters, a minority were familiar with the formal workings of such meetings. For some, loyalty to a candidate lasted only until the first ballot, and some supporters left the meeting when their candidate was defeated.

Encouraged by the belief that whoever won the Tory nomination would win the subsequent election, many of the candidates ran expensive campaigns. John Keery, a reporter for the Kelowna *Daily Courier,* thought that the campaign of newcomer David Richter was the best organized. Troy Schmidt, an experienced local Conservative who led a group of committed pro-life activists within the association, masterminded Richter's nomination. This team created a carnival atmosphere, playing songs through loudspeakers and offering food and drink to their supporters. Not to be outdone, Al Horning hired public relations expert Brian Lightburn to run his campaign. Although more modest than that of his main opponent, it too was highly effective. Lightburn made good use of his extensive business connections with members of the local Conservative community to rally support for Horning.

Richter led Horning by just 86 votes on the first ballot. The official tally on the first vote had Richter at 791 and Horning at 705, with the next candidate 500 votes back. This was a shock to many association members, particularly those who did not want a single-issue candidate and relative newcomer to win. Horning and his supporters lobbied the other candidates for their support on the second ballot, noting the limited nature of Richter's platform and his lack of history in the riding. These other candidates withdrew from the race, leaving Horning and Richter to battle it out. The public support of these other candidates was enough to give Horning the edge over Richter by 1,038 votes to 809. In recognition of the organizational strength of Richter's campaign, Lightburn asked Richter's campaign manager, Schmidt, to join the campaign team, which he did. In reporting the nomination, the *Daily Courier* reinforced the presumption that the Tory nominee would win the upcoming election by captioning its story of the nomination "Horning headed for Ottawa."

Horning's success is a classic case of local democracy at work. The Tory association was highly competitive and very appealing. Its permeability was such that the two leading candidates and many of their supporters joined the party just prior to the nomination. This permeability was heightened by the instability engendered by new riding boundaries and the uneven organizational presence of the Conservatives in British Columbia. Unlike the NDP, there was relatively little central coordination of activity within the Tory party in the province. Rather, local conditions dictated the form of the nomination. In a newly organized association such as that in Okanagan Centre, there was little chance for members to identify and woo a preferred candidate. Moreover, cadre-style associations do not place the same emphasis on formal searches as do mass parties. The nomination was wide open. Such nominations favour well-known local notables who have good contacts in the community and can rely on family and friends to help organize their nomination bid.

Changing electoral boundaries can make once uncompetitive associations more competitive, or at least appear so. New circumstances offer hope for improved electoral performance, which members are likely to play on to attract candidates, and there is no entrenched party hierarchy bent on restricting access to the nomination. This improves an association's appeal to candidates, may encourage members to seek out candidates, and can lead to an open, contested nomination. The impact of new boundaries in the Okanagan can be seen in all local nominations. Even the new Reform Party attracted three candidates and 300 members.[1]

Members of the previously moribund Liberal association in the riding came to believe that the riding would elect a Liberal member. They even managed to organize a formal search for candidates – an achievement for any Liberal association west of the Rockies. The new association was permeable, and the nomination wide open. Other than a desire to find a well-known individual to run for the party, the search committee did not attempt to define precisely the sort of candidate it wished to attract. It approached a number of local notables, informing them that the new electoral circumstances favoured the Liberal Party. They were successful in attracting three candidates to the race. One of these, Murli Pendharkar – a well-known ex-school superintendent and a one-time New Democrat supporter – considered the matter for several months. When about fifty of his friends pledged their support at a meeting he called in late 1987, Pendharkar decided that his chances of winning the nomination, and the level of interest in the Liberal Party, warranted his entering the race.

Pendharkar had never been a party member but knew that the nomination could be won by recruiting members. He did this, making use of his contacts within the local Indo-Canadian community. With the other two candidates recruiting as well, the association grew to about 780 members. Over 500 voters attended the nomination meeting in June of the election year. Pendharkar took 278 votes on the first ballot to become the nominee, with his nearest opponent about 100 votes behind. There was some tension within the association over Pendharkar's success in gaining control of the nomination with strong support from the local Indo-Canadian community. But he was the sort of well-known local that the party had hoped to entice into running for the riding.

The number of ballots needed to select a nominee determines the logic of success at a nomination meeting. Heavy recruitment is often critical if a candidate is to win on the first ballot. Winning on subsequent ballots may require the additional support of long-time party members and the recruits of other candidates. The more ballots needed, the greater the value of the coalition-building abilities of experienced candidates and association members in comparison to the recruiting abilities of candidates. In particular, superior coalition-building abilities are needed to overcome insurgent candidates who may have recruited the largest single group of supporters. Victory goes to the candidate – such as Tory nominee Al Horning in Okanagan Centre – who can convince members recruited by other candidates who drop out of the race to stay, and then attract their support. This type of nominee requires wide popular support within the association. A high profile either in the local community or among association members is crucial to success.

Because recruitment is so important in open, contested nominations, the ability to sign up members, particularly among organized groups in the community, can play a pivotal role in determining the outcome. Successful recruiting of members by any candidate forces the others to follow suit. Even candidates who have been long-time members and who have strong support within the association must conduct a recruitment drive to avoid being swamped at the nomination meeting. Consequently, the relationship between the candidate and the local community and interest groups can be critical to victory. Candidates often woo the leaders of groups in the hope that they can deliver support from among their members (Scarrow 1964, 55). Candidates who are leaders in their local community, such as Pendharkar, have a special advantage in this regard. So too do those affiliated with interest groups.

If a recruitment drive develops into a contest, there is plenty of room for conflict, and open, contested nominations often exhibit all the acrimony of an election campaign. This is particularly true if any candidate manages to obtain the support of an interest group or a segment of an ethnic minority. In particular, long-time members may feel they are losing control of their association to new recruits, while the latter resent attempts to control the process by the old hands and are concerned only with the simple calculus of popular democracy. Being permeable, cadre-style associations are susceptible to this type of insurgent candidate.

In Surrey North, some of Cliff Blair's opponents for the Tory nomination were unhappy with his recruitment of Indo-Canadians and pro-life activists. Burnaby-Kingsway Tory candidate John Bitonti used his extensive contacts in the local Italian community to recruit members. He too had support from pro-life activists. Bitonti felt that his victory over the association secretary in this way alienated members who might otherwise have worked on the local campaign.

In some cases, community groups offer their own candidates up for selection.[2] These candidates then have access to a ready-made pool of supporters from which to sign up members. In the Fraser Valley, an association member with links to the pro-life movement challenged Tory MP Bob Wenman for the nomination.

The retirement of an incumbent opens up a nomination and often produces local democracy. The retirement of Tory MP Allan McKinnon provided a nomination in an association that, despite facing a worsening electoral situation, was well financed and retained electoral appeal. McKinnon failed in his attempts to install by acclamation a candidate from among local luminaries. One such possible candidate, former provincial cabinet minister Brian Smith, thought the Tories would lose the seat. The nomination process was thrown wide open, and beyond the association's direct control. Local strategists believed they had a better chance of electoral success if they avoided nominating local councillors and high-profile business people. However, they were unsuccessful in this regard, and two councillors, one from Victoria (a high-profile businessman) and another from Saanich, entered the race along with four other candidates. Local businessman Geoff Young won the nomination on the third ballot.

While competitive, permeable, cadre-style associations are capable of running candidate searches, their appeal helps them attract candidates and undercuts some of the need for a search. Moreover, they do not have the commitment to formal organizational structures such as search committees nor the ideological consistency found in mass parties, and are therefore not as inclined to impose a definition of a preferred type of candidate. Where they do impose such a definition, it is likely to be through an informal search process conducted by a group of association insiders. Participants in the Liberal and Conservative nominations generally noted that the association did not seem to have a particular type of candidate in mind (other than in the broad sense of someone whose beliefs were consistent with party policy). Most believed the nomination process had been fair and open.

Historically, the Liberal and Conservative Parties have accounted for most local-democracy-style nominations. These cadre-style parties are permeable, with open searches, and, having usually formed either the government or opposition for the last century, tend to have greater electoral appeal; that is, to be more competitive. Whichever one goes into an election as the major opposition party experiences more such nominations because it has fewer incumbents and a greater number of open nominations. That is, permeable, competitive, cadre-style associations account for most cases of local democracy.

Party Democracy
The internal competition of nominations that exhibit party democracy is synonymous with the relatively impermeable, well-organized associations of mass parties that run closed, contested nominations. Four of seven New Democrat nominations studied were contested compared with only five of the fourteen in Liberal and Conservative associations. This in part reflects the greater number of incumbents in Tory associations and the weakness of many Liberal associations in the group. But it also points to the effectiveness of NDP associations in attracting party members to their nominations. In contrast to the contested Tory and Liberal nominations, which were relatively open, contested NDP nominations were closed. Newcomers won the contested Liberal and Conservative nominations, while long-term party members won all the contested NDP nominations.

New Democrat associations in British Columbia have substantial appeal for party members contemplating nomination. Many associations are highly competitive, and the provincial party is well organized and has extensive political expertise and resources. The feeling that the NDP would do well at the Tories' expense in British Columbia added to the appeal of its nominations. Although search committees were organized in most NDP associations, there were usually a number of members willing to run for the nomination. No NDP nomination was uncontested because of a lack of interest.

In Surrey North, Okanagan Centre, and Kootenay West-Revelstoke, NDP associations experienced hotly contested nominations that produced internal conflict. In each case, changing electoral boundaries created ridings that gave the party a chance of winning (or doing well in) a seat it did not hold. Surrey North and Okanagan Centre were new ridings and offered local associations a chance to take advantage of this break in local political history. In the Kootenays, the addition of Revelstoke to the Tory-held riding of Kootenay West gave the NDP a real chance of beating the incumbent. Unlike Liberal and Conservative associations, the more permanent NDP associations quickly reassigned the assets and members of old associations to the new ones produced by the 1987 changes to federal electoral boundaries. This continuity, and the assistance of a powerful provincial party, helped NDP associations organize for the election.

Internal competition in NDP nominations reflects in part the development of informal factions within associations. These groups coalesce around issues such as feminism, unionism, and environmentalism. Factions may each enter a candidate in the nomination race. Here, the candidates' strategic goal is not recruitment but gaining support from long-time members and bolstering the organizational strength of sympathetic factions. This accounts for the reduced recruitment found in NDP associations (Carty 1991a, 111-7). This nomination strategy favours candidates who have built up some organizational credibility in the party. This is in stark contrast to the more volatile, often outsider, insurgent groups that support candidates in open, contested nomination, and which provoke vigorous recruitment drives.

New Democrat candidate search committees reinforce the bias towards members with a record of extensive work in the party or union movement. And given that NDP associations are more likely to have formal search committees than their cadre-style cousins, the exclusion of outsiders is more common. The nomination meetings produced under these conditions are often smaller in terms of voters, though not candidates, than those in their openly contested counterparts. But they can be just as fractious and acrimonious if factional candidates square off against each other.

In Okanagan Centre, the New Democrat nomination involved a spirited and sometimes bitter contest between the two leading candidates, each supported by a faction within the local association. The 250 members who attended the meeting divided into two camps: one consisting mainly of older union members, and the other of younger environmentalists. The selection of Bryan McIver as its nominee, a local insurance broker and relative newcomer who had once been a Conservative Party member, was a win for the second of these two groups. The outcome was not popular with many long-standing members, in part because of McIver's chequered partisan background.

In the NDP association in Kootenay West-Revelstoke, the addition of unionists from Revelstoke as a result of newly drawn boundaries strengthened the hand of the union faction against those members who would have put environmental and other issues at the top of the association agenda. As free trade was seen to threaten employment in local heavy industry such as the Cominco smelter in Trail (which is highly unionized), as well as in the transport and forestry industries, unionists in many local communities had added incentive to become involved in association politics.

The formal candidate search committee identified five candidates, each with union and party backgrounds. The nomination meeting attracted about 1,200 members and was hotly contested. Some candidates stressed social and environmental issues, but these were pushed aside by concern over the impact of free trade on the local economy. Lyle Kristiansen, a high-profile union member who had led a local experiment in union management of a timber mill, captured the nomination. In addition to his union involvement, Kristiansen had held the old seat of Kootenay West. While his parliamentary experience was an important factor in this win, some of Kristiansen's supporters admitted that other candidates had better personal qualifications for the job but lost because they lacked institutional links with the union movement.

The NDP candidate in Surrey North, Jack Karpoff, attributed his nomination success to the support of women and feminists in the association. This support was the result of his high public profile on issues affecting women during his eight years as a local NDP municipal councillor. He estimated that women filled about 80 percent of the key organizational positions in the association. Unlike candidates in more open nominations, he did not expend much energy signing up members but aimed at strengthening his support among women members during the nomination campaign. With their backing, he overcame several candidates whose policy emphasis favoured traditional New Democrat industrial and economic concerns. In Fraser Valley West, Lynn Fairall, a union shop steward and long-time party worker, attracted the interest of the search committee. She melded support from women and local unionists to win a close race over the secretary of the association, a union-supported male candidate.

The impermeability and narrowly focused searches of these mass-party associations dampen the upward impact of competitiveness on membership numbers and the downward pressure that accompanies lack of competitiveness. In a contest between party insiders with few or no insurgent candidates, there is less pressure for strong recruitment drives, so candidates turn their attention to wooing the existing membership and fighting opposing factions and their candidates. This compounds the effects of impermeability and further reduces the volatility of membership numbers. It also means that these associations have fewer links to their surrounding community. Reasonably competitive NDP associations account for most such nominations.

Latent Democracy

Latent democracy is found in permeable associations that lack appeal and struggle to find candidates, and which experience open, uncontested nominations. Occasionally, these nominations do attract two candidates, but the contest lacks vigour. This situation confronted many Liberal associations in British Columbia. In the Fraser Valley, the Liberal nomination was not very appealing, as the association had little chance of success. Lawyer Tony Wattie, a long-time Liberal worker who had held the presidency of two associations, easily won the nomination on the first ballot over one other candidate. His position in the party all but guaranteed this outcome. Wattie made it clear that his goal was to strengthen the local association in the hope of future success.[3]

In Kootenay West-Revelstoke, local doctor Garry Jenkins built the small Liberal association from the ground up and was its president. The nomination was very permeable but had little appeal as the party had no chance of success in the Kootenays. Jenkins believed the party should field a candidate in the riding and that his position as a family doctor in the local community would help him win votes. As the only candidate, he won the nomination by acclamation.

Uncompetitive, permeable associations often fail to attract party members to their nomination and must look beyond the association for candidates. They may search for the best candidate they can find, preferably someone with a public profile who has no knowledge of the frailty of the association. Party members may inflate the chances of electoral success and the campaign help they can provide, and encourage candidates to believe that their public profile can be translated into electoral support. Using these arguments, and pointing to the lack of an incumbent as an advantage, the Liberal search committee in the new riding of Surrey North convinced two candidates to run. One of these, ex-mayor of Surrey Don Ross, had a high public profile. Ross believed not only the claims of local members regarding his competitiveness but also that his links with the local Social Credit establishment would help him run a strong campaign. He easily beat his one opponent at the nomination meeting attended by over 100 newly recruited party members.

In cases where no candidate can be found, the party may appoint a candidate from among its loyal workers. This standard bearer is unlikely to be a local party member but someone from the national or provincial office of the party – perhaps a young person with political aspirations. The Liberal association in Burnaby-Kingsway was both unappealing and incapable of finding its own candidate. Sam Stevens from the party's provincial office was parachuted in as a candidate. He had no connection with the association or riding and was simply fulfilling an organizational directive aimed at ensuring that the party fielded election candidates in as many ridings as possible. As a result, this association barely stirred from its inter-election dormancy during the campaign.

The poorly contested Reform Party nominations in Fraser Valley West, Surrey North, and Victoria reflect the fact that the party was not yet fully organized. In general, those nominations consisted of a few friends agreeing to support one among them as the candidate so as to show the party flag in the riding. As with their Liberal counterparts, the associations were ciphers for the personal ambitions of a candidate and a few of his or her friends.

Latent democracy occurs in uncompetitive, weak, cadre-style associations that are open. Because the nomination is either uncontested or nominally contested, it is likely to be a quiet affair (Carty and Erickson 1991, Table 3.11). If there is a nomination meeting, the low level of recruitment means that the victor can win with a handful of supporters. The successful nominee fills a gap in a party's roster of candidates but has little chance of winning.

Limited Democracy

Limited democracy occurs in high-profile nominations that, because of the efforts of party strategists to limit candidate access, are closed and uncontested. Because of the lack of real competition for the nomination, it does not drive recruitment of new members. These nominations occur in a few high-profile ridings in every province, such as Vancouver Centre. Centre has a history of electing important MPs, and prior to the election was held by the Conservative cabinet minister Pat Carney who had been heavily involved in free trade negotiations with the United States. She had decided to retire just before the election. Conservative strategists expected to lose seats in British Columbia but hoped to retain a few so as to maintain a presence in the province. Strategists believed their only hope of winning Centre was to run an outstanding candidate.[4]

Local and nonlocal Tory strategists worked together to control the nomination process by conducting a directed search for a high-profile candidate. This coincidence of interest reflects the belief of local members that the association deserved a high-profile candidate, and that an elite search committee would have the best chance of finding one. The committee was willing to restrict access to one candidate in order to make the nomination more appealing, and promised prospective candidates help from both local and nonlocal elements of the party. The eventual successor to Carney, provincial Social Credit MLA Kim Campbell, accepted the nomination only after personally receiving Carney's endorsement. The search stopped and Campbell was acclaimed the candidate well after the election writ had been issued.

While there was a formal candidate search for the NDP nomination, it was stymied by party president Johanna den Hertog's well-known intention to run again in a seat she had contested in 1984. When party leader Ed Broadbent was invited to attend the nomination, his office indicated that the leader would do so only if there was no controversy. This was partly to protect his image as a caring leader that was so crucial to the New Democrat campaign. Den Hertog's overwhelming institutional support meant the other candidate had no chance of winning. The nomination did not develop into a real contest, and Broadbent attended.

Tex Enemark won the Liberal nomination in Vancouver Centre. His experience in Ottawa as a deputy minister in a Trudeau Liberal government and his work for one-time Liberal MP Ron Basford from Vancouver made him one of the few high-profile Liberals running in British Columbia. He was also well known in business circles in Vancouver and had personal ties to Liberal leader John Turner. With this profile, he easily beat his less well-known opponent on the first ballot.

As in Vancouver Centre, the presence of a high-profile party insider stymied competition for the New Democrat nomination in Victoria. John Brewin had run for the seat in 1984, was association president, a past president of the BC NDP, and was married to the NDP mayor of Victoria. As well, he had run for the party in Ontario at the provincial level, where his father had been a member of Parliament for the NDP. As in Vancouver, Ed Broadbent's office made it clear that he would attend only a well-managed nomination meeting. Although there was a candidate search and a nominal opponent, Brewin's profile in the party and in the riding helped secure him an easy nomination victory. The nominal opposition faced by Brewin and den Hertog is evidence of the NDP's commitment to procedural democracy that makes closing access to nominations more difficult than in the less formally organized cadre-style Liberal and Conservative Parties.

There was a functioning Liberal association in Victoria, but its lack of competitiveness limited its appeal for aspiring candidates. Association president Michael O'Connor agreed to the request of his friend and party leader John Turner to run in order to ensure a high-profile candidate in the riding. Turner's endorsement stifled whatever chance there was of a contested nomination. In addition, O'Connor was a well-known and well-liked local lawyer with strong contacts in the community. He won the nomination unopposed.

Most incumbents are renominated with little or no opposition. These nominations exhibit limited democracy. Loyal party members, and those that recognize the value of backing a winner, do not wish to see the incumbent challenged for the nomination. This limits the appeal of the nomination and the impetus for a candidate search. As well, incumbents exercise a great deal of influence over local associations, which are often organized from the candidates' electoral office using the MP's financial resources and professional staff. Incumbents or their representatives often control the rules by which the nomination is run, rules which can be manipulated to complicate a challenger's task, reducing access to the nomination. Finally, if the nomination does entail a vote, the incumbent is in a powerful position to lobby for support. This strong form of association impermeability explains why few incumbents lose nominations (Carty and Erickson 1991, 133).

Svend Robinson in Burnaby-Kingsway was an example of a well-respected MP who had the support of the association executive and membership and was unlikely to be challenged. His office staff was strongly committed to him personally, and his position as a local boy with a national profile gave him extraordinary influence over the local association. His organizational links stretched to the very top of the party as the national spokesperson on defence. He also had a special role in the party and in the country as an activist and opinion leader on issues affecting gays and lesbians. He was nominated unopposed.

On those occasions where an incumbent is challenged, the nomination is likely to be controversial, and the meeting large (Carty and Erickson 1991). Challengers threaten the status quo and often elicit a hostile response from many association members. To have any chance of winning, a challenger must open up the contest and then recruit large numbers of members, or attract support from among disaffected association members. This is very difficult given that the incumbent has great influence over the association, its members, and the rules governing the nomination.

In Fraser Valley West, an association member challenged the long-serving Tory incumbent Bob Wenman. His pro-life opponent felt that Wenman had not been forceful enough in his opposition to abortion in Parliament and was too focused on national politics. Association rules dictate that candidates must nominate a month before the meeting. Aware of the threat of a challenge, Wenman announced the date of the meeting a month and a day in advance. This gave his opponent one day to submit his name as a candidate, and only a month to find enough new and disaffected current members to threaten Wenman's hold on the nomination. In the end, he failed to attract enough support to take the nomination from Wenman.

Nominations in high-profile ridings and the renomination of incumbents account for most cases of limited democracy. Because high-profile ridings are important to the election campaign of the wider party, party strategists attempt to ensure a preferred candidate wins the nomination by limiting competition. In the case of an incumbent, his or her control of the association, and the advantage of having been successful, works in his or her favour and limits competition for the nomination.

Nominations, Candidates, and Campaign Teams

Four types of nominations have been identified on the basis of whether they are appealing and open to potential candidates. They are variants of local democratic politics. The filters that control access to each type of nomination operate in distinct ways and combinations to exclude some candidates. The twenty-five campaigns in this study are categorized using these criteria in Table 4.2. To be successful, nomination candidates must identify and capture the resources that are critical to success given the constraints produced by the filters on the nomination process. Nomination winners or nominees can be considered to embody the logic of these filters, and each type of nomination tends to produce one of four archetypal candidates who construct distinctive campaign teams.

Open, contested nominations are examples of local democracy. The associations are permeable and organize permissive, often informal, candidate searches. Such nominations appeal to a range of potential candidates who find them easily accessible. This type of contest is likely to occur in competitive, cadre-style associations. They are highly contested, involve heavy recruitment drives, and attract candidates from within and without the association. Local notables who have the support of large numbers of new members, many of whom the candidate has signed up to the association and who know him or her personally, often win these nominations. The campaign teams that result from these nominations are large and have access to substantial financial and other resources, though they may lack experienced campaigners.

Closed, contested nominations have some appeal but are not easily accessible to candidates from outside the party and are therefore a form of party democracy. Such nominations occur most frequently in mass-party associations. These mass-party associations are impermeable and focus their formal candidate searches on current party members. Even in less competitive associations of this type, members may contest the nomination out of a sense of obligation to the party. The focus on a competition between current party members reduces the incentive for candidates to recruit new members. The winner is likely to be an association member or party insider with a history of strong commitment to the party, and for whom other members in good standing are willing to vote. This type of nomination results in a campaign team made up of committed party workers, at least some of whom have campaign experience.

Table 4.2

Types of nominations

Riding	Contested nominations[a]		Uncontested nominations[b]	
	Open	Closed	Open	Closed
	Local democracy	Party democracy	Latent democracy	Limited democracy
Burnaby-Kingsway	PC (3)	—	Lib (1)	NDP[c] (1)
Fraser Valley West	—	NDP (3)	Lib (2) RP (1)	PC[c] (2)
Kootenay West-Revelstoke	—	NDP (6)	Lib (1)	PC[c] (1)
Okanagan Centre[d]	Lib (4) PC (6) RP (4)	NDP (3)	—	—
Surrey North[d]	PC (6)	NDP (4)	Lib(2) RP (1)	—
Vancouver Centre	—	—	Lib (2)	PC[e] (1) NDP (2)
Victoria	PC[e] (6)	NDP (1)	Lib (1) RP (1)	—

Notes: Figures in parentheses denote number of candidates contesting nomination.
[a] Average number of candidates greater than 4.
[b] Average number of candidates less than 2.
[c] Incumbent nomination.
[d] New riding, no incumbent.
[e] Retiring incumbent.

Open, uncontested nominations are accessible to potential candidates, but the association is so uncompetitive, and the nomination so unappealing, that they may fail to attract a candidate and are best thought of as a form of evanescent or latent democracy. The association is permeable but too weak to run a thorough, formal search for candidates. Most such nominations occur in uncompetitive, cadre-style associations. Being weakly contested, there is usually little or no recruitment. Candidates may be either outsiders ignorant of the weakness of the association or party stalwarts anxious to ensure the party has a candidate in the riding. These nominations can be won with a handful of supporters. Sometimes, the party appoints a nominee. These are stopgap nominees who fill holes in a party's nationwide list of candidates. The campaign teams that result from these types of nominations are small and lack resources.

Closed, uncontested nominations are the final type explored in this chapter. Access to these nominations is restricted, and as such they exhibit a form of limited democracy. The association is impermeable and the search is directed at a specific sort of candidate (though it may still be informal). Although these associations are often competitive and should appeal to prospective candidates, this appeal is muted by the wide-held belief that only a certain candidate, or type of candidate, has a chance of winning. This suggests that appeal has more than a competitive element, but there is also a need for prospective candidates to believe they have a chance of gaining access to the types of resources necessary to win. These nominations occur in high-profile or strategically important ridings. Cadre-style associations seem more susceptible to such nominations than their mass-party counterparts. These ridings are found disproportionately in urban centres and attract high-profile candidates. Associations that renominate incumbents are also included in this group. This brings a great diversity of associations into the category, as incumbents may be in rural, suburban, or urban ridings. In general, the campaign teams formed following these nominations are strong. They are well financed and staffed, with access to experienced campaigners and professional assistance.[5]

This chapter noted the relationship between nominations, nominees, and the type of campaign teams that are formed following a nomination. The next chapter looks more closely at the nature of campaign teams and how they vary as a result of the nomination experience.

5
Campaign Teams

Many of the activities pursued by local campaigns are much the same from one campaign team to the next. These activities are generated by the need to identify supporters, communicate a message, and mobilize support on election day. But close inspection uncovers myriad differences in the forms local campaigns actually take. These differences reflect variations in the character of campaign teams, the relationship between the local campaign and its national party, and the nature of the local contest. That is, these three factors determine the style and content of a local campaign.

The next three chapters systematically explore each of these factors. This one considers the structure of a campaign team, and how its size and composition are critical to the style and content of local campaigns. Central to the team is the candidate and the volunteers who fill its important organizational positions. Because nominations are crucial in deciding the composition of this group, they have profound implications for the way in which campaigns are organized.

The Structure of Campaign Teams

About half of all associations engage in regular election campaign planning between elections, and one-third have a campaign team in place prior to the nomination (Carty 1991a, Table 3.17 and Figure 7.1). But there is a decided quickening of the pace of these efforts as nominations are organized and completed, most of which happens in the six months prior to the calling of an election (Carty and Erickson 1991, 112 and Table 3.5). The volunteers who make up the campaign team are the central resource of any campaign. They are also the most difficult to bring into the campaign process. Across the three major parties, the appeal of the candidate is the most important factor in attracting volunteers to work in a local campaign (Carty 1991a, Table 7.13). Their relationship to the candidate and the skills they possess shape the character of the team (see Carty 1991a, 151-62).

Campaign teams must be large enough to fulfil the labour-intensive activities of a campaign, including door-knocking, putting up signs, and dropping leaflets. They must also be smart enough to deal with the more subtle complexities of campaigning, such as advertising, making national party policy relevant to local concerns, presenting the party and candidate in the best light, and responding to other campaigns. This requires a division of labour that places the most experienced campaigners and those with skills well suited to organizing campaigns at the centre, while those with less experience and perhaps less commitment act as foot soldiers, doing the trench work of the campaign.

Campaign teams consist of three types of workers. At the periphery are those who sympathize with the party but whose commitment may stretch only to putting up a lawn sign or helping on election day. Closer to the centre are secondary workers, who participate in the campaign a number of times during the election, handing out leaflets and perhaps doing some canvassing. At the centre are the core workers – the inner circle – who develop and implement strategy. This inner circle includes the candidate. They may be left to do critical administrative chores or canvassing, depending on the number and expertise of other campaign workers. A campaign organization can thus be thought of as consisting of three concentric rings of campaign workers, which surround and encompass the candidate as shown in Figure 5.1.

Figure 5.1

Campaign workers

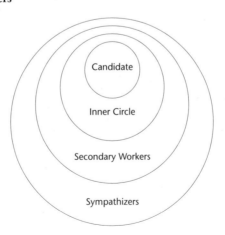

Note: Inner circle: 10 to 40 in number. Secondary workers: 20 to 50 in number. Sypathizers: 50 to 300 in number (in a few cases, up to 1,000).

Having a good mix of each type is important if a candidate hopes to win a marginal seat or turn an apparently hopeless situation into a real contest. Jim Karpoff, who won the election to become the Surrey North NDP MP, suggested that his success in a riding that might have gone to the Tories had much to do with the mix of supporters found in his campaign team. Large numbers of volunteers from a strong local association supported his campaign and long-time acquaintances with provincial and federal campaign experience formed the inner circle.

Sympathizers

Sympathizers may help once or twice during the campaign period, erecting signs, folding flyers, attending fund-raising events, driving voters to polling booths on election day, and perhaps working as a scrutineer on election day. While some are members of the local association, others are not. Their attachment may be to the candidate and/or the party, but is more likely to the latter. Campaigns that appear to be doing well may attract sympathizers as the election progresses.

The skills and commitment that sympathizers bring to the campaign are not crucial given the sympathizers' sporadic involvement. However, the size of this group can have an impact on the effectiveness of the campaign, and on the atmosphere it generates. A large team gives a campaign an aura of competitiveness, and sympathizers' normal social contacts can influence the way in which a campaign is discussed in the local community. Sympathizers may be particularly useful when a campaign requires a large, short-term workforce, such as when it tries to flood a riding with campaign signs. The number of such campaign workers reported by candidates in this study varied from none to over 1,000.[1] In any one riding, the successful campaign team is usually larger than its opponents.

Secondary Workers

Secondary workers form an intermediate ring around the candidate consisting of regular campaign office workers and canvassers. Some work a few times during the campaign while others help out several times a week throughout the campaign. They may be unwilling or unable to fill major roles in the campaign that require full-time work. These individuals suit tasks that do not require consistent work but demand skill and commitment, such as canvassing by phone or foot, doing mail-outs, or helping with administrative tasks. Unlike sympathizers, they must be reliable if a campaign is to get its work done. They may number anywhere from half a dozen to 100. Some urban campaigns claimed they had access to up to 300 secondary workers but that difficulties in coordinating such a large number of volunteers placed a limit on how many could be used.

Both the number and skills of secondary workers are important to a campaign. Members in this group often deal with the public and implement campaign strategies. By doing many of the mundane but crucial campaign tasks, they free up the inner circle of strategy makers to concentrate on the more esoteric aspects of campaigning. A lack of secondary workers places great strains on the inner circle, which is forced to complete labour-intensive campaign chores that sympathizers are unable or unwilling to do.

Most secondary workers are party members. They may be people who have played a more active role in earlier campaigns but are now reducing their commitment, as well as those who are moving the other way and becoming more involved with campaigning.[2] This tier of workers exchanges important anecdotal information about campaigning. As with sympathizers, a large number of secondary workers gives the impression that the campaign is electorally competitive, not only because of their direct campaign efforts but also because the campaign is widely discussed by these workers among their friends and neighbours in the riding. This can help give a candidate's claims about being competitive added credibility.

The Inner Circle
Inner circle workers fill the key positions in the campaign organization shown in Figure 5.2. Members work consistently part time (at least a few times a week, perhaps daily) or full time on the campaign. In this group, the central organizational role is that of campaign manager, who takes responsibility for the day-to-day running of the campaign.[3] This includes making key strategic decisions, sometimes with little assistance or advice. In the words of Ron Stipp, campaign manager for Vancouver Centre New Democrat candidate Johanna den Hertog, a manager "guides the entire campaign, helps develop and ensures its strategic direction, acts as the peak organizer, and oversees important functional elements of the campaign such as media relations, the candidate's schedule, spending ... with the final say on most things."

The most legally onerous position is that of official agent, who is responsible for managing campaign funds. He or she must ensure that campaign contributions and expenditures comply with the demands of the Canada Elections Act, and must make an official report of campaign revenues and expenditures to Elections Canada. Campaigns often try to find a professional such as an accountant or lawyer to fill this position. In fact, the Conservatives explicitly recommend this (Carty 1991b, 83). Because of their greater access to the social strata that includes professionals, the cadre-style Liberal and Conservative associations are much better at finding such volunteers than is the NDP.[4] But all parties usually offer some access to centralized legal and accounting advice, including schools designed to train official agents. All campaigns must also hire a qualified

Figure 5.2

Structure of a campaign team

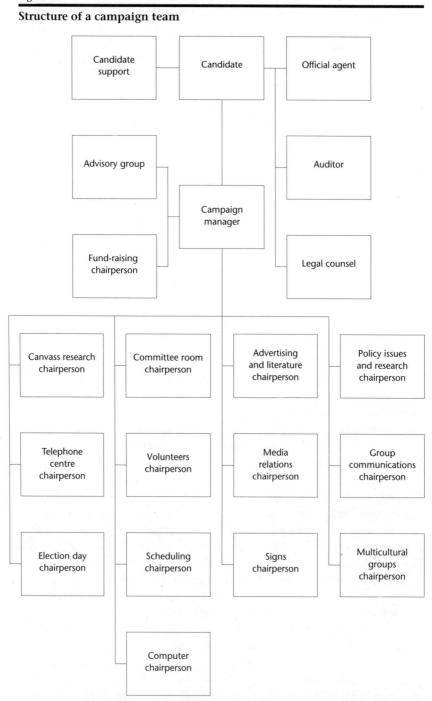

Source: Progressive Conservative Campaign Manual, 1987

accountant to audit the accounts kept by the official agent and to certify their accuracy.

There can be up to forty people in this inner group, but it is often smaller (between ten and twenty people), and may include the spouse or other relatives of the candidate. They are involved in critical campaign functions, such as planning strategies, arranging the candidate's schedule, dealing with press releases and the media, and raising funds (see Figure 5.2). Members of the inner circle chair committees dedicated to these tasks and coordinate the work of volunteers in these areas. If there is a lack of workers, its members are called on to make sure the basic elements of campaigning – canvassing, literature dropping, organizing the candidate's schedule, and dealing with the media – are covered.

Because of differences in the strength and competitiveness of local associations, and their nomination experiences, campaign teams vary across ridings and parties. The nomination shapes these campaign teams and influences the mix of workers, skills, and resources available to them. In particular, it brings a distinctive flavour to relations among the inner circle of campaign volunteers that surround the candidate.

Candidates and Their Campaign Teams

Most associations form campaign teams during the period between the nomination and the election (Carty 1991a, Figure 7.1), though New Democrat associations have a greater tendency to have some elements in place before the nomination. As well as choosing the candidate, the nomination governs the size and nature of the pool of workers and the method by which these workers find their way into the campaign team. Candidates and campaign teams can be classified by reference to their nomination experiences.

The four types of nominations presented in previous chapters are each associated with a different sort of candidate. The campaign teams that surround each type of candidate differ consistently in four important characteristics: the relationship among the inner circle campaign workers; the composition of the campaign team, particularly the inner circle, in terms of the type and number of workers and the financial resources available to it; the locus of decision making with respect to building the campaign team; and, finally, how the inner circle, including the candidate, perceives the task of running a campaign and its main strategic focus. These factors help determine the style and content of the campaign.

Local Notable Candidates

Local notable candidates generally win local-democracy-type nominations held in competitive associations of cadre-style parties (see Figure 5.3). In winning these open, contested nominations, local notables use their public profiles to recruit many new members. They and their supporters see the candidate as central to the campaign team, a team held together by personal ties. The candidates are often new to the party and may be inclined to rely on other new members and personal acquaintances to help run their campaigns. With a strong association and plenty of funds to work with, these are competent campaigns. Decision making with respect to shaping the campaign team and choosing strategies is localized. Campaigners' perceptions of the character of the local riding play an important role in their decisions.

Figure 5.3

Local notables

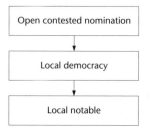

The manner in which a local notable chooses a campaign team resembles that of a leader choosing a support team after winning a party leadership. Because success in the nomination is strongly affected by the performance of the candidate, and his or her support base is somewhat independent of the local association, the winning candidate has a good deal of freedom in building a campaign team. Friendships and acquaintances are likely to play an important role in shaping the candidate's decisions. In Surrey North, Tory candidate Cliff Blair chose Scott Thompson as his campaign manager mainly because they knew each other from previous campaigns and were also close personal friends and business partners.

Local executives in cadre-style associations are more likely to defer to the candidate over important organizational decisions than are those in the NDP (Carty 1991a, Table 7.1). This is part of the separation between the association and campaign organization that is common in cadre-style parties in which local notables are invariably nominated (Scarrow 1964, 61). The nonlocal party is only very rarely involved in selecting campaign team members in any party. This type of intervention is slightly more common in the NDP than in either the Liberals or Conservatives (Carty 1991a, Table 7.2). This in part reflects a willingness of local NDP organizers to accept the dictates of the national party about association matters even when they disagree with the national strategies (Smith 1964, 73).

Occasionally, where the association is well organized or the candidate is inexperienced, the local association executive may have some say in the selection of people to fill important campaign positions. In the Okanagan, the inexperienced Liberal candidate Murli Pendharkar relied on the few local Liberals with campaign experience to fill crucial campaign positions. Thus, the position of campaign manager was shared between two long-time members of the association who had helped search out prospective nomination candidates.

The relationship among members of the inner circle, and in particular between the candidate and volunteers, is quite personal. Personal bonds between team members may be formed during the nomination process, from relations built up inside a strong, competitive association or as a result of shared membership of groups and service organizations outside the association. Successful insurgent candidates – that is, those who are new to the association – are disinclined to choose existing association members to fill important campaign roles, preferring to rely on friends brought into the association during the nomination process. Insurgent Burnaby-Kingsway Tory John Bitonti chose a campaign team composed mainly of personal friends and family.

In general, volunteers in local notable campaigns have a personality-driven view of politics and see personal attributes as more important than party platforms or policies in deciding the outcome of an election. Local notables and their volunteers consistently rate the role of the candidate in the campaign as very important. This is not surprising, as the candidate plays a crucial role in attracting volunteers to campaigns in cadre-style associations (Carty 1991a, Tables 7.13 and 7.14). Only the party leader tends to be seen as more important to the outcome of the local election. Moreover, candidates in these associations claim to have known about 80 percent of the volunteers prior to the election.

The campaign teams of local notables are usually highly competent. They usually have access to an adequate supply of well-qualified workers from the association and among new recruits (in part as a function of the social strata that cadre-style parties appeal to). Where workers are lacking, the campaign is wealthy enough to hire help in critical areas such as fund-raising, writing advertisements, or opinion polling. Because most local notables win in associations that are competitive and hence strong, their membership is large. As a result, winning candidates have a considerable pool of potential workers from which to build a campaign team. Inner circles of forty volunteers are common, and the campaign team may have over 100 members, and up to 1,000 workers. Cliff Blair in Surrey North and

Al Horning in Okanagan Centre claim to have had access to between 500 and 1,000 workers, many recruited during the nomination process.

If relations between the candidate and members of the association who supported other candidates have remained cordial, members with election experience are nearly always invited to play an important role in the campaign. This was the case in the Tory association in Okanagan Centre. The organizer of one losing nomination campaign, Troy Schmidt, became the campaign manager for candidate Al Horning.

Effective fund-raising by strong local organizations is common in these campaigns, and party headquarters is usually willing to provide added financial assistance if necessary. Within the same party, the campaigns of local notables attracted more and larger donations than their less competitive counterparts. There is, however, some tension between the independence of most local notables and the need to find funds and workers. If a candidate alienates party members, or an insurgent hijacks an association, they may have trouble raising funds from traditional party supporters and attracting experienced campaigners. This is always a danger in open, contested nominations, and is another reason insurgents may rely on volunteers they know or have brought into the association.

As it is, insurgent candidates are more likely to win in weaker, if still competitive, associations that are very permeable. These associations may have limited resources to offer a candidate, and party strategists may not feel they are competitive enough to warrant federal support. John Bitonti in Burnaby-Kingsway and Cliff Blair in Surrey North, both to some degree insurgent, pro-life Conservative candidates, struggled to find adequate campaign funds. Bitonti raised just $20,775 – only a little more than the party-appointed Liberal candidate in the riding. Blair raised a paltry $14,948, half that of the Liberal candidate, and one-third of his NDP opponent.

There are qualitative differences in the pool of volunteers that local notables have access to in comparison with many other candidates. By encouraging recruitment drives and casting a wide net for candidates, competitive, cadre-style associations attract a diversity of candidates and members, thus multiplying the connections between the association and ethnic and interest groups in the riding. These groups may even support a particular candidate, or nominate one of their own, adding to the heterogeneity of the association.

Being in cadre-style associations, these campaigns are likely to have a disproportionate number of professionals drawn from the social strata that support the Liberals and Conservatives. Their skills are well suited to the technical and management tasks required of the inner circle. Furthermore, these professionals often have flexible work arrangements that allow them to take leave without pay from their firms. Not only can they commit themselves full time to the campaign, but their normal salary is not considered by law to be a campaign expense. Thus, the campaigns of local notables often receive expert advice that is not subject to the limits on local campaign spending dictated by law. Consequently, campaign activities that might otherwise be too expensive are accessible to the campaign. While most Liberal and Tory campaigns in this study had lawyers and accountants on their campaign staff, only a minority of New Democrat campaigns – those in high-profile ridings where the national NDP helped to provide such workers – had direct access to this type of assistance.

With access to workers and funds, the local campaign is in the enviable position of being able to choose its election strategies and determine its organizational style. It can develop its own strategies and organizational form, or follow those offered by the party. This decision has implications for every aspect of the campaign, from the focus of literature to the public events the candidate attends.

The choice of campaign strategies is greatly influenced by the relationship between the various members of the inner circle as well as the style of the candidate. For local notables, the personal nature of relations among the inner circle, and the fact that the candidate often welds the team together, results in the candidate being the linchpin of the campaign. In Surrey North, Scott Thompson, campaign manager for Conservative Cliff Blair, speaks about campaign strategy entirely in terms of the role of the candidate: "We saw the candidate as very important to success. Our strategy revolved around increasing Cliff's profile. The most important poll results for us were those that showed us the level of name recognition we had gained for Cliff."

This role for local notables distinguishes them from many other candidates and is not surprising given that permeable associations in nonprogrammatical cadre-style parties select them. In contrast, NDP campaigners in Surrey North ranked national and regional issues, as well as the party leader, higher than they did the candidate when listing factors affecting their campaign.

Given that local notables are central to the campaign team and usually have an intimate knowledge of local conditions, the campaign is likely to have a local focus. This local impulse makes the campaign susceptible to parochial styles of politics and local interest groups. Local control of the campaign – the development and implementation of its own strategies – is an identifying characteristic of this sort of campaign. Local organizers in cadre-style parties view with suspicion any intervention by the national party. In contrast, NDP campaigns place greater emphasis on national and regional issues and are often closely linked with national party strategy.

Party-Insider Candidates

Impermeable associations whose nominations are examples of party democracy select committed (usually local) party members, or party insiders, as their candidates (see Figure 5.4). These associations are found mostly in mass parties such as the NDP. Party insiders often perceive themselves as first among equals, a sentiment that fits well with the organizational ethos of a mass party such as the New Democrats. In contrast to the personal style of local notable campaigns, party-insider campaigns have a bureaucratic/ organizational approach to team building.

This approach identifies a standard operating procedure for every campaign job and fills it with the best-qualified party member. A committee of executive members regularly assigns positions on the campaign team – including the campaigner manager – often before the nomination is completed. This approach, or some variant of it, is more common in the NDP than in the cadre-style major parties. The latter rely on the traditional form of organizing, with candidates appointing positions such as campaign manager (Carty 1991a, Figure 7.4) often on their own judgment, and often on the basis of friendship.

Experienced NDP candidates have more discretion in choosing a campaign team. This is particularly true in competitive associations, where a history of working for the party at a high level is often critical to nomination success. But these cases are the minority. NDP candidates appointed official agents in 44.2 percent of the ridings the party contested, compared with 74.8 percent and 82.5 percent in the case of the Liberals and Conservatives (Carty 1991a, Figure 7.4). In Kootenay West-Revelstoke, the official agent for the NDP hardly knew the candidate but was a long-time party member. Neither the Conservative or Liberal official agents were party members, and both were appointed by the respective candidates.

Relations among the members of teams constructed by these associations are less personal and more institutionalized than in local notable campaigns. The manner in which volunteers are assigned to positions on

Figure 5.4

Party insiders

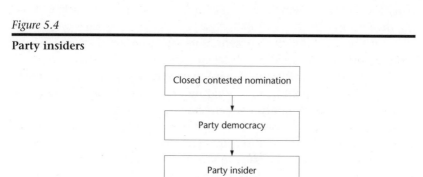

the campaign team favours loyal party members over those brought into the association by the nomination. While some may be friends of the candidate, it is their commitment to the party that underpins workers' willingness to join the campaign (Carty 1991a, Tables 7.13 and 7.14).

The impermeable nature of NDP associations restricts access to and exit from the party, dictating the organizational ethos of local campaigns. The association builds a repertoire of behaviour that becomes entrenched over time. Formal rules and committee decision making tend to dominate NDP inner circles. Commitment to the party and formalized job descriptions take the place of the friendships and transient organizational arrangements found in cadre-style parties. In Fraser Valley West, a losing nomination candidate, Charles Bradford, was appointed campaign manager to Lynn Fairall because he was considered to be the best person for the job.

Another corollary of the impermeability of NDP associations, and the related lack of large recruitment drives during the nomination, is that links between the association and the local community can be relatively limited. This reduces the ability of mass-party associations to respond to local political sentiment.

But solidarity has its rewards. Competitive associations maintain a core group of experienced, competent campaign volunteers who work on local campaigns from one election to the next. This allows them to pursue labour-intensive methods of canvassing and campaigning, but it also means that impermeable NDP associations rely heavily on long-time members to fill important campaign positions. This facilitates the early formation of campaign teams (Carty 1991a, 156) but reduces the incentive to find new members to help run the campaign. Even associations that are only minimally competitive are likely to have a group of committed members with some experience who are willing to organize the campaign. The Okanagan Centre NDP had no chance of success but managed to construct a team of experienced campaigners.

Just as with the Liberal and Conservative Parties, the nature of the social groups and strata that an association appeals to influences the composition of the campaign team. The NDP in British Columbia appeals disproportionately to bureaucrats, nonprofessionals, and union members (see Blake 1985). Its inner circles have fewer professionals than cadre-style campaigns, and find it harder to locate suitable workers to fill demanding positions such as that of official agent. And unlike the many professionals found in Liberal and Conservative campaigns, many wage-earning NDP volunteers do not have flexible working hours and as a result have to balance their jobs with their commitment to the campaign.

On the other hand, if NDP workers are professional organizers employed by a union (which is common in NDP campaigns), and thus are able to devote themselves full time to the campaign, their wages must be included as an election expense, which limits the campaign's financial flexibility. In comparison with their Liberal and Conservative counterparts, NDP campaigns are more than twice as likely to have a paid managers and half again as likely to have paid staff of some kind (Carty 1991a, Tables 7.3 and 7.4).

Party-insider campaigns place more emphasis on party policy than on the local candidate, both organizationally and strategically. This is in part a function of the greater role played by the association executive. New Democrats in Fraser Valley West had hired office space, begun fund-raising, and made important decisions about the conduct of the local campaign well before Lynn Fairall won the nomination. This pattern is evident throughout NDP associations. The constituency executive appointed 41.1 percent of all NDP official agents, while this was true for 19.7 percent of Liberal and 9.6 percent of Conservative agents (Carty 1991b, Table 3.2).

Unlike workers in the campaign teams of local notables, volunteers in party-insider campaign teams perceive their task to be inextricably connected with the goals and policies of the wider party. They believe that there is strength in unity and that a local campaign can be most effective by being part of a coordinated effort. Local campaigns have formalized links with the rest of the party, and internal party modes of behaviour greatly influence the manner in which they operate. The universal use of the NDP-developed three-canvass method in all campaigns with sufficient workers is evidence of this.

When asked to rank factors that influence election outcomes, campaign workers such as those in Jim Karpoff's campaign in Surrey North rated issues and party platforms and policies more highly than the efforts of candidates. Even NDP candidates see their job in this way. Fraser Valley West candidate Lynn Fairall notes that "Ours was just one of 290 odd campaigns ... our strength comes from presenting the same policies across the country."

This monolithic view of campaigning is not conducive to the influence of idiosyncratic local styles of politics on campaigning. Even when campaigns make an attempt to focus on local issues, they do so with an eye to the party platform. John Brewin notes that "We felt that peace issues, which the party platform is strong on but which were not central to the wider campaign, would play well in Victoria, so we emphasized them."

Linkages between the local and national branches of the party are evident in their financial relations. There are set levels of funding that must be provided to the national party by constituencies via provincial organizations. The national party tries to ensure that as many local campaigns as possible have adequate funding to fulfil the demands of campaigning by redistributing money to provincial sections that are weak (Stanbury 1991,

156-7). This means that different elements of the party are involved in a web of financial relations.

Because the appeal of the nominations that lead to party-insider campaigns is not driven solely by the electoral appeal of the association, there is a great deal of variation in the competitiveness of campaigns in this group. The more competitive (appealing) the nomination, the more likely it is that the association will insist that the candidate have a reputation as a good party member. As with other parties, more competitive associations in this group tend to be larger, better financed, and as a result, may be more strategically independent of their national campaign.

Competitive party-insider campaigns also have enough money to hire experienced campaigners for some jobs. But unlike other parties, these outsiders will be NDP members in good standing and are likely to come from the group of professional campaign organizers within the NDP. Members of this group regularly cross provincial boundaries and levels of government to work on campaigns, and may share their time between party work and union organizing.

Stopgap Candidates

Stopgap candidates win latent-democracy-style nominations in permeable and uncompetitive associations that organize a weak candidate search (see Figure 5.5). Most such nominations occur in cadre-style associations. In very weak associations, the party appoints a candidate, and a few local party faithful, working with whatever guidance the provincial or national party is willing to offer, run the campaign. On occasion, the successful candidate is a public figure who is not a member of the association but has been convinced by party members that the association has some chance of success. As such, there are two kinds of stopgap candidates: the faithful party member, and the insurgent or outsider.

Party faithful candidates can take one of two forms: a local party member willing to run in an uncompetitive association, or a candidate

Figure 5.5

Stopgap candidates

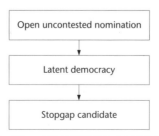

appointed by the party because no local candidate can be found. Insur-
gent/outsider candidates believe that their charisma is enough to attract
campaign workers and funds, as well as votes. If they lose the election, they
invariably claim that they were unaware of the acute weakness of the association. Given their limited contact with the association, this may be
credible. But it is difficult to determine whether it is this ignorance, or their
belief in their own appeal, which plays a bigger role in their decision to
run for the nomination.

The campaign teams of stopgap candidates are built locally. Faithful
party members and appointed candidates usually see themselves as filling
a gap in the party's national election roster and have few delusions about
their role in the campaign. They have modest expectations about the size
and competence of their teams. Candidates who are local party members
draw on acquaintances in the association in building their teams. Local
association president and Liberal candidate in Fraser Valley West Tony
Wattie was an experienced party organizer. He did not expect to win but
believed the party would benefit in future elections if it ran a candidate.
He relied on his contacts within the party and on his being a well-known
local lawyer to find volunteers.

Appointed candidates are often party members from outside the local
association who are willing to follow the directions of the party or local
members on how best to construct the campaign team. The construction
of the campaign team has little to do with the candidate. Rather, the team's
size and quality depends on how many local party members are willing to
work on what is nearly certain to be a losing campaign. In Burnaby-
Kingsway, the Liberals were forced to appoint Sam Stevens – a young party
worker from the provincial office – as the candidate. A few local party
members were willing to direct Stevens and help out with the campaign.
The candidate is nearly irrelevant in this type of campaign.

Charismatic candidates using the local association as a vehicle for their
own ends see themselves as the centre of the campaign. Given that the
association is likely to be weak, the candidate often builds the campaign
team. The campaign team consists of party stalwarts willing to support an
outsider and new members the candidate has brought into the association.
But as with appointed candidates, there is usually a lack of volunteers,
which severely constrains the team's ability to meet the demands of campaigning. If there are very few volunteers, the candidate must rely on
friends and family to fill campaign positions. Most such candidacies are in
cadre-style parties, inflating the number of their associations that report
candidate control of the campaign organization.

The relationship among the members of stopgap-candidate campaign
teams is quite intimate. This is a result of the small size of such teams and,
on occasion, members knowing each other well. The inner circle of insur-

gent/outsider candidates, which is made up of family members, is the most intimate of all. Don Ross, Liberal candidate in Surrey North and ex-mayor of Surrey, had to rely on his son to manage his campaign. His son notes just how limited the campaign inner circle was: "Strategy meetings consisted of mum and dad and my brother and I sitting around the table after dinner discussing what had to be done the next day."

Long-time Liberal member and local candidate Tex Enemark in Vancouver Centre found the association was too weak to provide experienced volunteers, and he relied on acquaintances and friends in building his team. Team members freely admitted it was their personal loyalty to Enemark rather than to the Liberals (though some had been members of the party in the 1970s and early 1980s) that led them to join the team. Fortunately for Enemark, many were professionals such as accountants and lawyers who had skills appropriate to campaigning. In Kootenay West-Revelstoke, candidate Garry Jenkins, his family, and a few friends ran the Liberal campaign and even provided most of its funding.

Most campaign teams in this group lack financial resources and cannot field a fully competent campaign team. There may be a core of workers to fill important positions but these workers will lack experience. Despite the presence of lawyers and accountants in Enemark's team, their lack of campaign experience proved to be a problem. The team's decision to discount the need to address the diverse ethnic and lifestyle groups in Vancouver Centre was seen by other campaigns as a strategic mistake born of political naïveté. Or there will be a small number of experienced campaigners who cannot meet all the labour-intensive demands of campaigning, as in Tony Wattie's campaign.

A lack of workers is the most reliable indicator of a campaign that has a limited electoral future. In Centre, the paucity of Liberal volunteers was particularly evident in a riding in which other campaigns had more than enough. With very few secondary workers and sympathizers, the Liberals could not complete all the labour-intensive tasks – such as canvassing the riding on foot – of campaigning. Campaign manager Allan Gould notes that they had to indulge in a "smoke and mirrors" strategy in an attempt to cover up this weakness. Moreover, Gould notes that a failure to attract adequate numbers of workers early on tends to be self-perpetuating once it becomes widely known. Even a strong media campaign in part funded by the national party to help out a candidate in a high-profile riding could not hide the fact that the Liberals were understaffed.[6]

However, most stopgap candidates do not have the luxury of special funding from their national party and usually work with limited funds. Ross in Surrey North was angry at his lack of support from the federal party, which saw Surrey North as both unwinnable and not important enough to warrant special treatment. The weak local association did not have a war chest prior to the nomination, and the lack of volunteers restricted Ross's capacity to raise funds. Party appointees, such as Stevens, may be able to attract basic funding from the party if the latter is concerned enough to help make the campaign appear viable. If the candidate has a public profile, as did Enemark and Ross, he or she may be able to attract funding through speaking engagements and personal appeals for support. But most such campaigns are doomed to impecuniosity and its difficulties.

Perceptions of what constitutes a campaign can vary among stopgap-candidate campaigns. Appointed candidates' understanding of the riding are of little consequence to the campaign. The candidate may have very little campaign experience and is often not well known to local volunteers or voters in the riding. This discourages a strong strategic focus on the candidate. Moreover, lacking resources, these campaigns rely on the national party for everything from campaign literature to election strategies. This general literature does not emphasize the candidate or local issues, but concentrates on party policy.

Local party members who run out of a sense of duty will also lack the resources to generate or implement a local strategy. There is either no real strategic focus to campaigns or they mimic that of the national party. The local campaign is a cipher for the national campaign, devoid of local issues or a direct role for the candidate's personality and abilities. So although they may have the necessary autonomy, these local campaigns are unable to implement a truly local strategy. For instance, Garry Jenkins relied heavily on nationally produced literature and followed the national campaign strategy, though he was personally opposed to the party's position on free trade.

Campaigns with better-known candidates attempt to develop a strategy that focuses on the candidate and may even ignore the national party. These candidates see themselves as strongly connected to the local community and able to read its pulse. They believe that voters will be sympathetic to a campaign based on their personal qualities and commitment to the riding. On occasion, they have some success with this approach. Ex-mayor of Surrey Don Ross focused on his links with the local community. Local campaign literature emphasized the candidate, and strategies were premised around making an impact at all-candidates debates. Ross managed to increase the Liberals' vote by 15 percentage points.

All the stopgap candidates in this study, even those with some financial backing, ran into the same major obstacle. They could not find enough volunteers to canvass the riding. Most campaigners believe that personal contact with the voters is the means by which candidates prove they are viable electoral alternatives. A failure to make this contact severely weakens the credibility of stopgap candidates. As a result of lack of resources, these campaigns either adopt or are swept up in the national strategy. They run parallel local campaigns; that is, campaigns that are not integrated into the national campaign but mirror its strategies.

High-Profile Candidates

High-profile candidates are successful in associations that are competitive and impermeable and run nominations that exhibit limited democracy (see Figure 5.6). What sets these associations apart is that party strategists believe their campaigns have an impact on the wider election. How well the campaign does, and the candidate's performance, sends signals to voters in surrounding ridings about the competence of the party and its chances of forming the government. This often occurs in ridings that, for a variety of reasons, receive extraordinary media coverage. This coverage may be a function of tradition, or even mundane factors such as the propinquity of the riding to major media headquarters. But it is often related to special features of the riding, such as its demographic character, the profile of the candidates or local MP, or the intensity of the local contest. This category also includes the campaign teams of most incumbents. While not all incumbents may be considered high profile, most have some public profile.

Figure 5.6

High-profile candidates

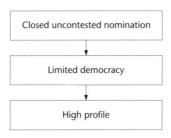

The selection of the campaign team for non-incumbents can depend on the interaction of a number of factors. Most of these associations are strong and can muster volunteers to help with the campaign. If local opinions have not been overridden in the process of having a high-profile candidate brought in to win the nomination, local association members can be expected to volunteer to work on the campaign. But if the candidate has been imposed by elite agreement, some local members may absent themselves from the campaign. Because the candidate is an important attraction for many workers, his or her very presence influences the composition of the campaign team. High-profile candidates often have strong links to various groups in the local community and perhaps the party, and bring their own personal supporters to the team. In Kim Campbell's case, her political experience enabled her to bring with her a protocampaign team from previous provincial elections.

Given the importance of the candidate to the campaign – evidenced by the party's pursuit of the candidate – he or she has some leverage within the party and possibly a veto over who holds important positions in the campaign team. But most candidates rely on a trusted strategist or acquaintance to organize the campaign team, freeing them to concentrate on campaigning rather than on the minutiae of organization. Local and nonlocal party members may negotiate on how best to fill campaign positions in order to meet both local and nonlocal objectives – often melding personal and partisan motivations – so as to produce the most effective campaign team. By comparison, a New Democrat candidate's role in selecting team members is circumscribed by the importance of the party platform and by the need for solidarity, which runs counter to the mercurial, candidate-centred campaigns found in high-profile, cadre-style associations.

Incumbents may rely on trusted advisors in their constituency office to assign positions on the campaign team. New Democrat MP Svend Robinson says of his constituency support staff: "They organize the campaign team and deal with all the details of campaigning. This leaves me free to concentrate on what I do best – meeting with voters." The use of advisors to organize the campaign team is evidence of one of the pitfalls of being an incumbent: being remote from local affairs because of the time spent fulfilling the duties of an MP (Land 1965, 72). In fewer cases, MPs who keep close tabs on their associations and local constituency office may be directly involved in selecting volunteers to fill campaign positions. Tory Bob Wenman in Fraser Valley West was one such incumbent.

An MP's constituency office provides a range of support for the campaign, including office space, equipment, and staff. Lists of campaign volunteers may be kept on record in the office. Before the election, staff can contact volunteers, begin fund-raising, and start the process of priming voters about election issues and party policies via direct mail and literature drops. The MP can use his or her office to hold informal gatherings of voters in order to get a sense of salient local issues.

Although the candidate may have a personal relationship with members of the inner circle, relations among volunteers in campaigns in this group are dominated by a professional ethic. Because of the candidate's profile, most workers know, or know of, the candidate. Some are close personal friends. But as these candidates are drawn from a political and social elite, many of these friends are professionals whose skills are useful to the campaign. On top of this, there are the professional campaigners attracted by the profile of the campaign or sent out by party headquarters. This, combined with the fact that the campaign has access to the latest demographic and polling information, as well as other technical assistance from the party, creates a sophisticated campaign team that sees its job in a technical, professional light.[7]

The size and composition of these campaign teams reflects the appeal of the candidate and the high-profile nature of the campaign. As well as a high level of expertise, these campaign teams are usually both large and well financed. Being attached to a strong association and having special appeal helps these campaigns attract upwards of 1,000 volunteers. They have access both to professionals in the wider community and to experienced organizers and campaigners in their respective parties. Legal advice is often provided by one or more lawyers, the official agent is an accountant, the communications chair is a trained journalist or public relations expert, fund-raising is done by an experienced party organizer, and industry professionals write the campaign advertisements.

In the case of cadre-style associations, this is due in part to the social strata from which these parties draw their supporters. But even within the NDP, a wider net is cast to catch campaign workers for these teams than for campaigns in less prestigious ridings. NDP members who make a living as professional campaign organizers are disproportionately assigned by head office to these sorts of campaigns. Or they may know the high-profile candidate personally and prefer to work on his or her campaign. In addition, party supporters who have useful skills (such as in broadcasting and advertising) are used in these campaigns, even though they may live outside the riding. These workers come largely from the public service and education sector. NDP teams rely more heavily on party members who have proven their commitment to the party, rewarding this where possible. A number of NDP strategists who played important roles in the federal election in British Columbia subsequently found work with the provincial NDP government.

The campaign teams of high-profile candidates either include important party strategists or have access to those who determine national strategies. The linkages between the local campaign and national strategists that develop during the nomination process, and go on into the campaign, help these candidates run effective campaigns. Kim Campbell's campaign used public relations experts and experienced campaigners from across the country. Patrick Kinsella, an old hand at Conservative and Social Credit campaigning, helped mastermind her campaign. Johanna den Hertog's key volunteers included communications chair Bill Bell, a lecturer in media studies who was well connected to the party hierarchy. She also had access to the NDP's provincial headquarters through her husband and NDP strategist Ron Johnson. In addition, den Hertog's campaign team included a lawyer and an accountant – rare commodities in most NDP campaigns.

Because these campaigns are often attached to competitive, strong associations, they are able to raise considerable funds for campaigning. The profile of the candidate and the attention given him or her by nonlocal strategists heighten the effectiveness of fund-raising efforts. Many such candidates are experienced in public fund-raising. The party usually reinforces the impression that the candidate is special by offering him or her extraordinary assistance. For example, Kim Campbell's campaign received ten times the financial assistance from the party than did the average Tory campaign in British Columbia. This focus on the local campaign reinforces the candidates' perceptions of their own importance.

Campaigners' perceptions of their jobs on the campaign teams of high-profile candidates are shaped by the centrality of the candidate to the campaign strategy, a professional ethic that permeates the campaign team, and the links between the local and nonlocal party. For their part, high-profile candidates have a clear understanding of their own worth, and having been wooed by the party, naturally see themselves at the centre of the local campaign effort.[8] Most live in or near the riding and have, or believe they have, a good sense of the local political terrain. They see themselves as influential and knowledgeable on a range of important issues and are often encouraged by parties to speak to local and national matters. On occasion, candidates are parachuted into the riding and rely on a campaign team and strategy constructed by the party. But even an interloper's view of the riding is informed by the latest technical wizardry available to the party. As such, the campaign should be able to identify effective campaign strategies and, with the resources at its command, implement them.

Despite the professionalism of campaign teams of high-profile candidates, their symbiotic relationship with their party's national campaign often confuses the local agenda. While a high-profile local campaign relies on the national campaign for technical, strategic, and financial support, it may have local issues it wants to promote, and a view of how the candidate should be presented to the public. It attempts to maximize the amount of media coverage it receives in order to present this agenda. For its part, the national campaign wishes to use the extraordinary regional and national media coverage these ridings receive for its own ends. It may wish to use the candidate as a national spokesperson and even as a symbol of what the party stands for. Not only might it be competing with the local campaign for space in the media, but its strategic objectives may also be at odds with those of the local party.

Given the close contacts between local and national strategists – in fact, one person can be doing both jobs – the tactics of each level often become intertwined, and the local campaign finds itself addressing local, regional, and national issues. This is possible only because of the vast array of personnel and resources available to it. Resolving tensions between the demands of each level of campaigning can consume a good deal of effort. PC and NDP strategists in Vancouver Centre argued with national organizers on numerous occasions that their campaigns needed to focus on local issues and strategies if they were to be successful.

Campaign Team Characteristics

The nomination experiences of candidates determine the character of campaign teams, and in particular, the core group of workers that control local campaigns. In turn, the character of campaign teams is critical in shaping the style and content of local campaigns. These teams vary in the four characteristics shown in Table 5.1: the relationship among the inner circle of campaign workers; the composition of the campaign team, particularly the inner circle, in terms of the type and number of workers and the financial resources available to it; the locus of decision making with respect to building the campaign team; and, finally, how the inner circle, including the candidate, perceives the task of running a campaign and its main strategic focus.

Table 5.1

Campaign team characteristics

| | Types of candidates and teams | | | |
	Local notable	Party insider	Stopgap	High profile
Inner circle	Personal	Bureaucratic	Intimate	Professional
Personnel and resources	Ample funds and volunteers	Adequate association funds and members	Lack of both funds and volunteers	Excess funds and ample volunteers
Locus of decision making	Candidate and local campaign organizers	Association executive and nonlocal strategists	Local campaign by default	Local and national strategists work together
Strategic focus	Candidate and local issues	Party policy and national issues	No focus; national by default	Candidate, local, provincial, and national issues

The strategic choices available to local campaigns can be described dichotomously: local versus nonlocal issues; party-centred versus riding-centred strategies; policy versus candidate; and so on. This is because local campaigns operate in two contexts. The first is an intraparty one, which is defined by the relationship between the national, regional, and local components of the party. The second context is defined by the local constituency contest and conditions. The next two chapters deal with these factors separately.

6
Toeing the Party Line

Just as the composition of the campaign team shapes the style and content of a local campaign, so too does the environment in which it operates. There are both intraparty and local constituency contest dimensions to this environment. This chapter deals with the nature of intraparty relations between the local and nonlocal campaigns.[1] The form this relationship takes depends on the desire and ability of the national party to intervene in local affairs on one the hand, and the willingness of the local campaign to accept national party involvement and its capacity to resist if it so chooses on the other.

Intervention in local affairs by national campaigns is a function of either a strategic interest in a particular campaign or a general commitment to providing assistance to local campaigns. Strategic interest is driven by how the national party sees the local campaign fitting into its overall strategy. A particular local candidate or set of local issues may attract national strategists. In general, cadre-style parties are less willing to impose a single strategic vision on local campaigns than are mass parties, and the latter may also be committed to equalizing resources across all campaigns in an attempt to ensure uniformity.

The strength and competitiveness of national parties influences their capacity to intervene in local affairs. Because Canadian parties struggle to maintain a consistent presence across the country, there are variations between provinces and ridings in the assistance they can offer local campaigns. This is also true for their capacity to hold local campaigns to central party strategies. The Liberals and Conservatives are the only two parties to have sustained any long-term capability to intervene in local campaigns across the country, though this may no longer be true given the electoral destruction of the latter in 1993.

In general, the capacity and desire of national parties to intervene have increased with the growth in the size and sophistication of their campaign organizations over the last decade, paralleling similar trends in other

Western democracies (Carty 1988a, 9-10; Panebianco 1988). This has resulted in more coherent national campaigns and encouraged a tendency among national strategists to intervene in riding campaigns. The Liberals and Conservatives, and to a lesser extent the NDP, were capable of supplying the basic tools of campaigning to local campaigns across the country. All, or nearly all, local campaigns receive some assistance from their national counterparts (see Preyra 1991, 144-55).

Although the availability of more resources holds out the chance for a local campaign to develop and implement its own strategies, these resources may come with strings attached or have embedded in them assumptions that limit the strategic freedom of a local campaign. In fact, a national party may provide assistance to a local campaign as a means of attaining specific strategic objectives of its own.[2] These may or may not be consistent with local goals. Each of the four types of campaign teams discussed in the previous chapter has different attitudes towards their nonlocal counterparts and their involvement in local affairs. These are determined in part by the team's organizational ethos, strategic focus, and the resources it has at its disposal.

The resources that constitute the relationship between different levels of a party include money, strategic advice, technical and professional assistance, visits from the party leader, and even the transfer of personnel. It is possible to categorize this relationship on the basis of what resources flow from the national to local level, and whether or not the local campaign is strategically subservient to its national counterpart. The first can be thought of as measuring the extent of the relationship, while the second is an attempt to measure its impact. Differences in the mix of resources flowing to a local campaign have direct implications for its style and content.

Intraparty Relations
Besides basic financial assistance, which may be in the form of loans or transfers, national campaigns may provide local campaigns with a range of resources. In an attempt to ensure local campaigns are well run and consistent with party expectations about the content and style of campaigning, all the major political parties conduct campaign schools at which candidates and campaign managers are given advice on electioneering. Candidates are encouraged to dress in ways that present a suitable image, trained how to deal with media interviews, and warned of the dangers of not toeing the party line on policy matters.

Party campaign and policy manuals also provide campaign information to local campaigners. They describe campaign organizations in detail and outline tasks such as fund-raising, finding office space, canvassing the riding, and dealing with the media. The size and sophistication of the packages provided to local campaigns by national parties varies. The

Liberal and Conservative Parties offer local campaigns a choice between a basic package or a more extended one. In 1988 and 1993 the Tories' extended package included the equipment needed for electronic mail. The NDP provided all campaigns with the same basic kit.

A direct link between national and local branches of a party during elections is the effort of regional or national organizers to keep in touch with local campaigns. Most campaign managers, and sometimes candidates, take part in a weekly conference call with counterparts in other ridings and strategists at either a provincial or national office to discuss tactics and the progress of the campaign. The party also provides access to lawyers and accountants who can advise local campaigns on electoral laws and campaign spending.

In addition to this basic level of assistance, a few campaigns in strategically important contests have a more extensive symbiotic relationship with their national counterparts. The national party provides technical and professional assistance – such as polling information, help with media relations, and trained personnel – to local campaigns. In return, the local campaign offers a conduit through which the national party can pursue its strategic objectives. While the objectives of the two levels are often congruent – both want the local campaign to do well – there are times when local and nonlocal goals clash. Although they are important to the national party, these local campaigns are usually strong, so the nonlocal party cannot easily impose its will on them.

The relationship between each of the four archetypal campaigns and their nonlocal counterparts is different and has a distinctive impact on the local campaign. The campaign team characteristics identified in the last chapter are useful guides for considering the impact of this relationship on the style and content of a local campaign. The relationship among members of the inner circle, the locus of decision making, the resources available to a local campaign, and its strategic focus influence, and are influenced by, relations between the two levels of the party.

Local Notables, Parochial Campaigns

Most local notable campaign teams are competitive and attached to strong associations. As such, they have access to ample local resources and do not usually require outside assistance (Carty 1991a, 209-17). They are suspicious of national party strategies, tending to focus on the candidate and local issues. National campaign organizers in cadre-style parties that nominate local notables feel no obligation to be involved in local affairs, except where it suits their direct strategic interests. The local team relies very little on its national counterpart and is not strategically subservient to it. Rather, the local campaign develops its own parochial style and content.

Parochial campaigns value their independence from the national party.

The suspicion that local notables have of national strategists is exempli-fied in Surrey North Conservative Cliff Blair's attitude to the national party candidate school that was supposed to help him run his campaign: "They treat you as if you are training to be prime minister and everything you say might be reported in the media. It is all about what you are not allowed to say, sticking to the party line, never upsetting anybody, dressing the right way ... I was seen as a 'loose cannon,' which suited me."

Local notable campaigns rarely lack volunteer support or funding. If there is a transfer of money from head office, it is modest (see Table 6.1). The five campaign teams in this category received an average of just over $1,000 from their head offices. Most of this money went to the Okanagan Centre Liberal campaign, which struggled after the nomination to main-tain its early momentum and asked for assistance from its national counterpart. Despite this assistance, local Liberal organizers felt they had free rein in shaping their campaign, mainly as a result of the party's orga-nizational weakness in the West.

Table 6.1

Intraparty resource flows in parochial campaigns

Campaign team	Funds received ($)	Contribution to total (%)	Other resources
Burnaby Kingsway (PC)	1,000	4.8	$5,000 loan
Okanagan Centre (PC)	137	0.2	Ministers and leader visits
Okanagan Centre (LIB)	4,253	16.0	Manuals
Surrey North (PC)	0	0	Leader visits; $5,000 loan
Victoria (PC)	0	0	Leader visits; $5,000 loan; strategic advice

With respect to other sorts of resource flows, these teams receive relatively little from their national party. One exception in Okanagan Centre was the willingness of the Progressive Conservative campaign to have visiting government ministers point out that the Tories would help local farmers adjust to the impact of free trade on agriculture in the region. Moreover, as a riding that the government expected to win against the tide in British Columbia, it was considered politic for the party hierarchy to visit when they were in western Canada.

Campaigners in parochial teams know each other, and there is usually a core of experienced local organizers who can direct the campaign. This creates cohesiveness and promotes independence. Decision making is local. This does not mean local organizers may not adopt national party resources and strategies. Rather, they are in a position to choose the degree to which they develop their own approach or follow the nonlocal campaign. They can assess how appropriate nonlocal strategies are to the local conditions. The capacity to make this choice sets their campaigns apart from other campaigns that lack the resources and personnel to control their own destiny or that wish to be integrated into the national campaign.

Parochial campaigns tend to focus on local issues and the candidate. Their intimate organizational style among the inner circle does not fit easily with the imposition of strategies from above. Tory Al Horning's Okanagan Centre campaign is a good example of a parochial campaign. The strength of the local association in a region that had sent many Conservative members to Ottawa meant the campaign had the money and skilled campaigners to develop and implement its own strategy. Campaign organizers agreed that the campaign should emphasize Horning's forty years of service to the local community in fields as diverse as sport and local government. This focus on the candidate and local issues suited the personal style in which politics is done in country communities such as Kelowna.

Given that Brian Mulroney was unpopular in the riding, some separation from the national party was considered advantageous. Although the senior party was happy to help out in one of the few ridings it looked likely to win in British Columbia, it was content to keep its involvement at the level of visits by party luminaries aimed at reinforcing the importance of the riding. This suited local organizers and gave them room to pursue their own version of the campaign. Decision making remained local, and the national party made no other major contribution to the resources of the campaign.

Of course, this separation of local and nonlocal campaigns works both ways. Conservative Cliff Blair's campaign was less competitive than Horning's in the Okanagan and had fewer resources with which to develop and implement its own strategies. Blair was a strong supporter of free trade and stridently promoted the deal. The national party was unsure of this tactic, preferring to soft-peddle free trade in British Columbia. In addition, Blair was passionately pro-life, an issue generally avoided by the party. Moreover, the party did not think he would win. For his part, Blair was unwilling to compromise on the style and content of the local campaign in order to attract national party assistance. Blair notes that his Surrey North campaign "hardly saw a party strategist," and that national strategists "felt no compunction to help the local campaign."

The gap between local and nonlocal PC party strategists in Surrey North was evident during the leader's tour. Mulroney ignored the advice of local strategists regarding important local issues and the value of not mentioning Quebec or speaking French. When the media heard campaign manager Scott Thompson criticize Mulroney for giving an extended press conference in French, his comments were reported, and he ended up on CBC's evening news show, *The National,* trying to explain his statement.

Unlike Horning, Blair would have welcomed help. He had access to plenty of workers with campaign experience and was able to generate a local strategy, but was short of the funds needed to deliver his message. Blair points out that things changed when party strategists came to believe he had a chance of winning: "We received hardly anything from the party until the last couple of weeks of the campaign, at which point they started to believe, as we did, that we had a chance of winning. Once they realized this, they made $5,000 available to us as well as key advisors. On election day the party sent workers out to help us organize. If that help had come earlier, and we had been able to widen the debate on free trade and talk about home ownership, we would have done better." Blair believes the party lost a riding it might have won because of some minor differences in opinion and its own poor judgment. His successful New Democrat opponent, Jim Karpoff, agreed, claiming to have "stolen" the riding from the Tories.

Liberal Murli Pendharkar's Okanagan Centre campaign stands out as one that raised relatively few funds and received a substantial proportion of its money from the national party. Although the Liberal nomination attracted several candidates, and Pendharkar was a local notable, it seems that the Liberals' chances in the riding were overestimated by local members and nomination candidates. When fund-raising began in earnest, it became clear that the campaign would not be able to match the efforts of the NDP and Tory campaigns. As a result, the Liberal campaign had to rely more heavily on national help than other local notable campaigns.

Misjudgment of a party's chances of winning a riding by candidates and even party strategists makes drawing the line between stopgap-candidate campaigns and weak local notable campaigns difficult. Whereas Pendharkar's campaign came to resemble that of a stopgap candidate, on the other side of this divide, Don Ross's stopgap candidacy came to resemble that of a local notable. As the ex-mayor of Surrey, Ross raised more money in Surrey North than his Tory opponent Cliff Blair. Blair, like Pendharkar, ran a local notable campaign that struggled and resembled that of a stopgap candidate. The line that separates stopgap candidates and local notables reflects the wider competitive position of the Liberal and Conservative Parties. Local notables are attracted to open nominations in cadre-style parties. Both Liberal and Conservative associations offer such nominations. Of the two parties, the one that looks like forming the government will have a larger number of strong associations and attract more local notables. Stopgap candidates are more likely to be needed in the party that does not look like it will win government.

Local notables and their parochial campaigns are in general left to their own devices, which provides them with the freedom to succeed or fail on their own terms. Because of their access to workers and resources, they are capable of developing and implementing either a local strategy or elements of the national campaign. While they have this option, the structure of the campaign team and the importance of the candidate as a unifying factor incline them to a local focus. This is consistent with the organizational and philosophical foundations of the cadre-style parties in which most such campaigns are found.

Party Insiders, Subsidiary Campaigns

Party-insider candidates have a close relationship with nonlocal campaign organizers. The ethos of solidarity in mass parties such as the NDP places a premium on ideological and organizational consistency across different levels of the party. The capacity to include local campaigns in regional and national strategies is to some degree seen as a measure of success. This involves substantial transfers of resources between levels of the party at the behest of national organizers. Strategically, the party tends to ensure consistency by running a top-down campaign (see Table 6.2). The party hierarchy constructs strategy and expects compliance at the local level. In general, acceptance of the need for solidarity leads most NDP campaigners to defer to the nonlocal party. In provinces where the party is successful, provincial strategists may also play a role in ensuring strategic consistency. Local campaigns are integrated with and subservient to the nonlocal campaign, having little influence over its direction (see Dyck 1989, 207-8). Party insiders, then, run subsidiary campaigns.

Unlike many of their counterparts from cadre-style parties, NDP candidates are generally positive about the party's attempts to influence the style and content of local campaigns. Lynn Fairall, a first-time candidate, thinks the school held for BC candidates at the University of British Columbia was helpful: "The campaign school was very good. It taught us some

Table 6.2

Intraparty resource flows in subsidiary campaigns

Campaign team	Funds received ($)	Contribution to total (%)	Other resources
Fraser Valley West (NDP)	17,639	66.5	Manuals; advice; coordinated media relations
Kootenay West-Revelstoke (NDP)	17,552	40.8	Manuals; advice; leader visits; national personnel
Okanagan Centre (NDP)	21,657	49.7	Manuals; advice; leader visits
Surrey North (NDP)	35,214	79.9	Manuals; advice; personnel; coordinated media relations
Victoria (NDP)	30,279	59.2	Manuals; nonlocal personnel; leader visits; coordinated media relations

useful skills, and brought us into contact with experienced campaigners, strategists, and other candidates ... the sense of comradeship helped motivate me."

The most profound indication of the integration of local and nonlocal campaigns in the NDP is the way in which the party collects and redistributes funds (see Table 6.2). Local associations send money to the provincial party, which then sends money to the federal party (Stanbury 1991, 156). Quotas are set for election and nonelection years. Up to 40 percent of what associations raise can end up going to the party (Morley 1991, 108). But the party also helps out weaker campaigns by subsidizing weaker provincial parties, which pass on the assistance at the local level. Incumbents' campaigns are excluded from any such extra assistance (Stanbury 1991, 159).

Because of this method of collection and redistribution, the amount given to local NDP campaigns cannot be compared with that found in other parties. It does not reflect the national party's strategic interest in the local riding as clearly as in the case of the Liberals and Conservatives; neither does it suggest clearly which campaigns are competitive and wealthy, and which need help. Because party transfers are calculated as a proportion of money raised, competitive campaigns that raise more funds send larger dollar amounts to the federal party and receive similarly larger amounts back through their provincial party than do weaker campaigns.

As well as this monetary integration, there is a great effort put into formalized strategic relations between various levels of the party. In attempting to offer a single vision of the campaign across the country, the national party provides manuals, advice, and even personnel to local campaigns. It also makes an effort to coordinate media relations across the different levels of the party. Where the party is weak, this is difficult. For example, campaigns in the Atlantic provinces are only nominally integrated into the national strategy.

The NDP's integrated organizational structure helps it to impose a single vision of the election on local campaigns across the country. The continuous existence of some NDP associations provides opportunities for volunteers to be schooled in the ways of the party. This is manifest in the more formal, less personal relations that characterize the inner circles of these teams. In Surrey North, municipal, provincial, and federal NDP campaigns relied on many of the same volunteers and even shared office space. This pattern of integration has long been a feature of NDP campaign organizations (see Peterson and Avakumovic 1964, 93-4). Federal candidate Jim Karpoff ran his campaign from the offices of the local New Democrat MLA Joan Smallwood. As a result, the local federal association was continuous in the sense that its members worked on campaigns at different levels year in and year out. As the example of the NDP demonstrates, not only are mass parties more likely to want to impose conformity than are cadre-style parties, but there are more mechanisms for doing so.

NDP candidates generally have a positive view of the party's efforts to help local campaigns, and emphasize the importance of consistency across ridings in the policies presented by the party. This involves allowing important strategic decisions to be made nonlocally. But this approach is not accepted without reservation. Lynn Fairall, NDP candidate in Fraser Valley West, had reservations about the degree of conformity expected: "The degree to which they wanted us to stick to the party line was much greater than I had expected. I think it is important for local candidates to be able to bring their own interests to the campaign."

Despite being concerned about the national campaign's emphasis on Ed Broadbent, and its failure to address tax issues (such as the goods and services tax proposed by the Conservative government), Fairall deferred to the party's judgment and followed the national script. The dominance of the centre reinforces the primacy of policy over local candidates and issues as the focus of local campaigns. In Kootenay West-Revelstoke, Lyle Kristiansen ran hard on opposition to free trade, in line with the strategic advice offered by the party. One of the key workers in his campaign team was a local man who worked in Ed Broadbent's office who returned to the riding for the duration of the election.

Attempts by the party to assist local candidates can move the strategic focus away from local issues and the candidate. The local campaign must expend time and effort fitting into a strategy that may take the candidate out of the riding, and which may or may not suit its local strategy. NDP candidates in British Columbia participated in a number of joint public events. Lynn Fairall from Fraser Valley West took part in group canvassing with other NDP candidates. As well, the party produced a suggested federal NDP cabinet made up entirely of women and had a press conference of women candidates from British Columbia. These group efforts occurred mainly in downtown ridings because they offered better access to the provincial and national media. They were invariably dominated by a few high-profile candidates, such as Johanna den Hertog, and by national issues. This emphasis on the collective nature of campaigning helps make local campaigns subservient to their national counterpart. Such events are uncommon in cadre-style parties.

Even in the NDP, there is some local cynicism about the value of the resources provided by the party. The sheer quantity of information can overwhelm the local campaign, and it is not always relevant to local circumstances. Gerald Rotering, an NDP organizer in Kootenay West-Revelstoke, notes that

> Central party literature predominates. Fact sheets sent out from head office during the campaign, issue sheets from the national party, faxes from head office, and literature from provincial headquarters inundate the campaign. [Yet] ... 99 percent of the material provided by the central office is junk ... [and] of only marginal value to the local campaign. But we feel obliged to use it. For example, we photocopy issue sheets and hand them out, and make some use of pamphlets if people are interested in a particular issue. We also create press releases to announce party policy, but these are largely ignored by the local media. By part way through the campaign, many of the releases from head office are ignored by local organizers.

Integration of local and nonlocal campaign strategies, with the former accepting the definitions offered by the latter, is characteristic of mass-party campaigns. This integration is driven by a belief in the need for a consistent campaign strategy across the country that flows from a view of politics that privileges class and economics over culture and region. Class-based views of politics treat geography as a second-order variable, and necessarily cut across those that emphasize the importance of localism. As a result, weak campaigns benefit from the redistribution of resources in their favour, while stronger ones pay a price for their strength. This means that there is less variation in NDP campaigns across different ridings both in terms of strength and strategic focus. This is not to say there is no variation. Well-financed and -staffed campaigns such as that of NDP candidate John Brewin in Victoria do have greater flexibility and autonomy.

Stopgap Candidates, Parallel Campaigns

Although the campaigns of stopgap candidates are weak and in need of campaign assistance, national organizers offer them little help (see Table 6.3). The cadre-style parties in which these campaigns are found have little commitment to helping weaker local campaigns. Resources spent on uncompetitive campaigns are seen as wasted. Any help the parties provide is minimal and generic. Because the resources are not suited to local conditions, they are unlikely to help these needy campaigns to reverse their fortunes. Unable to control their own fortunes, stopgap candidates run parallel campaigns that mimic the national campaign but have no important interaction with it. The local campaign is strategically subservient to its national counterpart.

The national party may provide a parallel campaign with funds, but only to avoid the embarrassment of a pathetic local campaign. The local association usually struggles to mount even a basic campaign or find a candidate. The national party is particularly obliged to help campaigns of candidates it has appointed, such as Liberal Sam Stevens in Burnaby-Kingsway. In fact, providing the candidate in these instances can be seen as a type of resource flow. Local campaigns in these circumstances must accept whatever assistance they are offered, even if it is not fully suited to local conditions. As a result, the average transfer to parallel campaigns is greater than for their parochial cousins.

In a few special cases, the price of avoiding embarrassment can be very high. Liberal Tex Enemark in Vancouver Centre received nearly $24,000 (more than ten times the average transfer to campaigns in British Columbia), or about 44 percent of his funding, from the national party. Enemark was competing in a high-profile riding against very well-financed Tory and New Democrat campaigns. Strategists didn't want the party to be

Table 6.3

Intraparty resource flows in parallel campaigns

Campaign team	Funds received ($)	Contribution to total (%)	Other resources
Burnaby-Kingsway (LIB)	5,454	30.2	Candidate; manuals
Fraser Valley West (LIB)	1,049	4.2	Manuals
Kootenay West-Revelstoke (LIB)	1,501	5.3	Manuals
Surrey North (LIB)	0	0	Manuals
Victoria (LIB)	23,945	44.3	Manuals; advice; leader visits
Victoria (LIB)	3,574	8.0	Manuals; leader visits

seen as out of its league in such a high-profile contest and knew it was necessary to have a presence if the party was to have any hope of winning the riding in subsequent elections. As well, knowing they might only win John Turner's seat of Vancouver Quadra in western Canada, strategists hoped the party's presence in the media coverage of this high-profile contest would reinforce its credentials as a national organization and help it seem competitive in British Columbia and western Canada.

Unfortunately, Enemark did not support Turner's position on free trade, and his campaign never reconciled this tension, heightened as it was by the amount of support given the campaign by the national party. Despite running by far the most expensive media campaign, Enemark's challenge was quickly dismissed by his opponents and the media. His campaign team was too small and inexperienced to match the NDP or Tory campaigns on the hustings, nor was it sure how to make proper use of the funding to which it had access. Like other parallel campaigns, it failed to generate a distinctive image for itself.

Some parallel campaigns, such as those of Liberals Tony Wattie in Fraser Valley West and Don Ross in Surrey North, raise sufficient money to mount a credible campaign, relieving the national party of any obligation to offer financial assistance. In both these cases, assistance was restricted to generic campaign manuals and literature. Strategic campaign advice was limited because of the Liberals' organizational weakness in British Columbia. The party would not even help Ross write advertisements or press releases, souring his attitude towards it.

Although they are weak, parallel campaigns in cadre-style parties share with parochial campaigns the desire to be somewhat independent of the national campaign and to focus on local issues. The small, intimate nature of these campaign teams also encourages them to think of the candidate and local issues as potential strategic foci. As Ross notes, the party's lack of involvement heightens this sense of independence: "Our literature was locally produced ... but we used those parts of the national platform where it agreed with our position. Because we had raised our own funds, we had a lot of independence from the national party. The party is weak in the West, and we had a good deal of latitude in the way we ran the campaign."

Unfortunately, this intimate, independent organizational style is a function of a lack of workers and resources. Although decision making is local, which encourages a local strategic focus, parallel campaigns are unable to fully develop and implement a local strategy. Despite his strong disagreement with Turner's position on free trade, Liberal candidate Garry Jenkins in Kootenay West-Revelstoke was unable to develop an alternative focus for his own campaign. This strategic subservience had profound implications for his electoral chances. Not only did he find it difficult to attack free trade during public debates, thus weakening his performance, but the NDP had sewn up all the opposition to free trade in the riding, and the Conservatives all the support. Jenkins needed the campaign to revolve around other issues. But his underfunded, understaffed campaign could not generate interest in other issues and was stuck with the national party's emphasis on free trade.

As with parochial campaigns, strategists in parallel campaigns often wish to go their own way but are incapable of doing so because of a lack of resources, and most important, an insufficient number of volunteers. Against strategists' will, the locus of strategic decision making is nonlocal, resulting in a national focus. Campaigns end up adopting the form and content of their national counterparts, handing out national literature and following national party strategies even when these are irrelevant or even damaging in the local context.

High-Profile Candidates, Component Campaigns
High-profile candidates have ample resources and experienced campaign teams capable of running strong local campaigns regardless of whether they receive any assistance from their national counterparts (see Table 6.4). But because of the strategic importance of the campaign – the high-profile nature of the riding, or the fact that the candidate is an MP – the national party has a direct interest in local affairs. The fortunes of the MPs in this group are inextricably linked with those of the national campaign, while high-profile candidates offer the party a chance to further its strategic interests. These local campaigns are components of the national campaign. Although there is a substantial flow of resources to the local campaign, it is not strategically subservient to its national counterpart. The relationship is symbiotic; the final mix of strategies employed in the local campaign depends on negotiations between the two levels of the party.

Table 6.4

Intraparty resource flows in component campaigns

Campaign team	Funds received ($)	Contribution to total (%)	Other resources
Burnaby Kingsway (NDP)	58,178	82.7	Personnel; strategic interaction
Fraser Valley West (PC)	3,029	5.0	Organizational and strategic node
Kootenay West-Revelstoke (PC)	5,161	8.4	Leader visits; $5,000 loan; advice
Victoria (PC)	19,540	16.7	Leader visits; strategic interaction
Victoria (NDP)	50,737	76.2	Leader visits; personnel; strategic interaction

Comparing intraparty transfers within the NDP with those in other parties is obviously difficult given the party's funding arrangements, but Johanna den Hertog's campaign in Vancouver Centre received much more than other New Democrat campaigns, both in proportion of its total funds and in absolute terms. Centre Tory candidate Kim Campbell also received assistance from the national party; more than ten times the average amount of funds provided to all BC campaigns. In both cases, national party strategists not only wanted to win in this high-profile contest but also hoped to use the media coverage of the contest for their own strategic ends.[3]

More important than financial assistance is the nonmonetary help provided to component campaigns by their national counterparts. National organizers have a number of reasons for providing help to these campaigns. A professionally run component campaign has a better chance of winning and gives a good impression of the competence of the party as a whole. It is also likely to attract more media coverage, thus widening the possibilities for national strategists wishing to get their message to voters via the local campaign. National party assistance helps the local campaign meet the extra demands placed on it by the party. National organizers expect the candidate to act as a national spokesperson, and the campaign to carry a disproportionate organizational burden, including tasks such as coordinating extensive media relations, sometimes for other candidates. To do this, the candidate and campaigners must make an effort to understand party policy and be able to communicate effectively with voters.

Party strategists were deeply involved in Campbell's campaign in Vancouver Centre. They brought both experience and connections with the rest of the party to the local campaign. In addition, the national party provided special polling information and technical advice, and the prime minister took a personal interest in the local campaign. As national party president, Johanna den Hertog was well connected to the strategic centre of the party, and her campaign was staffed with experienced NDP campaigners. Bill Bell, a community college instructor in communications and experienced NDP campaign organizer, ran den Hertog's media relations. Lynda Young, an accountant, and Michael McEvoy, a lawyer, helped out with the professional demands of the campaign. Her campaign manager, Ron Stipp, had managed a number of municipal, provincial, and federal campaigns for the NDP, and her husband, Ron Johnson, was a provincial NDP strategist.

The candidate is a primary strategic focus for component campaigns. Campbell's campaign worked hard to gain media coverage of her efforts at all-candidates debates and media conferences. Daily strategies were built around her public appearances, and the party made use of her as a spokesperson. Campbell and Prime Minister Brian Mulroney campaigned together a number of times. Den Hertog played a similar role for the NDP. Her campaign orchestrated a number of media events in which she was the central spokesperson, and the party used her access to the media to gain exposure for its other BC candidates. The party arranged events for her with Ed Broadbent when he was in British Columbia. National strategists thought she was good for the party's image throughout Canada, and den Hertog felt Broadbent's presence helped her campaign.

   Component campaigns have access to money and experienced campaigners, and can generate and implement their own strategies. But given the involvement of the national party in providing assistance, and its strategic interest in the local contest, the strategies employed and the locus of decision making are the result of negotiations between local and nonlocal strategists. There is always the possibility of conflict between the two levels, in both how the candidates' time is used (Land 1965, 87) and the strategies adopted. The outcome depends on the abilities and determination of strategists at both levels. Sometimes local campaigns are crowded out of their own local contest by the intervention of nonlocal strategies. On other occasions, the national party seems subordinate to the local campaign. Tory campaign manager in Vancouver Centre Lyall Knott noted that local and national strategists had a bitter dispute over the local campaign's decision to defy national strategy and have Campbell forcefully defend the North American Free Trade Agreement, in part using national party resources (Sayers 1991, 44).

   The New Democrat campaign manager in Vancouver Centre, Ron Stipp, was upset with the degree to which the campaign was forced to focus on national matters at the expense of local issues. He blamed this in part on den Hertog's association with the party hierarchy in her role as national party president. The party's reliance on Broadbent as a central strategic focus exacerbated the problem, because he visited Centre several times and always appeared publicly with den Hertog. As the election proceeded and Broadbent's fortunes declined, so did those of the local campaign.

   The campaign of an incumbent is a type of component campaign. In these cases, the linkages between the local and nonlocal party are a function of the MP's time in Ottawa, and of public perceptions that hold incumbents responsible for party policy, while those from the governing party may be held responsible for government decisions. Such campaigns can occur anywhere in a province, as opposed to the component campaigns run in high-profile, usually urban, ridings.

   Svend Robinson also received inordinate assistance from the national party. The NDP always tries to protect its relatively small base of sitting members. An incumbent is important to any party, and his or her own resources provide an MP with more freedom to move than other candidates, even in a mass party such as the NDP. Strategically, Robinson's campaign was intimately connected with the national party. Robinson was a national spokesperson and had been important in shaping party policy in a range of areas, notably gay and lesbian concerns, as well as peace and environmental issues.

The Tories support of free trade and local resistance to Brian Mulroney's leadership made Progressive Conservative incumbent Bob Brisco's job of winning Kootenay West-Revelstoke very difficult. The campaign tried to avoid these issues and focused instead on Brisco's success in bringing government money into towns in the riding. This independence was possible only because of the resources available to Brisco, which enabled him to produce distinctive campaign literature and advertising in each town in the riding. Brisco wanted and received little direct help from the party, other than strategic advice: "Seventy-five percent of national literature was party oriented. This required that we use it selectively. We created our own literature, put local issues first, modified these to suit each of the towns in the riding, noted my own record on local issues and things I had done for the riding." Despite this, the links between Brisco as an incumbent and the national party were strong and overpowered this local strategy. Voters continued to see his campaign as a component of the national Tory campaign and to connect it with the issues and personalities that were so damaging.

The Tory incumbent in Fraser Valley West, Bob Wenman, received little help from the party but was in one of the safest Progressive Conservative ridings in the country. His campaign acted as an organizational node for the Tories in British Columbia, filling the role of the nearly defunct provincial Conservative Party. The campaigns of other experienced Tory MPs such as Chuck Cook in North Vancouver and Tom Siddon in South Vancouver played a similar role. These candidates and their teams advised other campaigns and acted as conduits for information from the national party to the local level and back.

As already noted, the relationship between a component campaign and its national counterpart is symbiotic. The national party provides resources to the local campaign in the hope of winning the riding and achieving wider strategic objectives. For its part, the local campaign provides a spokesperson for the party, even on national issues, and can be an important regional organizational node. As well, the party may hope to use the media coverage it receives to influence other contests in the region, or perhaps the country. If local and nonlocal organizers agree on the general strategic thrust of the campaign and how resources should be used, this relationship can be amicable. But there is no guarantee that this assistance will be of a sort that is considered useful by local campaigners. The chances of this are heightened if local campaigners lack a sense of partisan solidarity that leads them to accept national party involvement. This may result

in bitter disagreement on how resources should be used and on the preferred style and content of the campaign. Working out these differences
makes for interesting intraparty politics.

Comparing Intraparty Relations

The relationship between a national party and its local counterpart influences the style and content of a local campaign. It shapes the nature of the
campaign team, the relationship between its members, its composition
and resources, the locus of decision making, and its strategic focus. In addition, it is also an environmental factor to which this team must respond.

For most local campaigns, regularized interactions, which may include the
transfer of funds from one level of a party to another and the provision of
campaign manuals and strategic advice to local campaigns, dominate their
relationship with the national party. A handful of campaigns have a more
complex relationship to their national counterparts. The nature of this
relationship varies across four archetypal candidates, depending on the
nature of the resources that flow from one level to the next and what this
means for the strategic direction of the local campaign (see Table 6.5).

Table 6.5

Intraparty relations

Resource flows	Strategically subservient	
	Yes	No
Yes	Party insider/ subsidiary campaign	High profile/ component campaign
No	Stopgap candidate/ parallel campaign	Local notable/ parochial campaign

The parochial campaigns of local notables tend to have limited linkages
to their national party. They are well financed and staffed and, being self-
sufficient, have little need for help from their nonlocal counterparts. They
are usually in cadre-style parties and view outside assistance with some suspicion. The personal nature of relations among the team, and its focus on
the candidate and local issues, does not sit easily with the imposition of
national party objectives. As a result, they resist the party's attempts to
impose strategies on them, but may selectively accept some help from the
nonlocal party. Overall, resource flows between the two levels of the party
are limited. Local organizers largely determine the nature of the relation-

ship. Their strategic focus remains centred on the candidate and local issues. Decisions are made locally, and the campaign team retains a distinctive style that is influenced by the personality of the candidate and relations between members of the team. That is, they remain strategically independent.

Party-insider campaigns occur mainly in mass parties such as the NDP, have formalized linkages with their party headquarters, and tend to run subsidiary campaigns. Funding, staffing, and other aspects of the local campaign have a national element, and thus the very character of the campaign team is shaped by its relationship to its nonlocal counterpart. Notions of solidarity synonymous with mass parties encourage the national party to impose uniformity on local campaigns and the latter to accept national involvement. Resource flows are extensive and may include money, campaign literature, strategic directions, and even personnel. Candidates and local strategists accept the dictates of the national campaign and allow these to shape the style and content of their campaign, making the campaign strategically subservient to its nonlocal counterpart. The same mass-party ethos that drives the national party to be involved in local affairs encourages local organizers to accept the imposition of national imperatives. The formalized structures of such parties provide the conduits for the transmission of these imperatives. There is a much greater reliance among NDP campaigns on paid organizers from outside the riding (Carty 1991a, Table 7.8).

Like parochial campaigns, it is the absence of a relationship that is noticeable in parallel campaigns. In this case, this is due to a lack of interest on the part of the nonlocal party. The campaigns of stopgap candidates have unidirectional linkages with their national counterpart. Limited resources flow to the local level from the provincial or national party. The national party has little direct interest in shaping the character of the team and its strategic decision making unless it is called on to build a team where the local party is too weak to do so. Parallel campaigns tend to mimic the strategic character of the national party campaign. Although the nonlocal party does not directly dictate local strategies, the dynamics of the federal election campaign tend to overwhelm the local campaign because it lacks the resources to develop its own strategic vision.

Local campaigns with high-profile candidates have a symbiotic relationship with their national counterpart. Local and national strategies often compete for space in these component campaigns. Local candidates may be expected to lead the national campaign in their riding or region, with the candidate acting as a party spokesperson, and party affairs coordinated through the local office. This is in addition to the obvious local objective – winning the riding. In attempting to achieve its objectives, the nonlocal party may provide extensive financial, technical, and personnel resources to the local campaign. This adds to the complexity of the relationship by increasing the resources available to the local campaign while at the same time tying it into a web of obligations to its national counterpart.

Because the local campaign usually has access to substantial resources of its own, it is not obliged to accept the dictates of the national party. The strategic focus and the locus of decision making are negotiated by the two levels of the party, and in this sense reflect their symbiotic relationship. Depending on the outcome of negotiations, the relationship between the local and nonlocal party may increase the organizational effectiveness of a local campaign, or hinder its efforts by imposing on it national party objectives that may not be suited to local conditions. The interpenetration of the two campaigns is determined by these negotiations.

The final factor that shapes the style and content of local campaigns is the most dynamic and contingent: the local electoral contest. It is to this that we turn in the next chapter.

7
The Constituency Contest

Along with the politics of the nomination that fashions the campaign team and the relationship between the local party and its nonlocal counterparts, the riding contest completes the triumvirate of forces that shape the style and content of local campaigns. The riding contest and intraparty relations determine the environment in which campaign teams operate. The character of the riding contest reflects the political community constituted by the riding, how the media report the contest, and how contested the race is. These factors help determine how local campaigns communicate with voters, the types of issues campaigns raise, and the way in which the candidate is presented to voters.

For the period of the election, ridings constitute a political community with its own set of interests. These interests, expressed in the local political agenda, are shaped by the physical, social, and economic character of the riding (see Blake 1978, 280). Campaigns must respond to the nature of this political community and its interests. This is a central force shaping the character of local campaigns.

News coverage plays a crucial role in shaping political agendas in these communities and has a profound impact on the elections (MacDermid 1991, 89). The types of media that cover a local contest, the access that local campaigns have to that media, and how much coverage a contest receives affect campaigners' strategic decisions, and in particular, the means by which they communicate with voters. Local campaigns compete for media attention to communicate with voters and shape the local political agenda. They tailor their advertising to suit the media to which they have access, and its coverage allows them to stay abreast of the activities of other campaigns.

The number of campaigns that are competitive in a particular riding has a direct impact on how local campaigns engage with each other, and on how attractive the contest appears to the media. The competitive position of the parties in previous elections often acts as a rule of thumb as to their present competitiveness, but this can change over the course of the campaign. Contests in which only one candidate has a chance of success are usually less intense than those where one or more may win. Campaigns are likely to try hard to engage with each other in close contests as each tries to gain some advantage. In cases where there is a clear front-running candidate, he or she may be able to choose to avoid such engagements.

Political Community

All campaigns must fulfil a range of tasks aimed a communicating with voters. These tasks include producing and distributing literature, campaign signs, and advertising; canvassing the riding by foot and phone; holding media interviews; attending all-candidates meetings; mainstreeting; and getting out the vote. In communicating with voters, campaigns identify and respond to the interests of the local political community, while at the same time try to manipulate them for their own strategic ends.

Given that geography remains at the core of any definition of community, it should not surprise us that the geographically defined single-member constituencies used in Canadian elections delimit distinctive communities. Just as politicians are aware of and respond to the nature of these communities (Blake 1976; 1978, 282; Munro 1975), so too do local campaigns at election time. With respect to factors that shape the character of local campaigns, a useful distinction can be made between country, suburban, and city ridings. The social, economic, and geographic features of each type of riding have direct implications for the conduct of local campaigns. While this categorization simplifies the complexity of riding communities in Canada, it is a useful heuristic for guiding a discussion of the impact of locality on election campaigns.[1]

Underpinning the country-city divide, and of crucial importance to the argument in this chapter, have been discussions over whether the growth of cities is associated with a shift from Gemeinschaft to Gesellschaft; that is, from a society based on communal attachments (idealized as those found in country areas) to one derived from associational relationships (as those found in large cities). The assumptions built into this model are complex and beyond the scope of this work. What is relevant is the body of evidence to support the claim, accepted here, that there is some greater reliance on associational relations in urban areas than in rural ones, where communal ties are more important (Kasarda and Janowitz 1974, 328-9).

The reasons for this difference across communities are a matter of controversy. Kasarda and Janowitz reject explanations based on population size and density. Rather, their evidence favours an explanation based on population transience.[2] The transience of voting populations is one of the factors that varies significantly across city and country ridings in Canada, in line with the predictions of this model. City voters in this study are more transient than their country cousins, with suburban voters somewhere in between (Canada, Statistics Canada 1987).

Similarly, Fischer (1982, 251-3) has noted that better educated people rely more on social networks outside the family, and they have wider webs of social relations. Moreover, they tend to be more sophisticated in the way in which they form opinions. Once again, differences in the underlying characteristic – education – coincide with the city-country divide. City voters in this study are generally better educated than their country counterparts, while suburban voters are again in between (Canada, Statistics Canada 1987).

Kasarda and Janowitz (1974, 231) note that a systemic approach – one that takes account of personal characteristics rather than population densities and sizes – suggests the importance of a process of socialization in the formation of opinions and social networks. This is congruent with the argument here that the nature of the riding community is likely to be affected by factors such as what media report local affairs, the profile of a riding, and its social heterogeneity.[3] Differences in the character of ridings with respect to these factors help shape the style and content of local campaigns (Blake 1978, 282).

Country Ridings

Country ridings include those that encompass large rural areas as well as those that encompass country cities and towns. Although there are differences among ridings in this group, they share a sense that they are on the periphery, separated by distance and interests from large urban centres. They are also often socially homogeneous. Together, these factors create a sense that political interests are better defined in these ridings than in socially heterogeneous city ridings.

Geographically, large country ridings that include a number of towns place special demands on rural campaigns. Tory incumbent in Kootenay West-Revelstoke Bob Brisco and his strategists decided to focus on local issues during the campaign. Kootenay West stretches over 500 kilometres from south to north and encompasses half a dozen towns. Nestled in valleys between rugged mountain ranges, these towns have developed distinct sets of interests. The campaign had to identify the interests of each town and adjust its campaign to suit each. This approach was made possible by the fact that advertising in the local media was affordable.[4] The strategy required special print runs and arrangements to deliver campaign literature and specifically designed press conferences and public announcements from one place to the next.

In order to cater to local conditions and distances, the Kootenay West-Revelstoke Tories established campaign offices in three towns. The successful NDP campaign had offices in four towns. The weak Liberal campaign had only one office. Although country rents are modest, staffing these offices was difficult and involved duplication of effort. The number of well-staffed offices a campaign could open came to be seen as a measure of its strength. Gaining the best positions for campaign signs along major roads and highways was also considered a measure of success.

Country ridings are in general socially homogeneous. They have relatively low rates of population turnover and are generally ethnically and even economically more homogeneous than city ridings. Disparities in income levels are less in country ridings than in city ridings. A great majority of country voters own their homes, while many city voters rent. While average education levels are lower than in city ridings, more of the population has a basic education. Country communities often have a clear sense of their political interests. The lack of social diversity reduces the relative importance of cultural and social issues in political debate. In combination with a shared sense of community, this encourages a focus on issues related to local economic development.

In any riding, there is a good chance that local issues that have been important before, or which remain unresolved, will appear again during the election. This is particularly true of country ridings, where communities and economies are somewhat self-contained. Local economic development is likely to be high on the agenda, in part because many rural areas have been in economic decline in recent times.[5] Candidates and campaigns need to address development and often act as local boosters. They are called on to indicate how their party's platform – and the candidate's incumbency if he or she wins – will ensure local prosperity. Of the candidates interviewed, only those in the Kootenays and Okanagan had local development issues at the top of their agendas.

Campaigns in country ridings try hard to bring national policy debates into local focus and to use this to their advantage. Because fruit growing in the Okanagan was likely to be affected by free trade, this wider national issue was localized in the riding. The NDP and Liberals argued that local intensive agriculture would suffer under free trade. In the Kootenays, unionists and the NDP made similar claims about the impact of free trade on the local Cominco smelter. Because of their clear opposition to free trade and a belief that the issue helped their campaigns, New Democrat candidates pursued this localization. However, many Liberal candidates who supported the idea of free trade (despite party opposition to the Free Trade Agreement) tried to avoid it.

In both ridings, PC candidates argued for the benefits of free trade in line with government policy, but tried to minimize their exposure on the issue. If they did mention it, they argued for its local benefits or highlighted government efforts to ameliorate its impact. In the Kootenays, Brisco tried to show that having an MP from the governing party brought in largesse that would boost the local economy in spite of free trade. In the Okanagan – a safer Tory riding – the local campaign tried to sell the deal by emphasizing the help offered to the agricultural sector by the government.

Given that country voters tend to be less mobile than their city or suburban cousins, informal information networks are often well developed in country ridings. These networks transmit campaign messages, and local campaigns try to take advantage of this. As well, and just as important, they transmit gossip about how well the local campaigns are performing. A sensible campaign seeds such networks with positive sentiment about its electoral chances. Liberal candidate Garry Jenkins used his personal contacts built up via his medical practice to promote his campaign in Kootenay West-Revelstoke, as had chiropractor Brisco.

The candidate's contacts with the area, his or her family history and involvement in community affairs, and the way in which he or she acts in public are all matter for comment in these campaigns. Put simply, voters in these communities know their candidates. Many candidates have occupations that give them strong local profiles and wide contact with the community. As well as the two doctors in Kootenay West, Tory Al Horning in Okanagan Centre was a local councillor who emphasized his familial links with the local community and his work with local organizations. His NDP opponent was a well-known local insurance broker, while the Liberal candidate, Murli Pendharkar, had been a school superintendent in the riding.

This emphasis on personal contact and history is linked to a set of commonly held expectations about how elections are conducted and how candidates should behave. Candidates are expected to behave in a dignified manner and are frowned on if they do not. Country campaigners regularly made note of the fact that local campaigns did not stoop to the sorts of bad manners seen in city contests. Campaigns should not attack an opponent's character or deeply held beliefs, which are considered beyond politics. In Kootenay West-Revelstoke, candidates tacitly agreed not to discuss abortion because it was considered too sensitive an issue.

Suburban Ridings

The geography of suburban ridings lends itself to the use of traditional forms of campaign communication, most notably, lawn signs. Getting to voters in these communities can be difficult and requires large teams of volunteers willing to canvass and drop literature. As well, like their city cousins, local campaigns in suburban ridings must reach voters in apartment buildings and must deal with a wide array of local issues.

Suburban ridings are large enough to encompass several metropolitan communities that may have distinct interests. In Surrey North, the riding was split along north-south lines, with the north around Whalley being less affluent than Newton in the south. Local campaigners considered the south of the riding to be more supportive of free trade and the Tories, while the north was seen as anti-free trade and pro-NDP. Campaigners tried to tailor their canvassing to suit these perceptions. For the NDP, this meant attacking free trade in the north, while focusing on Ed Broadbent's appeal in the south. Tories followed the reverse strategy.

Suburban voters are more mobile than their country cousins, but less so than city dwellers. Many of them work outside the riding in the downtown core. On average, they have lived in the riding for a shorter period than country voters, and are unlikely to have a shared history of social or familial relations. Frequent changes to boundaries in suburban areas that are growing in population reduce the chance that a sense of community like that found in country ridings will develop. Rather than any traditional ties to the riding, associational elements of community life, which are not necessarily connected to any one riding, such as membership of churches, school boards, and sports clubs, link members of these communities. Defining truly local issues can be a struggle for local campaigns as they get lost in the larger metropolitan agenda.

These ridings are increasingly culturally heterogeneous, and in the Vancouver lower mainland, may include ethnic subgroups with identifiable associations, such as Indo-Canadian, Chinese Canadian, and Italian Canadian communities. They are, however, economically homogenous in comparison to city ridings, being largely middle class. The interests and life cycles of many suburbanites are similar across subgroups within these ridings. General issues such as taxes, mortgage rates, crime rates, schooling, and other government services that affect families are important. As well, commuters who work outside the riding have interests that are not strongly tied to the local community, as is the case with country voters. Rather, they have a general interest in a healthy economy that produces jobs, helps pay the mortgage, and maintains the property value of the family home.

A number of suburban campaigns focused on general social issues. The increasing number of women in the workforce, and their politicization over recent decades, has highlighted a range of issues such as day care, payment for home-making, and abortion. There was hostility between church sponsored pro-life groups and pro-choice advocates wishing to protect access to abortion in a number of suburban ridings. In recent years, the growth in cultural diversity in these areas has meant that immigration and multicultural policies are also of interest to some suburban voters. The perennial Canadian questions regarding the state of Confederation and Quebec's role therein received regular mention. Because of the general nature of these concerns, political debate lacks focus, a fact made worse by the absence of an influential local media capable of defining a political agenda.

The lack of local focus in suburban campaigns makes the development of distinctive riding contests less likely. Rather than being attached to a particular local issue, the opposing sides take on the positions of the major parties, producing often idealogically charged and sometimes bitter battles. The candidate is often viewed as a party representative rather than as an individual. Voters may expect relatively little from the candidates in terms of personal exposure. It is not so much that national issues are localized in suburban ridings but rather that they tend to dominate local agendas in these ridings.

City Ridings

Population densities in city ridings complicate the task of communicating with voters. These ridings often have substantial numbers of voters living in high-rise apartments. Access to apartment blocks is often impossible. When they do gain access, campaigners may receive a cool reception. Canvassing in apartment buildings is often felt to be more invasive than dealing with voters at the front door of a country or suburban house.[6] City ridings have a high proportion of households in which all members are full-time workers. This adds to the difficulty of reaching them, as canvassing has to be done outside work hours. In some downtown locations, the need to visit in the evening when voters are home can be daunting if the area is dangerous after dark. The alternatives, such as campaign literature dropped in the bank of mail slots of an apartment, are a necessary but poor substitute for direct contact with voters.

The main tactical response by campaigns facing these problems is to make extensive use of phone banks. If the voter shows interest, a time for a personal visit can be arranged, and the canvasser (often the candidate) can be let into the building. If the campaign is well organized, it may also follow up with letters dealing with particular concerns voiced by the voter. The Tories in Vancouver Centre had a well-orchestrated direct mail campaign of this sort. Such a response is also highly flexible, as it can be modified to suit each household in ridings as socially and culturally diverse as Centre.

A second response is to make use of organizations within the community through which voters can be reached. Seniors' homes, local ethnic organizations, churches, interest groups, even sports clubs and universities can be used to communicate a campaign message, and take on particular importance when candidates find it hard to meet voters in person (Land 1965, 81). A university offers candidates a chance to speak to education policy and an ethnic association meeting is an ideal place to broach policies dealing with multiculturalism. Events in such places also hold out the opportunity for media coverage. Svend Robinson made a point of visiting many institutions catering to seniors' needs in his riding. The media coverage of these events helped paint him as a sympathetic candidate interested in local voters.

Just as country campaigns face particular problems, city campaigns face myriad difficulties peculiar to city life. The cost of renting office space in the downtown, providing security for these offices, and the need to have advertising and press releases in a number of languages are just some. As an indication of the different cost structures facing campaigns, an office in downtown Vancouver is about three times more expensive than one in a country riding. This means less money for other campaign activities, which shapes the structure of the local campaign team.

Party volunteers are able to work for any one of several campaigns in adjacent city and suburban seats. This not only means that workers are more mobile but that there is a greater likelihood that a party member will be able to identify a candidate for whom he or she wishes to work who may or may not be running in the worker's own constituency. Such movement can be a matter of preference. A volunteer may prefer a certain candidate to another, or prefer to work on a campaign that looks like it will win. A number of NDP workers in Vancouver Centre who might have worked for Johanna den Hertog moved to Svend Robinson's campaign to help him win reelection following his public announcement of his homosexuality. His campaign was a cause célèbre for some New Democrats. Given that Kim Campbell beat den Hertog by only 269 votes, these defections may have been costly. Similarly, Vancouver Centre Liberal candidate Tex Enemark lost volunteers to neighbouring Vancouver Quadra, where Liberal leader John Turner was running for reelection.

Volunteers may also move around to assist weaker campaigns or deal with emergencies. Parties have major headquarters in urban centres that can provide workers to metropolitan campaigns. Experienced Progressive Conservative campaign organizers and workers moved around to assist inexperienced campaigns in Vancouver's lower mainland. As well, parties redistribute workers to important campaigns. The NDP supplied Johanna den Hertog with experienced campaign manager Ron Stipp, a party organizer with no particular commitment to den Hertog. Experienced Liberals from across the country assisted in John Turner's Quadra campaign.

The voting populations of city ridings are typically more socially heterogeneous than those in suburban or country seats. They are relatively mobile, ethnically mixed, and encompass a number of lifestyle and socioeconomic groups. There are groups that rely on the state for income security that are not found in large numbers in most suburban or country ridings. Many city voters are single or part of a working couple. There is a relatively large proportion of poor renters, but also a sizeable middle-class, homeowning minority. Despite high levels of renting and poverty, education levels among voters in these ridings are above average. Such apparently anomalous characteristics point to the social complexity of inner city ridings.

As a result of transience and heterogeneity, many voters do not share a common history in the riding. Their understanding of elections and campaigning, and even of the nature of their local political community, is as likely to come from the media as it is to be informed by local tradition. In an increasingly group-oriented political culture, city voters are likely to identify with one or more of the groups that are involved in debating public policy rather than with a traditional, geographically defined local community.

Not surprisingly, heterogeneous city communities have a range of interests and a broad local agenda. Campaigns in these ridings must address many issues, and candidates must be familiar with a range of matters and policy, often acting as spokespeople for their party. Many of the groups that have members in city ridings, and may have regional headquarters there, have members spread across the country. They see elections as an opportunity to have their concerns canvassed and often use the media in cities to raise issues. In Vancouver Centre, dealing with the local gay and lesbian communities meant that candidates spoke to national party policy on these matters. Greenpeace used its headquarters in the city to raise environmental concerns, and the media prompted candidates for their responses. It is national public policy that concerns groups like these. This adds to the size of the local agenda and creates linkages to issues of provincial and national concern.

The same is true of economic issues in city ridings. Although there may be local economic issues of some weight, candidates often address the national economy as a way of speaking to the downtown business community, and the business and union organizations that have headquarters in these ridings. Local and provincial economic issues are not forgotten, but compete with national concerns. This is encouraged by the media attention that is given to candidates in these ridings. A very general debate about the merits of free trade was central to the Vancouver Centre contest, with some reference to its direct impact on the local riding. In Victoria, the presence of a naval base allowed candidates to address peace issues that affected the whole country. National issues are not strictly localized, but rather, there is an interweaving of national and local agendas.

There is an air of professionalism about many city campaigns as they attempt to ensure their candidate is capable of dealing with these demands. The riding contest is very much about campaigns developing positive, high public profiles for their candidates. The media play a crucial role in transmitting the personal qualities of candidates in these ridings, and in allowing them to address the many issues that make up the political agenda in the local and sometimes national community. This vital means of communicating with voters is crucial to the nature of local riding contests, and the style and content of local campaigns.

The Media

The media that cover a riding contest are crucial to the way the local election unfolds and to the style and content of local campaigns (Fletcher 1987, 1991a, 1991b). Campaigns compete for whatever media coverage is available. They also measure their performance, as well as the progress of the federal election, through the media. Both the quantity and content of this coverage gives some indication of the performance of the campaigns. Letters to the editors of local newspapers are often logged, to see who is winning the war of words. To test whether their candidate is receiving equal treatment, local campaigners measure column centimetres in newspapers and minutes of coverage on television and radio. Less airtime or coverage for their own candidate often leads to claims of media bias.

Campaigns are aware that some media organizations are more influential than others, and try to gain the best-quality coverage possible. The quality of news coverage is related to size in the eyes of many local campaigners. Strategists often see major media organizations with large newsrooms and distribution areas as more credible and influential than smaller, local media outlets. Candidates crave credibility and influence, and expend enormous effort in trying to gain such coverage. The diversity of media available to campaigners shapes their communication strategies as they try to gain the best exposure possible with limited resources. Campaigns may also advertise in the media. In general, the more influential a news outlet, the less affordable its advertising rates. This determines the amount of advertising a local campaign can do. In large cities, the cost of advertising in the major metropolitan media puts it beyond the reach of local campaigns.

The type of media that covers a local contest depends very much on whether there is a distinct local community within the riding that can support its own media organizations and the newsworthiness of the race (Fletcher 1987, 363-7). The latter can be affected both by the profile of the candidates and by the competitiveness of the local contest. The nature of the media in a riding also plays a crucial role in the degree to which national issues are localized. It is only through the media – whether local or nonlocal – that national issues are aired across the country and can come to be seen as relevant to or even dominate a riding contest.

To some extent, this localization captures the competition between local and nonlocal media for control of the local political agenda. A weak riding media unable to identify and pursue local issues may simply mimic those offered by the national media from where most wire services originate. In contrast, ridings in which the local media can identify local issues and concerns – and even local angles to national issues – produce more robust local political agendas.

With the advent of new technologies, the national media increasingly intrude on ridings in all parts of the country. The growth in the importance of opinion polling, leaders' debates, and tours – all elements of news coverage that are the province of national media – has increased the impact of national news on local ridings and strengthened the dominance of the major media organizations and national campaigns (Fletcher 1987, 363-7). Regardless of the capacity of the local media to generate their own stories, if voters get their news mainly from nonlocal media sources, the local political agenda reflects this outside influence.

The profile of candidates and the influence wielded by the media that report the local contest are positively related. There are patterns across country, suburban, and city ridings in the quantity and quality of the media that cover a riding contest. This has implications for the nature of the local contest and campaigns. Whereas both city and country contests receive coverage they can call their own, suburban campaigns receive relatively little attention. It is noteworthy that controversies surrounding all-candidates debates – perhaps the most local of all campaign stories – tend to occur mainly in country and city ridings where there is media interested in reporting the contest.

Country Ridings
The media in country ridings is a means around some of the difficulties of canvassing large ridings in person. Most country towns have local media that cover the riding contest and in which campaigns can afford to advertise. The self-contained nature of these towns makes viable small local media outlets. Campaigns split their advertising budgets between newspapers and radio. As well as advertising in local community papers, which all campaigns do, campaigns in Kootenay West-Revelstoke, Okanagan Centre, and Fraser Valley West ran some form of electronic media advertising. In contrast, campaigns in most city and suburban ridings could not afford this form of advertising because of the rates charged by the large electronic media in these areas.

The only medium that covered the whole riding (towns and countryside) in Kootenay West-Revelstoke was radio. The Kootenay Broadcasting Service (KBS) runs a number of stations that share news across the region, and its broadcast area is nearly contiguous with the riding. This service has a news-format style and is considered influential by local campaigners. In fact, KBS had the most comprehensive coverage of the local campaign of any media, attending most all-candidates debates. Because radio reaches listeners throughout this large, mountainous riding, it is an ideal medium for news coverage and campaign advertising in country areas. It is also affordable, and local campaigns spent about one-third of their advertising budgets on this network. Most of the advertising budget went to newspapers in the four large towns in the riding.

In many country ridings, newspapers are based in relatively small towns. They have limited circulation and, though affordable, are not considered to be influential. This is in part because the resources of these papers are modest and their coverage of the campaign is basic. This affects both the weight that campaigns place on news coverage in their strategies and the value they see in advertising. In Kootenay West-Revelstoke, each of four large towns has at least one newspaper. As a result, local campaigns had to deal with several newspapers at once, often tailoring their message and advertising to suit each town. As well, papers in the riding use a number of different typesetting methods, forcing campaigns to expend resources rewriting advertising to suit different technical standards.

The city of Kelowna, which accounts for about half the polls in the riding of Okanagan Centre, is big enough to have its own influential local television, radio, and newspaper organizations, yet these are small enough that local campaigns can afford to advertise in them. Riding campaigns worked very hard to garner news coverage and attract editorial support. They advertised extensively and put a lot of energy into developing professional advertisements. Locally produced radio and television advertisements featured Okanagan Centre candidates speaking to national and regional issues, and the local cable station aired an all-candidates debate held at the Kelowna Chamber of Commerce.

The availability of influential media made the Kelowna campaign distinctive. The media's interest in the contest and their capacity to follow up news stories allowed local stories to develop into election issues, while campaigns had a number of ways of delivering their campaign message. In stark contrast to ridings where there was little local media, the public debating performance of the candidates, and in particular of Tory Al Horning, became important in the campaign. In response to negative coverage of his efforts, the Tory campaign restricted Horning's public appearances and used local television, radio, and newspapers to promote its message via advertisements and written press releases, thus freeing Horning from the need to speak in public.

The spread of national and major city media into country areas provides voters with an alternative source of information about the major issues. Local country contests receive little if any coverage in these media. Added to this has been the growth in the reach of sophisticated news services from which local news organizations can get bulletins about national or regional issues. This can crowd out space in the local media. Although most country reporters still rate a good local story as more important than one from outside the riding, reductions in the number of journalists on these newspapers over recent years limits their capacity to run local stories. The growth in the extent and importance of cable networks is also changing local contests. Cable stations often host all-candidates debates that other media organizations are invited to attend.

Local media coverage in country ridings focuses the local political agenda. In cases where the riding is made up of several distinct towns, this may mean several local agendas. Truly local media allow for discussion of local issues and allow regional and national issues to be related to local conditions. The fact that there is a local media which can focus on the local candidates also strengthens the candidate-centred nature of campaigning in country ridings. Where there is some localization of national issues, such as the relevance of free trade to intensive agriculture in Okanagan Centre or metal smelting in Kootenay West-Revelstoke, the local media give a local tilt to the issue.

Media interest spurs campaigns to organize local advertising, news conferences, press releases, and news events, which often focus on local issues. This brings a sense of local purpose to a contest. Local campaigns invariably have communications organizers who chair the media committee. In Kootenay West-Revelstoke, Tory committee members wrote letters to the editor to ensure equal space with other campaigns. Organizers tried to ensure editorial endorsement by lobbying editors, or spending their advertising budgets in order to gain this support. Most campaign managers and candidates suggested that placing advertising in local papers was an attempt to ensure equal treatment. That is, it was a defensive strategy aimed at trying to prevent negative editorial judgments.

National campaigns can also afford to advertise in the media in country ridings. This brings the imperatives of the national campaign into the local contest. In Kootenay West-Revelstoke, the Tory campaign tried to avoid any mention of free trade and Brian Mulroney's leadership. Yet the national party placed significant amounts of advertising in the local media focusing on these aspects of the campaign. In fact, it spent more than twice as much as the local campaign advertising on the major radio network in the riding, angering local strategists.

The presence of local media gives a focus to contests in country ridings. It provides local campaigns with an array of means for communicating with voters. This encourages the development of local strategies to address riding concerns, balancing out the impact of the national media on local affairs. This alone can help give the local contest a more substantial, as well as idiosyncratic, ambience.

Suburban Ridings

Suburban campaigns operate in what is nearly a vacuum of media coverage as a result of being caught in the distribution areas of major metropolitan media. This media does not, in general, consider suburban contests newsworthy, and none of the metropolitan campaigns can afford the advertising rates charged by these large media organizations. The only coverage these campaigns receive, and the only advertising they can afford, is in local community newspapers. Partly because of competition from major media outlets, and partly because of the population densities of suburban areas, these newspapers often cover several ridings. As such, they can give only minimal treatment to any one contest. Campaigners believe that neither the community media that do report the riding contest nor the campaign advertising in these newspapers have much influence on political debate.

In Surrey North, the *Leader* and *Now* provided local coverage. These newspapers struggled to cover the campaign, as they had to report on three constituency contests that occurred within their distribution areas. Moreover, they had very limited resources and numbers of journalists. The problem of coverage was exacerbated by the concurrent holding of a municipal election, which further strained the resources of these papers. As noted previously, two years after the election, reporters could not even recall the names of some major party candidates.

Occasionally, these campaigns can afford to advertise on a minor radio station, sometimes broadcasting from the riding itself. Local cable stations may also run all-candidates debates. But much like community newspapers, there is little faith in the impact of these media. They are poorly targeted, reaching well beyond any single suburban riding. The difficulty of attracting media coverage forces campaigns to rely on labour-intensive, traditional forms of campaigning. Campaign structures reflect this. Relatively little effort is put into media relations compared with city or country ridings. Personnel focus on organizing foot canvassing, literature drops, signs, phone banks, and getting the candidate to meet groups in the riding.

A lack of local media coverage can also stymie efforts by local campaigns to pursue their own strategies. Liberal candidate Don Ross in Surrey North believes a lack of media interest prevented him from using all-candidates debates to further his campaign. Polling results showed Ross, an ex-mayor of Surrey, to be the best-known candidate in the riding, with New Democrat and former councillor Jim Karpoff second, and Tory Cliff Blair third. Yet Ross was running a poor third in terms of vote share, with Karpoff leading. He hoped to score some points by engaging his opponents in public debate. Ross was able to convince Blair to attend debates, but Karpoff, considered a relatively poor performer, would agree to attend only one. Ross did well in this debate but could not convince the local media to pursue Karpoff about his refusal to attend other debates. This undercut Ross's preferred campaign strategy of embarrassing his New Democrat opponent for avoiding debates in the hope of forcing his opponents to debate him.

Suburban campaigns can expect to be covered in the riding features run by most major city news organizations. At some time during the campaign, the *Vancouver Sun,* the *Province,* CTV, CBC television, and CBC radio do a story on each of the Vancouver suburban contests. In most cases, these nearly obligatory reports have little impact on local contests. A leader's visit can help single out a riding and lend credibility to a local campaign, but the reporting tends to focus on the leader, and is only fleeting. Unfortunately for suburban campaigns, it may take a crisis or impolitic comment before they are reported in the major media. This was the case when Burnaby-Kingsway Tory John Bitonti made comments critical of his opponent Svend Robinson's personal morality.

Suburban voters are inundated with national advertising and reporting on radio and television, and in major metropolitan newspapers. Advertising by local campaigns and the limited campaign coverage in community newspapers pale by comparison. The dominance of national media and campaigns in suburban ridings means that there is no distinct local political agenda; rather, the national agenda is reproduced. The lack of media coverage of suburban contests exacerbates the apparent anonymity of campaigns in these ridings and may help explain why candidates appear to be less important in these contests: they are not well known. Candidates represent the national parties and policies that are found in the influential major media that dominate news reporting in metropolitan areas.

City Ridings

The relationship between the media and the candidates in city campaigns distinguishes them from their country or suburban cousins. In contrast to their suburban counterparts, city campaigns receive regular media coverage, which, unlike country ridings, appears in influential major metropolitan media. For example, the *Vancouver Sun,* the *Province,* and the *Globe and Mail* newspapers, as well as CBC radio and television, BCTV, and other private radio and television stations, all paid special attention to the Vancouver Centre contest.

Although they received substantial media coverage, these campaigns could not afford to advertise in major media outlets. In most cases, if they could, it would be wasted on voters in other ridings. Instead, like their suburban counterparts, city campaigns advertise mainly in the local community newspapers in their riding. Victoria is an exception, as the Tory and Liberal campaigns could afford a couple of television advertisements. This reflects the size of the city. Advertising space is less expensive than in bigger cities, and there is less wastage, as a single riding accounts for much of the area covered by the city media.

There are a number of reasons why city campaigns attract media attention. Ridings centred on the downtown core encompass diverse social groups and organizations, each of which aims to get its interests onto the political agenda. Publications directed at lifestyle and ethnic groups are often based in these ridings, and candidates use them to advertise and discuss party policy. Candidates in Victoria and Vancouver regularly spoke to multiculturalism, environmental concerns, issues of particular interest to women, and gay and lesbian issues. Members of these groups across the country are made aware of these city candidates. As well, the downtown business elite is an important local constituency. It has a direct interest in the economic policies of the major parties, and encourages candidates to speak to the local, provincial, and national economies. In particular, companies and organizations with headquarters in the riding expect candidates to be cognizant of the issues in their sector of the economy.

Using these issues and groups as a backdrop, reporters can generate a range of stories by contacting the spokespeople for these various groups, and can expect local candidates to respond to these matters. City candidates are easily reached and ideally placed to provide a comment or press conference in short order. The logistics of television reporting in particular demand that pictures be brought back to the station and edited for the nightly news. It is not surprising that these candidates appear disproportionately in election media coverage.

As many of these candidates from the major parties go on to play important roles in government and the opposition, the media are used to treating them as party spokespeople. Party strategists encourage and train city candidates to play this role, and may provide assistance to help them master the media. In doing so, they aim to use candidates to promote their wider campaigns. This involves local campaigns in a web of relations with the media and local groups, and raises the profile of the local contest.

Population densities in city areas mean that the distribution area for community newspapers is small. Newspapers such as the *Vancouver Courier* and the *WestEnder* in Vancouver Centre are closely identified with the local community. Advertising and news coverage in these newspapers is not wasted on voters outside the riding, as can happen with suburban community newspapers that cover wide areas. As a result, although community newspapers are not considered influential by city campaigners, they give such newspapers more weight than do campaigners in suburban ridings. Campaigners in Vancouver Centre, Victoria, and Burnaby-Kingsway all hoped to gain editorial support of the community newspapers, and hoped their advertising budgets would assist in this goal.

The competition between campaigns for media coverage can be intense. Candidates participate in "bermashave" events, standing on busy street corners with supporters waving at peak-hour commuters; visit an educational institution; and meet with leaders of a cultural community or interest group, all in a single day. In Vancouver Centre, a visit to the city's Chinatown and the University of British Columbia, and walks through the downtown district meeting business workers – often with the party leader

– are obligatory for the candidates. Writing press conferences and news releases, playing host to the party leader, and responding to media requests for interviews take up a sizeable portion of the local campaign effort in both personnel and money terms. Many campaigns have a full-time media relations expert in the inner circle.

Regular coverage of city candidates and contests gives a focus to the political agenda in these ridings. The logic of suburban campaigns is reversed in their city counterparts. The media presentation of candidates means that national parties come to be understood through their candidates. As a result, there is a clearer sense that voters are choosing between candidates with particular strengths and weaknesses. Candidates play a role in explaining or transmitting the national contest to the local and even provincial arenas because of the media, and the national media often explain regional politics to the rest of the country by focusing on a high-profile candidate or city contest.

Media reporting of city riding contests leads to an integration of the local and nonlocal campaigns. New Democrat Johanna den Hertog's comments on issues in Vancouver Centre were carried across the country and linked the local and national agendas. The media does not so much localize national issues as integrate local, provincial, and national issues into a single web. Although this complicates the local political agenda, the amount of media available in the riding means it can accommodate a wide range of issues. The candidate embodies this integration. Although for different reasons, city candidates, like their country counterparts, have an identifiable public image. In this sense, it is suburban candidates who are the exception, lost in the anonymity of suburbia.

Contestedness and Competitiveness

The contestedness of a local riding race – how many campaigns are competitive – has a profound impact on the way in which local campaigns engage with each other, as well as on voter participation in the election process (Blake 1978, 296-301). This needs to be distinguished from the competitiveness of any single campaign team in a contest. This allows us to distinguish between a team that has no chance of winning from those that do, and between campaigns caught up in local contests from those that are "also rans" (see Table 7.1).

If a constituency campaign is uncontested, only the front-runner is competitive and has a chance of winning the riding. All the other campaigns in such a riding are uncompetitive and excluded from the contest. In contested ridings, all those campaigns that have a chance of winning are engaged in the contest. A campaign team that is uncompetitive and involved in a contested constituency is marginalized from the contest, having no impact on the battle that rages around it.

Table 7.1

Contestedness and competitiveness

	Type of constituency election	
Campaign competitiveness	Contested	Uncontested
Competitive	Engaged	Front-runner
Uncompetitive	Marginalized	Excluded

Contests where only one party has a real chance of success are likely to be gentler affairs than those in ridings where two or more parties have a chance of winning. There is a tendency among front-running campaigns to avoid engaging their opponents (Land 1965, 78). This defensive strategy is aimed at limiting the opportunities for competitors to score points at the expense of the front-runner. Moreover, poorly contested local races may attract little media coverage and voter interest may be low. The excluded campaigns can be ignored by the front-running campaign, and there may be no all-candidates debates as the front-runner attempts to avoid contact with other campaigns. In contrast, close contests with two or more competitive, engaged campaigns are likely to produce large campaign teams, good media coverage, and high voter turnout. Marginalized campaigns receive more attention than excluded campaigns, as there is a local contest that attracts media and voter interest. They are usually involved in the all-candidates debates at which the competitive parties vie for advantage.

Individual campaign team competitiveness helps determine the quality of the candidate, the size and composition of the campaign team, and media interest. Parties that have experienced little or no success in a riding have more difficulty attracting good candidates and running strong campaigns, and their supporters may be unwilling to vote.[7] Moreover, it is ensuring competitiveness that is the prime goal of local campaigns. On occasion, a closely fought battle can work to the advantage of all campaigns by attracting media attention and, subsequently, volunteers and resources.

Past electoral performances are the best guide to competitiveness and contestedness. However, there is an element of uncertainty in most local contests that even sophisticated polling techniques cannot dispel entirely. Workers in trailing campaigns know that different parties at one time or another (Blake 1991) have held most ridings. This volatility underpins the vigour of local campaigning. The clearest opportunity for a local campaign to engage with its opponents comes at all-candidates debates, which can have a profound impact on the campaigns' competitive positions. But this local effort occurs within the ebb and flow of the wider federal election, which can carry campaigns along in its wake, complementing or sabotaging their well-laid plans. This influence is transmitted via the media, which use national opinion polls, leaders' tours, and national leaders' debates to help tell the story of the campaign (Fletcher 1987, 205-9). The impact of national events on local campaigning depends on the influence of nonlocal media and the salience of national issues to the local contest. Both local and nonlocal factors shape the contestedness of a riding election and the competitiveness of any one campaign team.

All-Candidates Debates

All-candidates debates can be trite events. Among other things, candidates bemoan the lack of real debate and the stacked meetings. Yet many candidates and campaigners recount stories that suggest these debates can have an impact on local contests, and nearly every campaign sends its candidate to these debates, which may number more than a dozen. It seems that the chance to engage other local campaigns cannot be foregone. In addition, the performance of the candidates and the number of supporters that can be induced to attend these meetings are seen as thermometers of the local contest. Finally, candidates must confront the public directly. Their capacity to deal with the situation may influence whatever personal vote is available in a riding (Ferejohn and Gaines 1991, 297-8).

Campaigns involved in real contests usually engage each other strongly in all-candidates debates. Kim Campbell and Johanna den Hertog ran neck-and-neck in Vancouver Centre. Unfortunately for Liberal Tex Enemark, the competitiveness of the Campbell and den Hertog campaigns highlighted his difficulties. While the two leading candidates heatedly disagreed over the merits of free trade, Enemark attempted to support the principle of free trade, but object to "the Mulroney deal." Unfortunately, there was no middle ground available to him. The debates served only to highlight that Centre was a two-candidate race; one in which his marginalized campaign was out of place.

For candidates with a clear lead, all-candidates debates may only provide an opportunity to lose votes. Front-runners may attempt to minimize the number of all-candidates debates, while the second- and third-place candidates hope for a maximum number of chances to embarrass or upstage the leading candidate. Fraser Valley West Tory MP Bob Wenman had one of the safest seats in the country. However, the Christian Heritage Party (CHP) tried to unseat him by appealing to conservative voters. The CHP stole several high-profile Tories from the local association, ran its national leader in the riding, and attacked Wenman's record on social issues. Wenman responded to this challenge by refusing to attend all-candidates debates. When he did not appear at the first meeting, the matter became an election issue. Wenman responded to public criticism by sending Tory MP for Surrey-White Rock Benno Friesen to the second debate. Other candidates and the media ridiculed Friesen for this, forcing Wenman to relent and attend a later debate where he attempted to explain his earlier absences.

Debates can also bring home to candidates and campaigns the true nature of the riding contest. In Kootenay West-Revelstoke, Bob Brisco was confronted with evidence of his likely electoral demise when he attended the all-candidates debate in Revelstoke, which had been added to the riding in the 1987 redistribution. His organization in the town was limited, and few of his supporters attended the meeting, leaving New Democrats in a clear majority in the audience. His difficulties and the lack of partisan support exposed his electoral vulnerability and damaged the morale of his campaign team.

All-candidates debates are central to the way in which candidates and campaigners understand the riding contest. Most of what local campaigns know of each other comes through the media and anecdotal information supplied by volunteers who come across information about opposing campaigns, and is not informed by precise polling data (Carty 1991a, 181-3). Debates bring all the strategies and conjectures of a campaign into sharp relief, and offer an opportunity to score points at the expense of other candidates. To size up one's opponents in the flesh is still important to local campaigns.

Media Reporting of the Federal Campaign

The national media, national election events, and national campaigns are increasingly intruding on local campaigns. National opinion polls, the leaders' tours, and the national leaders' debates are used to tell the story of the campaign in both the local and nonlocal media. Unfortunately for riding campaigns, none of these storytelling techniques has much local content, and they rarely give a true rendering of the nature of the riding contest. Ridings with little or no indigenous media and in which the media tend to simply repeat wire stories are particularly susceptible to this form of reporting. At its worst, it may distort local agendas and the competitive positions of candidates. The impact of national events on local campaigns is often lagged as it occurs only after a consensus emerges in the media as to voter perceptions of the incident.

Local campaigners note that the reporting of the national election and opinion polls alters the mood of their campaign and the reception they receive in the riding. Positive assessments by the media of John Turner's debate performance fed into subsequent opinion polls and created a bandwagon effect (see Johnston et al. 1992, Chapter 7) which was felt by local campaigns. For example, a discussion of the possibility of a Liberal government in an article in *Maclean's* mentioned Vancouver Centre Liberal candidate Tex Enemark as a potential cabinet member. Morale in Enemark's campaign went up, volunteer numbers went up, canvassers met with a more positive reception, and donations increased.

This national effect was, however, at odds with local circumstances, where Enemark trailed the NDP and Tory candidates by a wide margin. It also managed to bring disaster to the local campaign. Greater media attention exposed Enemark's opposition to Turner's position on free trade. Enemark's campaign initially refused to hand out anti-free trade literature or get involved in debating the issue, but later reversed this decision after being challenged by the media and his opponents. What began as a potentially positive mood change turned into a disaster, highlighting the split in the party over free trade and destroying the local campaign strategy.

The BC NDP campaign was deflated after Broadbent was all but ignored in the debates. This encouraged the provincial party to refocus campaigns away from Broadbent and towards the free trade issue. Tory campaigns were mixed in their reaction to Mulroney's performance, recognizing that he had not won, but may not have lost either.

The progress of leaders' tours is used by the media as a vehicle for telling the story of the federal election campaign (see Dion 1964, 111). General assessments of a leader's performance can influence local campaigns, as can the presence of the tour in a riding. With their bands of roving reporters, these tours briefly focus national attention on a particular riding, or on an issue that may affect a riding. This can change the nature of the local contest, enhancing the credibility of a local campaign or threatening its strategy.

NDP campaigns tried to take advantage of Ed Broadbent's popularity. Local campaigners welcomed him and tried to create media events at which local NDP candidates were seen standing next to Broadbent. The refocusing of the BC NDP campaign after Broadbent's poor electoral performance meant that although local campaigns were still happy to have him in the riding, he became less central to the provincial strategy. There were some rumblings in Victoria and Vancouver Centre where workers believed he took attention away from important local issues and undercut the provincial strategy while he was in the riding.

Tory campaigners had to deal with one of the least popular leaders in Canadian history. Local strategists generally believed that Mulroney was a liability. Many also wanted to avoid discussion of free trade, with which the leader was closely identified. After intense debate, the Tory campaign in Kootenay West-Revelstoke worked to minimize its contact with the visiting leader. To its dismay, Mulroney's presence in the riding inflamed the free trade debate and hurt its campaign. In Surrey North, campaigners tried to direct Mulroney towards local issues, but he refused. As well, he ignored the wishes of local strategists and spoke in French at the press conference.

John Turner's tour in British Columbia was limited. Local campaigners were mixed in their feelings towards his visits. While many saw Turner as a sympathetic figure in the context of the campaign, many did not support his position on free trade. This meant they did not seek out Turner to help bolster their campaigns.

As Preyra points out (1991), local campaigns ride the waves of the federal elections. These ebbs and flows can have profound implications for the strategies, tactics, and content of riding campaigns as they adapt to the dynamics of the federal election as reported in the media. The manner in which campaigns engage with each other, the impact of all-candidates debates, and other local and national strategies are influenced by the balance between reporting of the local and national campaigns. In ridings where reporting of national issues is not modified to take account of local conditions, the dynamic of the federal election may greatly shape the local agenda and the perceived competitiveness of local campaigns. In this sense, city and country ridings that often have their own media are distinct from suburban ridings that are caught within the distribution area of large city ridings that do not report the local contest in any depth. Where local strategies are reported, and in this sense taken seriously, elections often have a distinctive local flavour.

The Role of Political Community in National Elections
There are identifiable differences in the nature of political communities defined by riding boundaries. These differences reflect the underlying sociodemographic nature of the riding and the media that report the local contest. As a result of shared conditions, local contests in each of three types of ridings – country, suburban, and city – exhibit similar characteristics.

Contests in country ridings focus on the local political agenda, which reflects the self-contained nature of local communities and economies. These communities are socially homogenous and stable in terms of population growth and movement. Central to their coherence is the presence of credible local media organizations that report on community events and underpin a parochial political agenda. In particular, such media reinterpret the national political agenda and the progress of the national election with reference to the local context. As a result, not only is there a coherent local political community, but it is protected from being overwhelmed by national and provincial political discourse. Local issues and personalities are important to these elections, and regional and national matters are interpreted through a local lens.

As a result, local campaigns in these ridings focus mainly on local issues, and in particular, on local economic development. This may reflect in part the general economic decline that has confronted country areas in recent decades. The intimacy of the local communities generates a personal style of politics that places a premium on the actions and beliefs of the candidates. This, and the presence of local media in the several communities that make up most country ridings, encourages local campaigns to focus on the qualities of candidates and to make use of all-candidates debates as strategic weapons. The impact and affordability of the media encourage local campaigns to spend more on advertising than their suburban cousins, and even many city campaigns. Insulation from national events and a local focus sets country campaigns apart.

In stark comparison, suburban ridings are often much less well defined, with boundaries that change markedly with every redistribution. The more amorphous nature of suburban communities is compounded by the lack of local media capable of focusing on local issues and of generating a truly parochial political agenda. Campaigns find it difficult to communicate with voters and to generate a distinctive image. This lack of exposure makes it difficult for campaigns to focus on their candidate or on using all-candidates debates as a strategic weapon. These contests are overwhelmed by provincial and national media reporting of the election campaign, and by nonlocal issues. As a result, suburban contests seem to be the most truly ideological, in that campaigns rely on the general campaign strategies, platforms, and literature provided by the parties. Being unable to generate a distinct local character, they trade ideological insults that reflect the antagonisms of national politics and Parliament.

City ridings are more like their country cousins in that there is a local political agenda. The large metropolitan and often national media in the riding or nearby that tend to focus on city contests underpins this. As well, there is often a range of local community newspapers in these ridings. Being socially diverse, and often home to the headquarters of businesses and interest groups, these ridings provide ample raw material for the development of a complex political agenda. As a result, campaigns deal with a range of local, provincial, and national issues.

The combination of a complex local agenda, access to high-profile media, and well-known candidates makes these city contests nodes in the national reporting of the election, with candidates regularly appearing on regional and national media discussing party policy. Local campaigns use the well-reported all-candidates debates to promote their candidates and strategies. This helps explain part of the appeal such ridings have for high-profile candidates, and the desire of party strategists to take advantage of this coverage by trying to have competent public figures run in these ridings in the hope that they can be used to help the wider party. The local campaign must often negotiate a balance between the competing demands of the local campaign and the demands of its party's national strategists.

The complex social and political composition of these ridings, along with a greater access to media, emphasizes the diversity of local opinion and leads voters and campaigns to see politics in personal and group terms (Regenstreil 1964, 239). This encourages local campaigns to focus on social issues in the campaign, with many candidates being on the liberal side of their parties on such matters. Given all this, the capacities, attitudes, and behaviour of the candidates are often central to these campaigns.

It is not clear that the distinction between country, suburban, and city campaigns describes differences in the contestedness of local campaigns. Although it is beyond the scope of this research, it is possible that the intimate nature of politics in country ridings would favour the development of personal electoral support for sitting members that may protect them to some degree from national and regional swings. This is unlikely to be true for suburban MPs but might also be the case for city MPs. Contestedness has an independent impact in that more closely contested campaigns are more likely to be reported than are one-sided contests. As well, close contests produce more intense electioneering and strategic manoeuvring by local campaigns, including a greater focus on events such as all-candidates debates. Front-runners often attempt to reduce opportunities for other campaigns to engage with them, while those running second or third try to maximize these engagements. Campaigns that have no chance of winning commonly struggle to attract workers and money, while those with a real chance of success are larger and better financed.

To some degree, the electoral character of local ridings relies on the presence of media willing to report the contests. It may be that we will always be more aware of close races in high-profile city ridings, while country voters will be able to remember closely fought contests in their ridings. On the other hand, suburban voters may never build up a sense of the history of their ridings just because it is so poorly reported. Over time, such tendencies may well produce identifiable patterns in the nature of local contests.

8
Winning Campaigns

The style and content of a local campaign have their genesis in the riding community (or style) and partisan organizational ethos of the association. The next two chapters discuss eight campaigns using the framework shown in Figure 8.1. Recognizing that contestedness and competitiveness are crucial to the resources available to a campaign and its final form, this chapter deals with winning teams, and the next with those that lost.

Riding style and partisanship shape nominations, determining whether they are open or closed, contested or uncontested. Open, contested nominations can be seen as a form of local democracy, while those closed (open to party members only) but still contested exhibit a form of party democracy. Open, uncontested nominations occur in uncompetitive associations that cannot attract candidates, and can best be described as latent democracy, while those that are closed and uncontested occur where parties wish to restrict access to a nomination, and are thus cases of limited democracy.

Each style of nomination produces a distinctive type of candidate and campaign team. Local democracy produces local notables, party democracy favours party insiders, latent democracy yields stopgap candidates, and limited democracy is associated with high-profile candidates. The campaign teams surrounding each of these types are distinctive in terms of the relationship between the members of the inner circle of the team, the personnel and resources available to the team, the locus of decision making, and the strategic focus of the campaign.

The character of the local campaign team and the organizational ethos of a party define the intraparty relations that develop between various levels of a party's campaign. Local riding conditions and the competitiveness of the local campaign play an important role in determining the interest that parties have in a riding contest or candidate. But the parameters of national or provincial involvement in local affairs are set by the organizational style of a party, with mass parties much more likely to be involved in shaping local strategies in pursuit of ideological consistency than cadre-style parties.

The complexity of relations between local and nonlocal campaigns varies, as evidenced by the size and direction of resource flows between levels of a party. Local notables run parochial campaigns that are capable of organizing their own affairs. Relations between the two levels are shaped by their mutual interest but controlled by the local level. Party insiders in mass parties are involved in subsidiary campaigns that purposefully adopt the strategies of their nonlocal counterparts. Stopgap candidates in weak associations are forced by circumstances to adopt national party strategies and run parallel campaigns. Finally, high-profile candidates are central players on the regional and national stage, and develop symbiotic relationships with their federal counterparts. Their campaigns are well organized and are components of the national party campaign effort.

The campaign environment in which local teams operate combines the dynamic of intraparty relations with that of the local contest. The local

Figure 8.1

Style and content of local campaigns

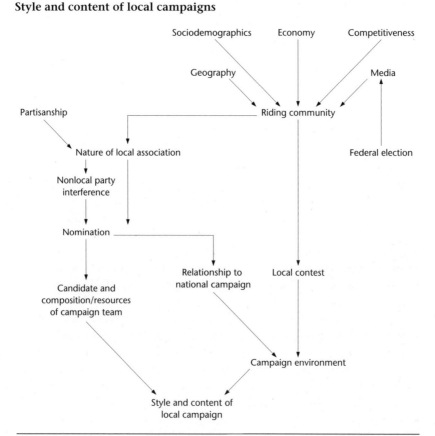

political community defined by the riding boundaries is the base unit for elections and politics in Canada. Campaigns in country, suburban, and city ridings share a number of characteristics due to similarities in the character of local political communities. Social heterogeneity, geography, the local economy, how campaigns engage each other, and the role of the local media in reporting the contest all impact on the final form of a constituency election. In reporting the national campaign, the media also introduce the dynamics of the federal election into the local contest.

In short, there are four types of campaigns found in three types of ridings. While there are clearly patterns in the types of campaigns that are found in a riding – for example, high-profile candidates and campaigns are most often found in city ridings – there is also an array of permutations. The eight case studies in the next two chapters present some of these and have been chosen because they illustrate the relationships discussed in earlier chapters, as well as being interesting stories in their own right. Each begins with an overview of the major campaigns in the local contest. The nomination process that chose the candidate is discussed, as is the nature of the resulting campaign team. This is followed by an analysis of intraparty relations and a final section on the local contest that explores how the campaign engaged with its competitors in the riding.

Kim Campbell: High-Profile Partisan

Vancouver Centre is the quintessential city riding, with a diverse, mobile population and good media coverage of local election contests. Facing a large swing to the NDP in British Columbia, Conservative Party organizers knew they needed a high-profile candidate to win the riding. Convincing Kim Campbell to run was a coup for the party. As a young, socially progressive woman, she suited the demographic profile of this cosmopolitan riding. She won a closed, uncontested nomination.

Having moved in conservative circles in Vancouver for many years, Campbell knew many of the local association members. Her supporters from provincial politics added to those already in the Tory association created a highly skilled and professional campaign team. The team had good contacts with national strategists, received substantial funds from the federal party, and was an important component of the national Tory campaign. Her campaign was competitive and engaged in a contested constituency election.

Although clearly a party insider, as the national president of the NDP, and having run for the riding before, Johanna den Hertog was also a high-profile candidate. The party was confident of success and put together a solid campaign team which included paid professional campaigners. However, there was some local annoyance at the party's support of den Hertog, and a number of local members decided to work on surrounding

NDP campaigns in Vancouver East and Burnaby-Kingsway. Despite this, the campaign had more than adequate funds and workers. Den Hertog's strong connections with the federal party, extensive media coverage of the contest with Kim Campbell, and the resources available to the campaign made the campaign a component of the national NDP effort. Den Hertog led in the polls prior to the election, and her campaign engaged with Campbell's.

Liberal Tex Enemark ran the weakest of the three major campaigns in the riding. Enemark had been an assistant to local MP Ron Basford, who was justice minister in the Trudeau government. Although there was one other candidate, Enemark had a stranglehold on the nomination, and it was essentially uncontested. Despite his contacts in the party, Enemark was really a stopgap candidate. The weak local Liberal association was unable to provide volunteers, so Enemark was forced to call on friends and acquaintances when building his campaign team. Only enormous financial support from the federal party, available to him because of the profile of the riding and his own contacts in the party, enabled Enemark to generate the semblance of a campaign. Despite his efforts to run a locally focused campaign, Enemark was drawn into the national Liberal strategy and ran a parallel campaign that was marginalized from the real contest between den Hertog and Campbell.

The Tory campaign used every available resource, particularly the candidate, to good effect. The NDP ran a solid campaign using its strong provincial resource base as well as that of the national party. In fact, this was one of the most hotly contested ridings in the country. In comparison with 1984, Tory support dropped by 4 percentage points, Liberal support was down 2 points, while the NDP picked up an extra 6 points. Campbell won by just 269 votes, or 0.4 percent of the vote.

The Candidate and Campaign Team
At the outset of the campaign, and without a candidate, the Conservatives' own polling showed them behind the NDP in Vancouver Centre. By the time Kim Campbell accepted the nomination in the third week of the campaign, the party's national fortunes had brightened. As well, Pat Carney's constituency office and a campaign team from previous elections had been at work since the summer preparing for an election. Campbell's guaranteed ride through the nomination, a perfect example of the limited democracy often found in associations in ridings such as Vancouver Centre, freed her to focus immediately on building a campaign team and getting out onto the hustings.

Campbell's name was immediately recognizable to local voters, and particularly to her constituents in Vancouver whom she had represented in the provincial legislature. She was clearly the central focus of the campaign team. Her feisty personality and obvious ability marked her as a high-profile candidate, and as a party spokesperson, she regularly appeared in the media, canvassing local, regional, and national issues. She was young, intelligent, experienced, socially progressive, and forceful – the sort of competent politician a high-profile riding deserved.

The ethos of the campaign team was a mix of personal and professional. Because of the overlap in the support base of the Socreds provincially and the Conservatives federally, Campbell had support among many Tory voters and organizers in the province. This meant she had good contacts with the sorts of people that ran Tory campaigns in British Columbia, including long-time Conservative and Social Credit campaigner Patrick Kinsella. To this she added her own group of provincial supporters. Thus, she had not only the support of the conservative elite in Vancouver but also a widely experienced group of professional campaigners, many of whom knew her personally, to draw on. As a result, the shape of her campaign team and strategies reflected the decisions of both local and national party workers.

Many of the campaigners were on leave from professional jobs in downtown Vancouver, and included advertising and public relations professionals, as well as graphic designers. From office management to advertising, the campaign had access to qualified help; for example, it used creative consultant Ray McCallister, a professional event-organizer, to oversee its publicity stunts. Many campaigners brought with them the expertise and resources of the companies they worked for. As well, the presence of a number of lawyers and accountants gave the team a professional air. Tories in other ridings saw the involvement of so many leading strategists as evidence of the party's fixation with Campbell at their expense.

With an inner circle of about twenty workers, and another fifty secondary workers, there was more than adequate help around the office. Campaign manager Lyall Knott estimates another 1,000 sympathizers helped at one time or another. While there is little doubt that the campaign contained people who were committed to the Conservative Party, the mindset of the team was very much one of electing a particularly well-qualified individual to the job of MP. Commitment to Campbell and to running a professional campaign in an important riding were powerful motivations for local campaigners.

The financial resources of the campaign team were stunning. It raised $116,488, more than twice the spending limit in the riding, and about twice that of its major opponents. With this money, the local campaign could afford to do polling of its own. In addition, the federal party did in-depth polling and analysis in the riding. Prime Minister Brian Mulroney took a special interest in the campaign, appearing a number of times in the riding. This was the epitome of a professional campaign team. Knott notes that it was a "textbook campaign, with a textbook campaign structure.

Every important campaign team position was filled by a knowledgeable campaigner. We had the money as well as the professional advice and assistance to ensure every aspect of campaigning was covered. These professional people were willing to work for nothing." Resources were plentiful, strategy making was done by experienced local and national strategists, and was implemented by committed, professional campaigners. The campaign's strategic focus was wide and included the candidate as well as local, regional, and national issues.

Intraparty Relations

Facing considerable losses in British Columbia, Conservative strategists saw Vancouver as a riding the party could win with a good campaign. The seat was considered high profile in the context of BC politics, and it was thought that a powerful campaign might have some spillover effect on other BC ridings. Moreover, holding onto the riding would bolster the party's claim that it represented all parts of Canada. Its profile ensured that it was a key component of the national party effort. But despite the involvement of national strategists, the powerful local Tory organization maintained control of the campaign.

The Tories had reason to be hopeful about the riding, as its considerable polling research suggested that the "right" candidate might do well. Strategists noted that the riding was relatively stable and could withstand the swing against the government expected throughout the province. The choice of Kim Campbell reflected the calculation that she was just such a candidate. Her appointment in late October after the campaign had begun reflected the difficulty of finding a strong candidate in a riding that the Tories might lose.

Focusing on the candidate was the party's response to the unpopularity of the federal government in British Columbia. The party offered her assistance at every level. In the words of campaign manager Lyall Knott, "The party put its considerable resources, both provincial and national, at our disposal, which, when added to those of the retiring Minister Pat Carney, made for a formidable campaign organization."

The Centre campaign was one of half a dozen identified for special treatment by the party, as evidenced by the moneys that flowed its way from the Progressive Conservative campaign fund. Whereas most other campaigns in British Columbia received a few thousand dollars, and usually via the provincial headquarters of the national campaign, Campbell received $19,490 from the national fund. By way of comparison, the losing Conservative incumbent in Kootenay West-Revelstoke received nothing from head office. Despite the assistance it received from head office, the local campaign maintained its independence.

Contrary to national party directions, local strategists decided that the local campaign had to address free trade, a potentially damaging issue for the Tories. Vancouver Centre, with its large media outlets and central location, was deeply embedded in both the regional and national debates over this major issue, which dominated the local riding context. Moreover, the NDP was willing to use the issue in British Columbia to cement its position as the main opponent to the Conservatives in the province. But national strategists wanted to avoid it. Knott outlines the local strategy in this way: "We ran a campaign that was 180 degrees away from the one the national party suggested. They had not factored in the BC effect – that is, we were running against the NDP more than the Liberals. We thought that in Centre, the anti-free trade vote would be split between the Liberals and New Democrats, and we could come up the middle. In fact, national strategists didn't even think free trade should be the main issue at the outset of the campaign."

As it happens, the national campaign asked for copies of the free trade literature produced in Centre after John Turner's strong performance in the leaders' debates raised interest in the issue. Campbell agrees that the campaign's independence was important: "Local control of campaign strategy allowed us to make the most of the fact that I was a different sort of PC candidate: a feminist, pro-choice candidate, interested in local issues but capable of dealing with national issues. We were able to take advantage of our maverick status. [We were] ... an antidote to the traditional power politics of the East."

Fortunately for the local campaign, it had enough resources to develop its own strategies. This and the abundance of media coverage and advertising outlets in the riding helped it implement this strategy successfully. The symbiotic relationship between component and national campaigns is reflected in the relative autonomy of the local campaign. But this autonomy came at a price, as Knott notes: "Relations with the national party office in Vancouver deteriorated as a result of our decision. They did not believe a PC campaign could win running on [free trade]." Yet at the same time, campaigners noted Campbell's campaign played a key role in the wider federal election. News stories by regional and national media concerning national issues often dealt with Campbell's campaign. She was also asked for her opinion on a range of local, regional, and national issues. The national campaign needed this sort of media attention and could not afford to alienate candidates such as Campbell, nor local campaign organizers.

The Local Contest
Even before the contest formally began, Pat Carney's local organization had been advertising in community newspapers with four-page inserts throughout the summer. Ostensibly presented as information packages on issues such as free trade, supplements were as much designed to sell the

government's policies as to enhance her reelection chances by touting her role in the free trade negotiations and the government. When Campbell became the Tory candidate, the local organization ran a similar advertisement in her name.

The nature of this city riding had profound implications for the Tory campaign. The political history of the riding held mixed signals. Many pundits, and certainly the polls, were predicting that the NDP would ride the anti-Tory wave to victory. The NDP held the two provincial seats in the area, and its federal performance had improved in recent elections. But the riding has often sent high-profile members to Ottawa, and had always been well reported in influential local, regional, and national media. This media profile was attractive to national strategists and held out the possibility of a high-profile campaign that might win the riding for the party.

Tory strategists worked hard to ensure that Campbell received maximum exposure in the major media based in Centre. Organizers had her appear wherever there might be media coverage, and constructed events for this purpose. The candidate had very little to do with the day-to-day running of the campaign, noting that she went where she was told and did what she enjoys and does well: speaking to people. One of the benefits of having a strategy built around a competent candidate with access to the media is that a campaign can quickly and effectively respond to the actions of its opponents. The very next press conference or public event provides an opportunity for the candidate to defend his or her position or attack the opponent's at very little cost to the campaign. The success of this strategy motivates campaigns to organize more press conferences and public events and drives the choice of campaign techniques.

The decision to focus on free trade presented problems for the local Tory campaign, in part because the issue was so closely linked to the unpopular Mulroney. Local strategists believed that it was impossible to avoid the issue in a sophisticated city riding. They decided to tackle the issue head-on. They knew that Campbell's profile and the media coverage she would attract would allow her to address this issue within a local context. They hoped that by addressing free trade locally, Campbell would prove herself to be both her own person – and therefore able to be elected against the anti-Tory tide in the province – and competent, worth sending to Ottawa.

Campbell's forceful defence of free trade at public forums helped her capture substantial media attention and highlighted her strength of character and intelligence. At the all-candidates debate in Christ Church Cathedral, she made headlines by challenging anti-free trade hecklers in the crowd, asking them "what [they were] afraid of," and suggesting that those voters with real faith in Canada should have no fear of American dominance due to the agreement. National party strategists more than once expressed their doubts that the local campaign was up to the challenge, but were proved wrong.

Party officials and the media agree that in a close contest, a good candidate can be crucial to success. Strong candidates are an attraction for the media, so their activities tend to be reported. Their personal qualities are a vital part of the campaign. This is particularly true for a member from Vancouver Centre, as he or she may well be in cabinet if his or her party wins office. Campbell had built up a working relationship with Vancouver journalists during her time as provincial MLA and minister. She was comfortable with them and they with her. One local journalist was so taken by her that he built an impressive pictorial record of her on the campaign trail.

The nature of Centre provided candidates with opportunities to canvass many issues. Companies and community organizations working in different sectors of the BC economy have head offices in Vancouver. Issues as diverse as fishing, forestry, mining, welfare, and immigration could be addressed as part of the public debate with the representatives of companies and associations with headquarters in Vancouver. By encouraging public debate in Centre, parties and the media simplify the logistical demands of conducting and reporting a province-wide campaign. Publicity of Campbell's pro-choice position on abortion and liberal views on homosexuality further enhanced her reputation as an unusual Tory.

Given that Vancouver Centre is home to most of the major media of British Columbia, coverage of the contest was extensive. All the major Vancouver-based media have extensive affiliation arrangements for receiving news from and distributing it to other parts of Canada, and most are relayed or published throughout British Columbia.[1] As with the Tories, other local campaigns in Centre seized every opportunity to gain exposure for their candidates, having them attend every all-candidates debate and make innumerable public appearances, both spontaneous and scripted. This heightened the sense that the campaigns, particularly those of the front-running NDP and PC candidates, were engaged in a close contest.

Media exposure gave Campbell's and den Hertog's campaigns the chance to set the local agenda and to act as components of their respective national campaigns. It is one of the paradoxes of component campaigns that they are in a position to selectively defy national party strategies; this was particularly true of Campbell's campaign. Local campaigns have the capacity to generate their own strategies, and because national campaigns need them, have the freedom to implement them. This symbiotic relationship means that the local campaigns are not at the whim of the federal campaigns.

Attempts by national strategists to take advantage of media coverage of this high-profile contest were criticized by some local campaigners, who thought that this distorted the media reporting of the election, skewing the content of the local issue space in favour of nonlocal concerns (Sayers 1991, 45). Campbell's narrow win in an area dominated by the NDP provincially was remarkable. Her personal campaign skills and her ability to attract to her a team of professional campaigners were crucial to this result.

Svend Robinson: Local Boy, National Hero

Svend Robinson is a high-profile politician closely associated with issues important to his party. Although the local NDP association in Burnaby-Kingsway was competitive, its impermeability and the presence of an incumbent forestalled a candidate search and any challenge to his renomination. He was acclaimed after a closed, uncontested nomination. With a mix of strong local and national support, Robinson built a professional, experienced, and well-financed campaign team whose members were strongly committed to his vision of politics; a vision that was seen as symbolic of the politics of the NDP. His strong connections to the national party as national spokesperson on defence and other issues helped ensure that his campaign was a component of the national NDP effort.

Robinson was expected to win, but strategists admitted some uncertainty as a result of his announcement of his homosexuality and because of changes to riding boundaries in the area. It is possible that in a socially diverse city riding such as Burnaby-Kingsway with a history of voting for the NDP, such an admission was never going to be a liability. With a powerful campaign team committed to both Robinson and the party, and extensive media coverage of the candidate, the NDP ran a professional front-runner campaign in an uncontested riding. Robinson recorded an easy victory, gaining 43 percent of the vote, well ahead of the Tories at 29.8 percent and the Liberals at 22.1 percent.

Robinson's Progressive Conservative opponent was John Bitonti, a local notable who had run for the BC Socreds in 1987. Although asked to run for the nomination by some local Tories, Bitonti was an insurgent candidate who joined the association only just prior to the nomination. He won the open, contested race with the support of relatives and acquaintances in the local Italian-Canadian community, but alienated a number of traditional association members, many of whom refused to help with his campaign. Most of Bitonti's supporters had little interest in politics. Moreover, he did not look like he was capable of winning the riding. As a result, few of his supporters were willing to join his campaign team, leaving him to rely on friends and relatives. With little support from the national party, which felt Bitonti could not win, the campaign suffered from a lack of funds and experienced workers. Despite that he was not interested in many of the main themes of the national campaign, Bitonti lacked the resources to run a parochial campaign. He tried to generate interest in what he thought was a local issue – Robinson's homosexuality – but which was in fact a national issue. Some national Tory strategists saw his anti-gay views as problematic for the party, fearing they would alienate the large gay community in Vancouver Centre, where Kim Campbell was involved in a tight race with the NDP. Bitonti's was a failed parochial campaign that was excluded from an uncontested constituency election by Robinson's strong electoral position and professional campaign.

The very weak local Liberal association could not find its own candidate. Although the nomination was open, it was uncontested, and party worker Sam Stevens was nominated as a stopgap candidate in the riding. The campaign team consisted of a few local party stalwarts who had little in the way of funds or other resources. The national party provided one-third of the paltry $18,071 raised by the campaign, substantially more than the average it offered other BC Liberal campaigns. This was a parallel campaign that was excluded from the constituency election and had little impact on the local contest.

Only Robinson's campaign was competitive in the local election, with his personality dominating the local political landscape. At no time did the local campaigns ever engage each other. Although Robinson received a great deal of provincial and national media attention, the local contest and his opponents did not.

The Candidate and Campaign Team

Robinson's high profile and political influence had a number of sources. He first won the riding in 1979, and is well known and respected as a hard-working MP. Robinson is very much at home in Burnaby-Kingsway, which has a history of voting NDP and takes pride in the fact that Robinson is a local boy – a graduate of Burnaby North High School who grew up in the area and became its member of Parliament. He makes much of his main street, storefront, constituency office in Burnaby as evidence of the access his constituents have to their local member.

Robinson believes he understands the riding, the local issues, and people who live there. As an incumbent, he has access to all the advantages of a constituency office. He has a place where he can meet voters, a coordination centre from which to begin campaigning, the capacity to maintain lists of volunteers and supporters, mailing privileges, and the advantages of continuity in seeking funds and voter support (see Heintzman 1991).

Robinson has also attracted attention as a national spokesperson for gay and lesbian communities across Canada and has been the NDP critic on a number of issues. His admission of his homosexuality has given him a high degree of moral credibility among voters interested in these issues. This national profile and his membership in the NDP executive means that he is intimately connected with policy making. He is both a powerful party insider and a high-profile public figure. It is not surprising that his renomination was by acclamation – a good example of the limited democracy found in most incumbent nominations.

Robinson enjoyed the support of both his partisan followers in Burnaby-Kingsway and an issue-oriented, national constituency. Gays and lesbians in particular, had, in Robinson's words, "a direct interest in [his] reelection." He is a standard-bearer for a minority that has suffered extensive discrimination, and for whom public admission of homosexuality is a politically charged issue. Not only does he offer practical political support for gay and lesbian concerns, he is a role model for their participation in Canadian public life. Many campaign team members exhibited a strong personal commitment to Robinson. Unlike in many other NDP campaigns, volunteers ranked the candidate as very important to the overall campaign strategy. Although the party platform and the candidate were considered of about equal importance, it appears that Robinson was an important symbol to workers and the party at large. For many members of the campaign inner circle, including those from his constituency office, Robinson's candidacy was of great symbolic value, showing the acceptance of homosexuals into mainstream Canada.

The inner circle of Robinson's campaign numbered around 15 and exhibited a high degree of solidarity and professionalism. The second circle of workers numbered about 50, but Robinson's high profile meant that he had access to a further 500 or so from the strong local association and among sympathizers. As well, Robinson's appeal as a national crusader meant he attracted workers from outside the riding. Some were experienced NDP organizers who work in critical campaigns both at the federal and provincial level and who chose to work with Robinson. One indication of the special appeal of the campaign was the syphoning of workers from other NDP campaigns in Vancouver. Party members interested in social policy and gay and lesbian issues moved from the Vancouver Centre campaign of Johanna den Hertog to Robinson's campaign.

Fund-raising efforts were extensive and effective, made easier by Robinson's national profile and the strength of the local association. He attracted money from political activists and gays and lesbians across Canada, which reinforced his image as an important politician. So too did the attendance of well-known television personality and environmentalist David Suzuki at a fund-raising event, helping to ensure that it was a success. Regular appearances on national television, often with important public figures, heightened Robinson's profile. This strengthened his local appeal and facilitated fund-raising in the riding. By the time of the election, the campaign had raised $70,331. This is three and one-half times what either the Conservative or Liberal campaigns were able to raise, and about twice the average fund-raising result for BC New Democrat campaigns.[2] The campaign managed to spend 93 percent of the $49,005 spending limit in the riding. In comparison, Robinson's PC opponent spent 69.2 percent of the limit, and the Liberal candidate 35.2 percent.

Robinson's profile ensured that his campaign was intertwined with the national NDP effort. Many of his organizers were experienced party workers and Robinson was a prominent figure in the national campaign, with wide interests and access to national media. His profile attracts national support to the NDP, making him important in the party's wider campaign and allowing him some discretion in how he campaigns. As well, the strength of his campaign team enabled him to maintain some independence from the national campaign and to address many issues. While the focus of Robinson's campaign moved across local and national issues, the locus of strategic decision making remained local.

Robinson was reasonably confident that he would hold the riding. He had substantial personal support, and the New Democrat's star was on the rise, particularly in British Columbia, where it expected to benefit from Conservative losses. Even the substantial redrawing of electoral boundaries in Burnaby just prior to the election appeared unlikely to affect Robinson adversely, as the whole area has a history of voting for the New Democrats. But he had not run as an openly declared homosexual before, and there was uncertainty as to how voters would respond to this. On the other hand, it gave his campaign something of the air of a crusade, which meant it attracted added financial and volunteer support.

Intraparty Relations
Robinson was a critical component of the NDP's drive to major party status. Many saw the election of a gay candidate as symbolically very important. Among gays and lesbians, it was a measure of their progress in accessing the political system and of their acceptance in wider society. It reinforced the NDP's position as champion of minority causes and leader on peace and environment issues, for which Robinson was a party spokesperson. As an important policy maker and opinion leader in the party, Robinson's profile attracted media coverage and helped cement the party's position on the political spectrum. And like any party, the NDP wanted to retain those seats it held.

The symbiotic relationship between local and national organizations found in component campaigns was clearly evident in Robinson's campaign. Being closely involved with national politics and party policy making, Robinson was invited to speak at regional and national press conferences organized by the party to deal with important issues as they arose during the campaign. He also advised party leader Ed Broadbent on a number of justice issues. He played a key role in the BC NDP campaign, helping to run the election school for provincial candidates and campaign managers, and offering them insights drawn from his campaign experience.

Robinson's campaign did not require financial or staffing support from the national party, which prefers to avoid offering such help to well-off incumbents in favour of less wealthy campaigns (Stanbury 1991, 151). However, the party made available technical support in the form of polling data, as well as assistance from professionals at party headquarters. As a result, the campaign was in close touch with national campaign strategists and privy to major tactical and strategic decision making in which Robinson was often personally involved.

A party wants candidates to speak to issues it sees as important, and to stick to the party line. Maverick candidates can be damaging to the national campaign. For their part, candidates who neglect local affairs, or support locally unpopular policies at the behest of their party, can damage their own local campaigns. The tension in this relationship is exacerbated in the case of high-profile candidates. This is just the sort of candidate a party wants to use as spokesperson, but such candidates have strong local campaigns and access to the media, and may be difficult to control.

In mass parties such as the NDP, which expect conformity from their members, the independence of high-profile candidates is particularly noticeable. Because of his strategic value to the party, and the fact that he could finance and operate a strong campaign, Robinson had some discretion in interpreting party policy. Although he shared the party's objectives, and the strategic focus of his campaign included local and nonlocal issues, it was not formally integrated into the national campaign. Says Robinson, "There was little contact between the local campaign and the national campaign, in part because we were so well organized, and because my riding was not seen as a priority. [That is, the party expected to win it.] For example, Broadbent did not visit Burnaby-Kingsway during the election campaign."

That Robinson could ask "Ed Broadbent to step aside and let [him] act as party spokesperson on a number of issues, including those affecting gays and lesbians," indicates that his is an exceptional case of this independence. Broadbent may have been willing to cede this role so as to maintain his appeal to a broad audience, avoiding antagonizing any anti-gay voters.

Despite their potential for independent action, component campaigns are embedded in party affairs. As a result, their strategic vision is likely to be similar to that of national strategists. As well, component campaigns receive enough media attention and have the opportunity to raise many issues, both local and nonlocal. While media coverage generates disputes over strategy between local and national campaigns, it is also a means for dealing with these differences.

The symbiotic relationship between component campaigns and the national party gives the former some autonomy. The national party needs these campaigns and does not wish to alienate high-profile candidates. How the centrifugal impulse of financial independence and access to media balance the centripetal forces of integration depend on the strength and organizational ethos of the party and the local campaign. In this case, although deeply embedded in NDP politics, Robinson's campaign was largely a world unto itself. Robinson's pursuit of his agenda and the party's willingness to accept this make him an unusual NDP candidate. In a party that prides itself on solidarity and uniformity, he is the exception that may prove the rule.

The Local Contest
Robinson's constituency office staff began to campaign well before the election was called. Lists of donors and volunteers from previous elections were dusted off and used to solicit volunteers and funds. Pamphlets extolling Robinson's virtues were distributed. And as is common among MPs, Robinson's office made a point of issuing "householders," the publicly funded newsletters MPs distribute to their constituents, just prior to the election, reminding voters of his work for the riding, his accessibility, and pointing to his leadership on high-profile issues.

Robinson ceded control of the campaign to a group of loyal, experienced inner circle workers: "I do what I am told; I trust their judgment. The most important thing for a candidate to know is how to take directions from his or her campaign team." Robinson's team canvassed the riding thoroughly on his behalf and ran the campaign office. By relying heavily on his campaign team to oversee the day-to-day organization of the office, Robinson was free to campaign in person about 80 to 90 percent of the time, though he did little door-to-door work, focusing instead on public events. This is common in the case of incumbents and high-profile candidates (Land 1965, 89).

Somewhat paradoxically then, the closeness of the relationship between Robinson and his team removed him from the everyday strategic decisions required of a campaign. This was possible only because the team had developed and demonstrated expertise in previous elections. Robinson not only trusts their judgment but has learned that this is the basis of a successful campaign. Winning campaigns tend to use the same style of campaigning that has been successful in the past.

Freedom from mundane tasks was critical in allowing Robinson to campaign in person across the country and in his own riding. His public profile became the central organizing theme of the campaign. The campaign revolved around him – where he went, what he did, the issues he stood for, the media he had access to, and the resources he brought with him. In a programmatical party such as the NDP, this emphasis on the candidate is a rarity and reveals the national party's willingness to deal with Robinson on his terms.

The most densely populated parts of Burnaby-Kingsway cannot be canvassed using traditional forms of campaigning, such as door-knocking and street signs. Robinson estimates that about 40 percent of the population live in high-rise apartments.[3] These apartments are difficult to canvass in person because canvassers have to get past security systems, and tenants are notoriously reluctant to allow this. As a result, it is especially important to city campaigns to work at other means of communicating their messages to voters. Campaigners worked to maximize Robinson's exposure to the major media in British Columbia and across the country, portraying him as a national political figure who took principled stands on a number of important issues. Because national media exposure is also seen in Burnaby-Kingsway, this was an effective strategy. The second element of the strategy to deal with voters living in apartments was a heavy reliance on phone banks. Phone banks allowed campaigners to get to voters, and were seen as much less intrusive than canvassing in person. The expense of phone banks and the need to staff them can place great demands on local campaigns. Neither of Robinson's opponents could afford this effort.

As a high-profile candidate, Robinson attracted the attention of the metropolitan media, including high-rating television stations such as BCTV. His campaign worked hard to provide him with the sorts of situations that are worth reporting. When he was in the riding, Robinson did most of his door-to-door campaigning in the mornings and attended events and other press conferences in the afternoon. In a typical day, with the morning spent canvassing and the afternoon at some event, Robinson would return to the campaign office at about 9 p.m. in the evening to answer questions from campaigners and see the schedule for the following day.

The campaign worked hard to show him as a concerned and effective local member. The Burnaby-Kingsway area has a large number of seniors' homes and two large educational institutions, Simon Fraser University (SFU) and the British Columbia Institute of Technology (BCIT). The campaign considered seniors to be very important, as they have a high propensity to vote, and meetings with seniors provide a good backdrop for media reporting. Robinson's campaign targeted (or "blitzed," as Robinson calls it) seniors' homes, meeting voters and providing a backdrop for media exposure that would be seen by other voters in the riding. He emphasized his local roots in the riding and interest in "people issues." Images of Robinson with senior citizens helped reinforce his standing as a respected, caring local member.

Local educational institutions also provided a useful backdrop for Robinson's campaign. His efforts at SFU and BCIT were designed to present, both directly and through the media, an image of a candidate concerned for young people and education. Although many of those attending these debates were not Burnaby-Kingsway voters, the debates were well covered by the media and hence seen by voters in the riding. Media scrums at public events meant Robinson, in his role as a party spokesperson and senior NDP member, was asked about national issues. This allowed him to address a wider audience and reaffirmed his national stature with local voters. However, such events pose some danger, as a difficult question or a gaffe by a candidate can damage a campaign.

Intensive phone canvassing aimed in particular at apartment dwellers followed a traditional pattern. Voters were classified as supporter, undecided, or hostile. This information, along with information on historical patterns of support, was collated by poll. The effort put into a certain poll, and the style of campaigning adopted, depended on how it was classified. Hostile polls received the least attention, while strongly supportive polls received attention in the form or requests for help and money. Supportive polls were targeted on election day in order to get out the vote. Polls where there were many undecided voters received the greatest attention and were subjected to the most aggressive campaigning.

Access to a phone bank meant that Robinson's campaign could call undecided voters several times during the election. Canvassers may have offered to send particular information or suggested a meeting with the candidate or campaign representative. The concerns of these voters were addressed through specifically designed letters signed by the candidate. Any voter who showed an interest in the campaign when approached personally or by phone was sent a detailed outline of the NDP platform and Robinson's particular interests.

The campaign used a mix of local, regional, and national issues to gain voters' attention. Major issues, such as human rights, social policy, free trade, and the goods and services tax, shared billing with local concerns such as pollution from a local refinery and transportation problems, the latter an acute concern for commuters. But it was Robinson's profile on national issues that dominated campaign literature and advertising. Robinson also saw national leadership as crucial to election outcomes. This view was not shared by many campaign workers in British Columbia, and is evidence of Robinson's strong ties to national party strategies that focused on Broadbent's leadership.

Relations between the media and the Robinson campaign were extensive. Even before his announcement of his homosexuality, Robinson's media profile was high. Events during the campaign, including ambiguous comments about his sexuality by his Conservative opponent and the prime minister, only heightened media interest. The major media reported his press conferences, and, in Robinson's estimation, used 75 percent of his press releases, the highest percentage reported by any campaign.

Robinson considers coverage by market leader BCTV to have been critical to his campaign. He also received extensive coverage in the *Vancouver Sun* and the *Province* newspapers, as well as on radio, including coverage on the most popular station, CKNW. His national profile was enhanced by coverage in the *Globe and Mail* and on national CBC and CTV television.

The local community newspapers in the riding include the *Burnaby NOW* (which reaches beyond the riding boundaries) and the *EastEnder* (covering the entire Vancouver east side). Both SFU and BCIT have student newspapers. All these newspapers ran profiles of the candidates and covered the election, but they were not considered influential. Robinson's access to major media coverage meant his campaign did not pay community newspapers much attention. He gave interviews to these newspapers, but they played little role in the campaign strategy. For their part, editors of local papers believe they must report the contest but know their papers' impact is limited by a lack of resources and investigative ability. Editors often dread the extra demands made of a federal election, particularly when, as in this instance, local municipal elections occur at about the same time.

Despite their lack of value as a news source, community newspapers are the main vehicles for campaign advertising, being the only advertising local campaigns can afford. Campaigners are conservative and averse to taking risks, and in general unwilling to miss an opportunity to advertise where they can afford to, even if the impact is dubious. All four local newspapers carried campaign advertising. The print advertisements, as well as the campaign brochures, were all locally produced. If anything, the lack of influential local media emphasized the need for campaigns to gain exposure in regional and national newspapers and television.

Robinson's campaign did not do any local polling. It is expensive, and campaigners believed they had a good sense of the local riding, and that Robinson was going to win. Rather, the campaign relied heavily on gaining a sense of voters' concerns through canvassing and, having identified undecided voters, concentrating on garnering their support. Robinson's confidence can also be seen in his attitude towards all-candidates debates, which indicates just how uncompetitive his opponents were and how little the local campaigns engaged with each other: "We agreed to attend one all-candidates meeting. I did not need the exposure, and these events are essentially boring. We get much better exposure at events organized for either myself, or a group of NDP candidates. We did half a dozen meet-the-candidate events, advertising them by dropping literature in the area first, and then reporting what was said at the meeting in the literature dropped after the event. I do not need to go head to head with my opponents – my electoral position does not require it."

The lack of engagement between the local campaigns was a defining characteristic of the local contest. The New Democrats did not need to engage with the other local campaigns and concentrated instead on keeping Robinson in the public eye as a means of communicating with voters.

Despite some concern in the NDP about the impact of Robinson's candour about his personal life on his chances, his national profile cemented Robinson's position as the only competitive candidate in an essentially uncontested riding. Robinson recounts how listless his opponents' campaigns were: "On election night, I went to visit my opponents. I could not find the Liberal headquarters, and tracked down Bitonti in a hotel room with his sister and bother-in-law and two other people; it was sad. Other than the all-candidates meeting, this is the only time I met or was aware of my opponents. Our campaign did not directly address them [as a serious challenge] at any stage."

In fact, not only was the Liberal campaign very weak, but it appears that local and nonlocal Tories gave their own candidate no chance of winning. John Bitonti believes that the party did not appreciate his controversial stand on family values and did not want him exposed to the media. He concludes that they were happy to see him lose the riding.

Robinson's campaign was a component of the national NDP effort, evident in the role he played in national affairs and the fact that his candidacy was seen as a symbol of ideas and issues important to the party. But while all Canadians knew Svend Robinson was the MP for Burnaby-Kingsway, his opponents went largely unnoticed. The national and local campaigns were intertwined through the person of Robinson. If one of his opponents had seriously challenged Robinson, there is little doubt that this would have been a major news story. Robinson's national profile suited city voters in the riding, who expect their candidates to have high profile and to see them reported in the major media. Moreover, his involvement in a range of local, regional, and national issues was commensurate with the interests of a heterogeneous, urban community.

While the campaign strategy was heavily loaded towards media events, and Robinson spent much of his time playing to a national audience, campaigners also paid close attention to local voters. They met all the demands of local campaigning – foot and phone canvassing, leaflet drops, placing signs, and so on. Full use was made of Robinson's time in the riding by having him meet with local voters, and press releases tied his national statements into local issues. Robinson combined his access to the national media with a strong riding campaign to reinforce his image as both a good local member – a local boy – and a powerful national political figure – a national hero.

Al Horning: Packaging a Local Notable
A local notable, Al Horning had served on the local council and was a

member of many local service organizations when he decided to run for the Tory nomination in the country riding of Okanagan Centre. Horning was new to both the party and national politics, but was well known among local Tories because of his work in the community and on sporting organizations. The area is strongly Conservative, and the nomination had a good deal of appeal for potential candidates. Constructed after the recent redrawing of boundaries, the cadre-style PC association was permeable and had an open search process.

Horning won a highly contested nomination by recruiting many members and convincing some of his opponents and stalwarts of the party to back him on the second ballot. These new members and some experienced party members formed the basis of a well-financed and -staffed campaign team that ran a highly parochial campaign based on Horning's personal connection to the riding. Horning bolstered the professionalism of the campaign team by hiring a public relations expert to deal with media relations. The intimate nature of the campaign team and the resources available to it allowed it to develop a locally directed, parochial campaign. Although a front-runner in what was in the main an uncontested constituency election, events during the campaign complicated Horning's electioneering.

Horning's main rival for the seat was NDP candidate and local businessman Bryan McIver. Despite the riding being new, the existing cohort of NDP members from the previous ridings was divided to fit the associations created by the new boundaries. Reassigning resources gave a fillip to new associations in those areas of Tory dominance such as Kelowna. The Okanagan Centre association was impermeable. Although McIver had been a member of the Tory party, he had been an NDP member for a number of years and was a party insider. The search committee managed to attract three existing members to run for the nomination. McIver won a classic closed but contested New Democrat nomination.

Given that the NDP has never done well in Kelowna, the local association was not one of the strongest in the province. Although it mustered enough workers and money to run a solid campaign, it was a subsidiary campaign, relying heavily on the regional and national strategies of the party for direction. Fortunately, the importance of intensive agriculture in the local economy, which looked likely to be damaged by the free trade deal, made these strategies relevant in the local context. However, given the strength of the Conservative campaign in the riding, the NDP was largely excluded from the constituency election, though there were brief moments during the campaign when the NDP did engage with the Tories.

Spurred on by the opportunity to reshape the political landscape out of the uncertainty generated by new riding boundaries, the Liberals conducted a candidate search that attracted four contenders who managed to sign up over a thousand members to the new association. Local notable Murli Pendharkar, a former school superintendent, won the nomination on the first ballot with the strong support of members from the local Indo-Canadian community.

Unfortunately, the Liberals' original optimism turned out to be misplaced, as the party struggled to raise money and to find experienced campaigners. The job of campaign manager had to be shared between two people, and despite trying to develop its own strategies, this was a parallel campaign that reflected the strategic moves of its national counterpart. In the end, it was largely swept up in the local free trade debate, a debate which better suited the NDP and Tory campaigns, and which excluded the Liberals from the local contest.

The rise of the Reform Party, led by candidate and original party member Werner Schmidt, was a shock to the local Tories. Schmidt won an open, contested nomination. Although his campaign lacked the resources and volunteers of the NDP and Tory campaigns, it attracted both money and people, as Schmidt did well at public events. Given the nascent quality of Reform at this election, it is difficult to assess the nature of its campaign or gauge its impact on the contest. Its appeal to right wing voters added some uncertainty into a contest that the Tories were expected to dominate.

The political community defined by Okanagan Centre had a set of interests associated with its major rural-based industries of intensive agriculture, water resource management, and tourism. Country ridings often have relatively undiversified economies, so anything that affects a major industry has ramifications for employment throughout the area. The potential impact of free trade on the local economy made this the major issue. Kelowna supports a number of medium-sized media organizations that are influential, capable of covering the campaign and able to reinterpret national debates using local lenses. Their detailed coverage of the local contest, including all-candidates debates, allowed local campaigns to engage with each other. Campaigns could afford to advertise in this media, implementing their own strategies and casting the free trade debate in local terms. All this meant that political debate had a sharp, local focus.

The NDP was somewhat competitive mainly as a result of Reform stealing PC votes. Reform had its strongest showing in British Columbia in this riding, polling 15.5 percent of the vote. Local Tories were more concerned about the Reform Party, whose position to the right of the Conservatives in a socially conservative riding such as Okanagan Centre was seen as a threat. In the end, the Tory vote dropped by about 20 percentage points from 1984, leaving Horning 7 points ahead of New Democrat Bryan McIver, who increased the NDP vote only marginally. That the NDP did not gain much ground meant that the riding was not highly contested.

Liberal candidate Murli Pendharkar garnered 17 percent of the vote, a modest improvement for the party.

The Candidate and Campaign Team

Al Horning focused all his efforts for a few months prior to the election on winning the highly contested Okanagan Centre Conservative nomination. Such endeavours are the hallmark of open, contested nominations. Although he had no federal campaign experience, and was not even a member of the party prior to the nomination, Horning had served in local politics in Kelowna for eight years. His intimate connections with the local community and social and business elites won him the nomination. This was seen as the most difficult task on the road to winning the seat, as the area had often returned Conservative MPs to Ottawa. In order to include volunteers who had supported his nomination opponents, Horning finalized his campaign team after he was nominated.

The success of a new party member such as Horning is a corollary of the permeability of the nomination process in this new Conservative association in British Columbia. It exhibits the cyclical growth and shrinkage in size typical of the associations of cadre-style parties. The Okanagan Centre Conservative nomination meeting attracted just over 2,000 voting members, most of whom were signed up by the candidates. The association lacked a coterie of well-placed members to act as gatekeepers for the nomination or build alliances aimed at guaranteeing a chosen candidate success. Winning the nomination required Horning to bring together a coalition of members he had recruited with supporters of candidates eliminated after the first ballot. Only after a single issue, anti-abortion candidate threatened to win the nomination did members rally behind Horning to give him victory on the second ballot.

Many new association members were only nominally committed to the party and were not experienced campaigners. Their first and sometimes only allegiance was to the candidate who signed them up, and many were unwilling to help with the campaign once their candidate had been eliminated. Despite this, the long tradition of support for the Conservatives in the area meant that the association was very large, and Horning had access to between 500 and 600 sympathizers. Most of the forty or so secondary workers were Horning's friends, who, lacking campaign experience, took directions from the inner circle.

The inner circle consisted of about a dozen experienced campaigners, some of whom had supported Horning's nomination rivals. Glenn Duncan ran the Kelowna campaign, while Troy Schmidt, who was much admired for his efforts in nearly winning the nomination for the pro-life Richter, ran the campaign in neighbouring Winfield. Horning had sufficient resources to hire Brian Lightburn as a full-time communications director.

Having worked for two provincial Socred cabinet ministers, and with twelve years' experience in the media, Lightburn was well suited to the job of overseeing media relations. He went on to become Horning's personal assistant after Horning was elected MP for Okanagan Centre.

The mix of friends and acquaintances with well-connected locals and experienced campaigners produced a strong team that retained a personal feel. Lightburn noted that about 80 percent of the team knew Horning well, having dealt with him in local civic affairs, sporting teams, or in business. Country ridings with their sense of local community lend themselves to this sort of campaign team.

The inner circle was the locus of strategic decision making, and, not surprisingly, the campaign focused on the candidate and local issues. With so little campaign experience, Horning did not feel able to challenge the strategic decisions of Duncan, Schmidt, and Lightburn. In fact, Lightburn actively prevented Horning from playing an organizational role: "I kept Al away from the organizational aspects of the campaign, and directed him to spend his time dealing one-on-one with voters. This is what he does best, and in terms of attracting votes, it helped offset his difficulty with public forums."

The strength of the association allowed the team to raise $54,974, $12,000 more than the campaign of its closest opponent, Bryan McIver of the NDP. Because of the close relations between workers and the local community, the campaign had access to other important resources. Rental equipment, sign painting services, and so forth were all arranged through acquaintances. The campaign produced literature, as well as radio, television, and newspaper advertisements, using local companies. Lightburn used his contacts with local media owners to facilitate the media campaign.

Focusing on Horning's connections to the riding and local issues presented some difficulties. After it became clear that Horning did not speak well in public, Schmidt, Duncan, and Lightburn redesigned the campaign to limit his attendance at public-speaking engagements. They pursued a strong media and advertising campaign to promote Horning and overcome his absence from public events that were reported in the media. As well, the campaign conducted a strong canvass of the riding. As the election progressed and media relations became more important, Lightburn became the central player, directing strategy and coordinating the actions of the two regional campaign managers.

This modification of campaign strategy is proof of how a candidate's abilities (or lack thereof) can impact on a campaign. The campaign was redesigned to minimize Horning's opportunities to alienate voters. The retention of a modified, candidate-centred strategy despite these difficulties points to the importance of local notables to their campaigns, the independence of these campaigns, and in this case, the nature of country ridings. Personal connections between local notables and voters are seen as powerful vote-getting qualities in a local campaign, particularly one in a country riding. Few campaigns would be willing to give away such an advantage. But Horning's campaign was able to do this only because it had access to a credible and affordable local media, and the flexibility of a parochial campaign to develop and implement its own strategies.

Horning was central to his campaign in a very different way than Robinson was to his. Public performances and a national profile were not the key to the local strategy; rather, Horning's connections with the riding were considered his greatest asset. This was confirmed by campaigners, who, when asked, ranked the candidate as very important – more so than issues or the party leader – noting that his links to the riding rather than his personality or abilities were critical to success. Given the intimate nature of community life in country ridings, the sort of community work done by Horning seems to be of particular value to a candidate.

Intraparty Relations
Intraparty relations were largely controlled by the local Tory campaign in Okanagan Centre. The campaign did not need financial assistance but requested that the national Tory government act to still local fears over free trade. As one of the few ridings in British Columbia where the Tories looked as though they would win, the local campaign was able to extract just the assistance it needed. During the campaign, visiting cabinet ministers announced a series of plans to encourage local fruit and wine growers to rationalize their production, as well as an adjustment fund to help them deal with the loss of tariff protection. This was consistent with attempts to localize discussion regarding free trade. The assistance offered by the national party enabled Tories in Centre to demonstrate that local concerns were important to the government and the party. They pointed to their effective lobbying as evidence of the advantage of having the ear of the cabinet.

Brian Mulroney made a brief visit following Horning's nomination but prior to the election being called, and not as a result of local requests. Other cabinet ministers including Joe Clark and Don Mazankowski visited just before and during the campaign in response to local requests. The emphasis on cabinet ministers other than the prime minister was intentional, as the free trade deal associated with Mulroney was controversial in the riding. Such attention also indicated the uncertainty generated by new riding boundaries and uneasiness about the growing Reform threat to the Tories' traditional support base. Wheeling out the big guns was a way of reminding the local faithful just how important they, and the riding, were to Tory fortunes in the West. The local campaign received further strategic assistance from the provincial campaign office in Vancouver. Glenn

Duncan, the campaign manager at the Kelowna office, was in daily contact with the provincial office. Using speaker phones, three or four strategists in Vancouver would speak to a number of campaign managers from different campaigns at the same time.

Despite the campaign's willingness to discuss free trade and links with the national party, these issues never overshadowed the campaign's strategic focus on the candidate. The campaign's success in emphasizing Horning was a function of its access to substantial financial and human resources, sound strategic advice from paid organizers and experienced campaigners, and an influential local media able to carry its campaign message. Horning's was a strong, parochial campaign. Although it received help to promote free trade, its financial strength and independence is evident in the fact that the national party provided it with just $137.

The Local Contest
Okanagan Centre is a relatively affluent country riding, with a high average age of voters, many of whom are retired and have moved there in recent years. Its population is relatively homogeneous, though mobile. It has been a Conservative stronghold and is the home of the Bennett Social Credit dynasty. As a result of its Tory pedigree, the strategic goal of Horning's campaign was to avoid making mistakes that might upset the expected outcome.

The initial interaction of local campaigns played a key role in shaping the local contest. Horning's poor public performance at the first all-candidates meeting in the Winfield Community Hall, a satellite city of Kelowna, created a crisis for his campaign. Horning's speech was poorly delivered, and he did not handle questions well. He was upset by heckling, and laughed at by the audience. His performance was widely reported in the local media and quickly became a major election issue. Reform Party candidate Werner Schmidt believes this hurt the Conservatives but helped his own campaign: "Horning did not speak well, and didn't understand the issues, ... his poor performance set him apart from the other candidates at the meeting. In a strong Conservative riding, we needed something like this to help us. It encouraged people to search out this curiosity, a new political party. We were the most likely alternative for Conservative voters. It was the beginning of a ground swell that [resulted] in people walking in off the street in the last few days of the campaign offering us help." Horning's poor performance dogged his campaign thereafter. When he refused to attend all-candidates debates, opponents taunted him and the media pursued the issue.

Early on in the campaign, the Tories focused on presenting the advantages of free trade and the protection offered by the government to local fruit and wine growers. They aimed to allay farmers' concerns about the free flow of agricultural goods, and to combat claims by environmentalists that the Free Trade Agreement would give the United States control over Canadian water resources. Horning's poor performance led to a rethinking of this strategy, as campaigners took more seriously the challenge from his opponents. The apparent strength of the Reform Party, which threatened the Tories on their right flank, gave added impetus to this change of heart. So concerned were Tories that they argued that Reform might split the conservative vote and allow the NDP to win.

Maintaining a focus on Horning seemed the best option, but he needed to be kept away from public meetings. In direct contrast to the Robinson campaign in Burnaby-Kingsway, Okanagan Conservatives kept Horning in the background. They limited his public appearances to meeting voters one on one during either door-to-door canvassing or phone canvassing. They also organized small group meetings at his campaign office and local civic associations, at which Horning excelled. Lightburn developed a series of briefing notes to help Horning understand the party platform and important issues, enabling him to discuss issues when canvassing. Horning spent most evenings going over these notes, and days canvassing by foot or phone. This took up nearly all his time.

With Horning unable to appear at public forums, yet central to the campaign strategy, local organizers had to devise ways of maintaining and improving his name recognition. They developed an advertising campaign that emphasized Horning's record of community service, and promised that he would extract action on local transportation, environmental, and agricultural problems from a federal Tory government if elected. The day before the election, the campaign placed a full-page advertisement in daily newspapers listing the community service of the four main candidates in columns beneath their names. His column ran the full length of the page, while the others had few or no entries.

The campaign made use of brochures and advertising on radio and television to spread its message. But most advertising was in newspapers because of a belief that they play a special role in the life of a country town. Newspapers are very strongly connected with a town's sense of itself in a way most other media are not. As Lightburn notes, "A newspaper will be left lying around home or the office or in a shop, and will be read throughout the day by a number of people. People can absorb and analyze information at their own pace." Radio advertising consisted mainly of tag-ons to national advertisements, naming the local candidate, interspersed with a few locally produced advertisements.

Television advertising played an important role in the last days of the election. The campaign faced two problems. Free trade had become a big issue, to which the campaign had not responded adequately, and Horning's absence from public forums had become an election issue. Strategists believed television could be used to help overcome both problems, but they knew they could afford only a few days' worth of such advertising.

Lightburn notes that "television is useful only if advertising is constant, from day to day and across the different time periods of any one day. Saturation advertising on television can be very effective in the short run." The campaign produced thirty-second advertisements emphasizing Horning's community service and responding to claims made about free trade by other campaigns. It used these to saturate television airtime in the last ten days of the campaign. This strategy, overseen by Lightburn and local radio station owner Walter Grey, shaped campaign spending, skewing it in favour of advertising and media events designed to attract news coverage.

An intensive advertising strategy is possible only in country ridings endowed with affordable, indigenous, and influential media outlets. There are two newspapers in Kelowna, the *Daily Courier* and the *Capital News,* and one in neighbouring Winfield, the *Westside Sun.* There are also three radio stations that cover the area, CKIQ, CILK, and CKOV. As well, the local television station is owned by BCTV but has a news affiliation with CBC, and Shaw Cable runs the local cable television system. Unlike the larger stations in Vancouver, rates for advertising on the local television and radio stations and in newspapers are within the reach of local campaigns. In a city such as Vancouver, where the media service a large number of ridings, their impact is diffuse, and is further compromised by the available news and entertainment alternatives. By contrast, the Kelowna media are more focused, and the city was particularly suited to covering the political community defined by the riding boundaries, which for this election were closely aligned with the city limits. The new boundaries emphasized Kelowna's growing size and importance, and the media were determined to cover the local contest in some detail.

The campaign also used staged events to gain media coverage. During the campaign, press releases were timed for between 7:30 a.m. and 8:00 a.m. to meet the 9:00 a.m. publication deadlines of the two daily papers. In the early part of the campaign, there was usually only one a week, but by the time of the election, they were at least daily, as the campaign tried to both direct the debate and respond to other parties' campaign propaganda. The campaign organized a number of heavily attended press conferences featuring seven or eight major local employers commenting that free trade would be good for the region. With his excellent contacts among the local media, Lightburn made sure these received extensive radio, newspaper, and, most important, television coverage.

In addition to a strong media campaign, Horning and his campaign used their connections among owners of local media outlets to ensure good coverage. Horning made use of his contacts among local notables, personally calling on friends and acquaintances in various community and sporting groups to lobby for support. Like most country towns, Kelowna has a well-developed network of informal information flows that can be used to disseminate election propaganda. Local foot and phone canvassers were used to reinforce this line of campaigning, though campaign organizers noted that this took its toll of volunteers, who began dropping out towards the end of the long, fifty-nine-day campaign. Some complained of the demoralizing effect of Horning's perceived poor performance.

The campaign used one other method to help overcome the image of Horning as incompetent. Lightburn and Horning contacted acquaintances in the Kelowna Chamber of Commerce and had them organize a strictly controlled all-candidates debate for cable television at the offices of the chamber just two days before the election. Initially, the NDP and Reform Party candidates refused to attend. But the influence of the chamber of commerce, the chance to confront Horning, and the opportunity to be on cable television proved too strong, and they attended. Three local journalists asked questions, and a moderator took questions from the audience. Each candidate was allowed to bring forty supporters into the chamber. Heckling was strictly controlled. Lightburn put Horning through extensive preparations for the event, which appear to have been successful. The candidate performed credibly, and classified it as the highlight of the campaign. Horning's good performance was reported on local television and radio as well as in local newspapers.

The ebb and flow of the national campaign did not play a big part in the local contest. In part, this reflects the ability of local campaigns and the local media to generate a truly local agenda. Where it did intrude, such as the localization of the free trade debate, there was enough local media to effectively defuse the issue by advertising adjustment policies and so forth. This further highlighted the existence of a coherent local agenda. This distinction between the local campaign and its national counterpart helped make Horning's parochial campaign a success, as his resources allowed him to dominate the local contest that was insulated from outside influences. This and the riding's Tory credentials helped Horning maintain his electoral position. That he could successfully avoid all-candidates debates is evidence that other local campaigns failed to engage his campaign effectively.

A well-developed local agenda not only defines the local contest, but it also redefines events that occur at the national level. Because the Tories were competing mainly with the NDP, and the Liberals held little threat for either, John Turner's strong showing in the national leaders' debate had only a minor impact on the contest. Local media did some of their own polling, which invariably showed the Tories in a strong position. Most national polls were useless, given the NDP-versus-PC contest in the riding, though BC polls showing the New Democrats in a strong position helped the local NDP campaign. In such political communities, local campaigns have a much greater impact on the conduct of the contest than their national counterparts.

John Brewin: Party Insider, Heir Apparent

With a strong upward trend in its vote in the previous three elections, and success at the provincial level in the area, the NDP knew it had a chance of winning the city riding of Victoria. This feeling was heightened when, during the summer, long-serving Conservative incumbent Allan McKinnon decided not to seek reelection. Although the New Democrat nomination was very appealing, John Brewin had a stranglehold on the nomination as a result of his strong campaign in the riding for the party in 1984 and his credentials as a well-connected party insider.

Transplanted from Ontario to British Columbia, Brewin was a member of the group of professional campaign organizers that work on NDP campaigns across the country. Brewin's father had been an important founding member of the NDP and an MP from Ontario. His wife, Gretchen, was the current NDP mayor of Victoria. Brewin had run for the Ontario provincial legislature in 1971 and had worked on other campaigns in Ontario and British Columbia. He had been president of the local association in Victoria and the provincial NDP, and held office in the provincial party in Ontario. Whereas most impermeable NDP associations produce closed, contested nominations, Brewin's position stifled competition, and he won a closed, uncontested nomination.

Brewin put together an experienced and well-organized campaign team. Typical of mass parties, the team was bureaucratic, with many volunteers working because of their interest in the party rather than in the candidate or particular issues. The team included experienced local campaigners, some with links to the party in other provinces. Brewin's party connections meant that his campaign was closely aligned with the NDP's national and provincial strategy. The strength of his campaign gave him some independence, but in general he was happy for the campaign to be a subsidiary of the national effort. His campaign was engaged in a contested constituency election.

The Conservative candidate was Victoria economist and alderman Geoff Young. Not a charismatic politician, he is best described as a local notable. Time spent as a local councillor and his local business connections as a management consultant gave him a profile. Among the five candidates was an insurgent pro-life advocate who mounted a spirited challenge. Association members finally supported the less charismatic but long-time party member and moderate Young, mainly out of a desire to reject the single-issue pro-life candidate. Young won an open, contested nomination in a permeable, cadre-style association, made all the more open by McKinnon's retirement.

The local association was aware that the tide was running against it but managed to build a solid campaign team, relying heavily on experienced campaigners and professionals from the local business community. Although strategic decision making was locally controlled in this parochial campaign, Young was determined to try to make free trade the major issue. Some volunteers thought that as an economist, he was convinced that he could persuade voters of the benefits of the deal. Although the Liberals' good performance hurt the Tories, its recent success in the riding meant that it felt itself to be engaged in a contest with the NDP, while defending itself from the insurgent Liberals.

Liberal candidate and local notable Michael O'Connor was president of the local party association, a respected local lawyer, sportsman, and member of innumerable local service associations. Unfortunately for Young, O'Connor had strong connections to the local Social Credit, a traditional base of Tory support in British Columbia. The lack of interest in the Liberal nomination in Victoria saw John Turner ask O'Connor to run for the party. The Liberals wanted a competent candidate in a riding that has a higher than average profile. A stopgap candidate, O'Connor won an open, uncontested nomination. Although he could rely on a few experienced local campaigners, the weakness of the local association caught up with the campaign, which lacked volunteers. This was a parallel campaign that tried to balance national and local issues, but failed. Despite a strong performance, it was largely marginalized from the local contest between the NDP and Tories.

The local contest was dominated by Brewin. His early start on campaigning emphasized the appearance of a ground swell in favour of the NDP and against the Tories; but, in fact, the NDP did not improve on its 1984 vote, maintaining its share at about 38 percent. This was enough to defeat the Tories by just over 8 percent. The win was made possible by a 16.5-point drop in the Tory vote share from 1984. Most of this went to the Liberals. The popular O'Connor garnered 21.4 percent of the vote, an increase of 8.3 points over 1984. The ascendancy of the NDP campaign over the struggling Tories took some of the fire out of the local contest. The Tory campaign was moderately competitive, and the Liberals' a little less so, leaving the NDP as the only truly competitive campaign.

The importance of a subsidiary NDP campaign in the riding meant that many national issues important to its federal strategy, such as free trade, were brought into the local contest. But influential media coverage of the local campaigns by the city media in Victoria gave them room to shape the local agenda. Both Brewin and O'Connor used this to introduce local issues, the latter doing so in his own television advertisement.

The Candidate and Campaign Team

The Conservatives beat the New Democrats in 1980 by over 7,000 votes, but Brewin cut this margin to 4,000 in 1984. He had begun to think about the next election soon after, spurred by the growing unpopularity of the Mulroney government. McKinnon's retirement, perhaps encouraged by the Tories' dismal showing in the polls, further strengthened Brewin's resolve to take advantage of his party and social contacts and their associated financial and human resources.

Believing he was assured of winning the nomination, Brewin started campaigning early in mid-1987, making use of his flexible working arrangements as a lawyer. He raised and spent about $15,000 by the time the election was announced. During this year, the campaign raised a further $51,177 to spend during the election, $3,000 more than the spending limit in the riding, but $5,000 less than his Tory opponent. With access to over $65,000, his was one of the best-financed NDP campaigns in the country.

As president of the strong local association, Brewin had a large number of volunteers he could call on. In addition, his links with the national party and personal contacts with professional campaigners gave him access to experienced volunteers from outside the riding. Most workers were committed NDP members willing to work for a good party member like Brewin. This team did not exhibit the same sort of personal friendships found in local notable campaigns, but was dominated by a bureaucratic professionalism. In true NDP fashion, Brewin worked with the local association executive in making the decision to begin early campaigning and when filling campaign positions. He and campaign manager Cyril Barkverd decided to get an early start to campaigning: "We began campaigning in 1987, forming an election planning committee. Our strategy was to present an NDP victory as inevitable in an area we controlled both locally and provincially."

The bureaucratic bent of NDP campaigners is clear in Brewin's assessment of the role of the candidate, which he sees in purely organizational terms: "Few voters will cross party lines because of a candidate, although a strong personal attachment may encourage it. The candidate has a cumulative effect, stimulating good organization, finding workers and donors, for example, and attracting attention to the campaign."

With a strategy that involved a long campaign, Barkverd and Brewin decided that it was necessary to have a small band of dedicated workers willing to put in six months to a year of work. More than most campaigns, it relied on a group of experienced, perhaps even hardened, campaigners to pursue a strategy that required extensive commitment. Brewin was able to find volunteers willing to stick with his campaign over a long period to fill inner circle positions. This organizational commitment meant that unlike the campaigns of many cadre-style associations, the same person filled key positions for an extended period. The inner circle of workers numbered about 20. About 75 workers helped less frequently as secondary workers, and there was a large coterie of NDP sympathizers on which the campaign team drew for additional help. Brewin claimed the campaign used 800 workers on election day.

The locus of decision making in Brewin's campaign reflected elements of the committee approach often adopted by the NDP. Because Brewin was influential in the local association and the wider party, he had a good deal of say regarding strategy. Nevertheless, strategy committees consisting of party members committed to the party rather than to the candidate made important decisions. As a result, the campaign largely followed the lead of the national party, emphasizing Ed Broadbent's leadership and opposition to free trade. Efforts were made to identify aspects of the national platform that affected local voters. Brewin considered opposition to nuclear energy and armaments, as well as the need to promote peace in the international system, to be issues of concern to local voters.

Intraparty Relations
In order to support such a long-running campaign, fund-raising was given a high priority. Brewin raised $15,000 by the summer prior to the election, using the lists of supporters and donors from previous campaigns, and those made available by local NDP MLAs Robyn Blencoe and Gordon Hansen. This is an example of the advantages of close contacts between different levels of a party. The candidate noted that successful fund-raising allowed his campaign some independence from its national counterpart. But for a subsidiary campaign in the NDP, this means choosing between party policies rather than focusing on strictly local issues or the candidate. As Brewin notes, "If you raise your own funds, and have your own organization, the party has no leverage on you. You control the campaign, choosing the mix of strategies and issues that suit the local circumstances best. [Thus], our locally produced leaflets contained some elements of the national campaign, adapted to local conditions."

The money was used to produce campaign leaflets and signs, and to support Brewin's foot canvassing throughout the year. The campaign also organized public-speaking events for a number of high-profile speakers. It could afford to hire venues and organize the publicity. It also helped finance a phone bank that was the central element of both the on-going fund-raising drive and the process of identifying voter support in the period leading up to the election. The phone bank, set up in the summer and staffed by about ten volunteers, had identified 5,000 supporters by the time the election was called. The continuation of this effort throughout the year and into the election proved very effective.

Although, like most NDP campaigns, this one focused on issues from the party platform, it had a greater capacity to pick and choose among them and to implement a multifaceted campaign strategy. This was because of its access to local funding, a strong campaign team, and an interested, influential media. Being able to afford office space and the other accoutrements of campaigning long before the election proper meant that rather like an incumbent, Brewin could invite voters to meet him at the campaign offices. He treated these meetings as focus groups, which, in combination with the party's preelection polling, allowed party strategists to explore the issues of importance to local voters. This was crucial to his strategy of acting as heir apparent to the retiring Tory incumbent.

More than in other parties, the structure of the NDP and its commitment to ideological politics ties New Democrat campaigns closely to the rest of the party. Unlike campaigns in other parties, NDP campaigns in British Columbia send questionnaires they receive from interest groups to the provincial head office, where they are filled out to ensure consistency across ridings and with party policy. Even well-organized campaigns such as Brewin's complied with this edict, though the party did allow media liaison officer Sue Stroud to deal with noncontroversial questionnaires. But those from a pro-life alliance and ethnic groups were all answered by head office.

The NDP campaign happily accepted visits from party leader Ed Broadbent. Brewin made a point of staying in contact with the federal party and encouraging the leader to visit Victoria. As a riding that the New Democrats had never held but had a good chance of winning, it was high on the list of places that Broadbent had to visit. He made two visits, which were highly publicized by the campaign. Brewin used these visits to highlight his good contacts with the party hierarchy and the likelihood that he would influence policy making in the NDP once elected. Consistent with his position as a party insider, Brewin ranked national issues and party strategy (such as Broadbent's performance) as the most important determinants of the outcome of the local contest. He ranked local factors, such as the performance of the candidates, his own strengths, and regional issues, as secondary.

Along with other NDP campaigns in British Columbia, Brewin's campaign placed greater emphasis on free trade than did the national campaign. This was because the provincial party had decided that in a politically polarized province, confronting the Tories over free trade took first priority over Broadbent's leadership qualities. The difference was a matter of degree rather than of direction, and reflects the strength of the provincial NDP. Brewin felt his prime goal was to ensure that the NDP was seen as the leading anti-free trade party, to forestall a Liberal challenge on this issue. The local organization followed the provincial party's lead, ahead of that offered by the national campaign.

The Local Contest

Victoria has a high number of government workers, many of whom can be persuaded to vote for the NDP (Blake 1985). As well, as the city has aged and become more densely populated, the riding has become more diverse in the distribution of wealth and its ethnic and age profile. This has replaced what was once a more homogeneous, affluent population. The sizeable number of low-income families and those receiving welfare are typically target audiences for the NDP. Although there are many senior citizens, a large number of these have moved to the riding from elsewhere, adding to the mobility of the population. Appearances at seniors' homes and local schools were mandatory elements of campaigning, attracting good media coverage. With 14 percent of the population having a university degree, Victoria, like Vancouver Centre, has a relatively well-educated population. As with most city ridings, there is enough room on the local political agenda for a range of issues. The metropolitan media canvassed issues from across the country and the province to which candidates were expected to speak on behalf of their parties.

The two provincial ridings in Victoria were held by the NDP at the time of the federal election, and it looked as though the area was going to the party at the national level. NDP support in the riding had grown steadily from the under 20 percent in the 1940s to 40 percent in the 1980s. Campaigners judged that the best strategy was to cultivate a sense of the inevitability of an NDP victory and to prevent the Liberals from stealing any anti-free trade votes. This could best be achieved by building and presenting to the public a competent campaign organization and candidate. Brewin had help from an unexpected quarter in his battle to defeat the Tories. Liberal candidate Michael O'Connor, perhaps the best-known candidate in the race, had strong connections to the Social Credit Party, undermining traditional Socred support for the Tories. As the Liberals had little chance of winning, their choice of candidate was fortuitous for Brewin.

The campaign system set up by Brewin and Barkverd was based on the tried and tested NDP three-canvass method. With known supporters, requests for support and donations were in the form of a letter, followed by one or two phone calls. The phone calls also gave campaigners the chance to ask for volunteers and gauge the concerns of the voters. Campaigners used past federal, provincial, and municipal results by poll in Victoria to guide the canvassing process. Polls were labelled on maps as "ours," "theirs," and "undecideds." With regard to the last of these, the campaign used more recent provincial and municipal returns to identify those polls that it thought the party should win, but in which it had not done well in the 1984 election.

Polls with many undecided voters in areas the campaign believed might vote NDP were singled out for special treatment. These areas were subjected to a literature drop, followed by the candidate or a campaign worker canvassing in person, and/or a phone call to enquire about the issues that concerned the voters and to ask for donations. Voters identified as undecided were called again in the hope of convincing them to support Brewin. Either a personal visit from a canvasser or the candidate or a personal phone call or letter were used to this end. In the last two weeks of the campaign, identifying the vote and concentrating on areas with high numbers of undecideds became a fixation of the campaign.

Phone canvassing was critical. Most campaigns lack adequate numbers of volunteers, and phone banks allow far fewer workers to canvass a much greater number of voters, including those that may have been missed by foot canvassing, such as apartment dwellers, than they would otherwise be able to. The early start to the phone bank improved the campaign's coverage of the riding, facilitated voter identification, and trained campaign workers in the subtleties of phone canvassing. Phone canvassers used canvassing scripts provided by the party. Barkverd estimates that phone canvassers reach about 75 percent of voters, requiring foot canvassers to reach the remaining 25 percent. The extensive phone campaign required about ten volunteers working full time on the phone bank, and ten more were needed for the foot canvass.

The organizational effort of the local NDP was enormous. Neither of the other campaigns could match it in terms of volunteer commitment. Brewin notes that the strict control of campaign workers and great demands made of them in pursuit of this professionalism had a debilitating effect: "The workers were burnt out by the time we finished. In fact, many volunteers did not last the distance. It was a gruelling exercise." Despite being well staffed in comparison with other campaigns, Brewin wished that he could have found more workers. Organizing campaign offices, signs, and foot canvassing was labour intensive. To alleviate some of the dislocation that such a long campaign might cause, computing and office facilities were placed in zone houses, which are homes of volunteers that acted as local offices throughout the riding. This enabled volunteers to work closer to or out of their homes.

To forestall any possible Liberal challenge, it was necessary to convince voters that the NDP was the leading anti-free trade party. The NDP attacked free trade and the Tories' tax proposals, echoing many of the themes of the national and provincial campaigns. Those local issues that were raised – such as water quality and disarmament – were related to wider concerns about the environment and the arms race. Meetings with the local labour council and discussions with anti-free trade groups and the Centre for Arms Control were important as evidence of the candidate's ideological commitment.

The strategy of presenting Brewin as the MP-in-waiting was designed to ensure other campaigns engaged with the NDP on its territory. Brewin was to have a superior position on those occasions when they did interact. All-candidates debates were considered suitable places to confront these other campaigns because of Brewin's strong public-speaking abilities, and he attended all ten such events. These meetings garnered considerable press coverage, much of which was positive towards O'Connor and Brewin. Indicative of their special utility for New Democrats, Brewin was the only candidate interviewed in Victoria who considered all-candidates meetings to be helpful to his campaign: "It helped us project an image as a public figure speaking on important issues that I was passionately engaged with."

The salience of all-candidates debates in Victoria was thought by Brewin to be a function of a sense of community in this city riding and an influential local media willing to report these debates. The media and a defined urban community help generate a local agenda and political debate. Members of the political community are interested in who will represent them in Parliament, and have daily access to reports of the candidate's performances and what their choice of representative will mean. Brewin used informal local information networks to boost his name recognition and credibility. As the local contest unfolded, Brewin became the clear front-runner, and engagements between the campaigns became tamer. With a little help from the Reform Party, which captured 8.2 percent of the vote, and the much-improved Liberals, who trailed the second-place Tories by only 8 points, the NDP easily won the local race with about the same vote share as in 1984.

The capacity of the local New Democrat campaign to canvass a wide range of issues was in part a function of the media environment in the city of Victoria. Barkverd notes that "there are walls around Victoria with respect to the media. It is somewhat isolated from the rest of the province and the country."

As the provincial capital and a large regional centre, Victoria has a well-developed media of its own. A sense of local community is reinforced by the thirty-kilometre gap between Vancouver Island and the mainland. Still, Vancouver dailies (the *Vancouver Sun* and the *Province*), as well as Vancouver television stations such as BCTV and CBC, and the Toronto-based national newspaper, the *Globe and Mail,* are all available in Victoria. The campaign was covered by the large city newspaper, the *Times Colonist,* and by city television, including CHEK TV (a CTV affiliate) and the local CBC.

The Victoria media covered a number of riding contests but reported the local contest in greatest depth. Candidates were regularly asked their opinion on policy issues, and their news conferences attracted media attention. For example, when there was an oil spill in the local harbour, they were given a chance to discuss their party's environmental policy. Like Vancouver Centre, the media density in Victoria meant the local agenda was diverse, taking account of local, regional, and national issues. The media played a dual role in reporting the federal election to local voters, and local and regional contests to the national media. The local campaigns were not components of their respective national party efforts to the same degree as those in Vancouver Centre but were still important given their high media profile.

Community newspapers covered the election in some detail, and the cable station organized an all-candidates debate, but local NDP organizers craved national media coverage. Being more influential, it was likely to reinforce the image of Brewin as a high-profile candidate and a sure winner in Victoria. A *Globe and Mail* reporter did spend a day canvassing with Brewin, which produced an article, and the campaign held three formal press conferences that attracted the media. Other than this, the campaign relied on Brewin being asked to talk shows and on the usual press releases. Campaigners hoped that by maintaining good personal relations with journalists and editors they could ensure that press releases were covered, and that reporters would seek out Brewin to discuss election issues.

The NDP was the only party not to make use of radio and television advertising in Victoria. Other campaigns advertised on CHEK TV and on several local radio stations. They also used the *Times Colonist*. Barkverd suggests that the New Democrats' decision to advertise only in community newspapers was a strategic one: "We advertised in community newspapers to keep 'in' with them. We used the advertising budget with local media in the hope of receiving positive editorials. The campaign received little strategic advantage from the advertisements per se, although we encouraged the committee dealing with advertising to think otherwise. Advertising was not central to our strategy of appearing as if we had already won the election; editorials were."

Rival campaigns in Victoria also tried to raise their profile by strategic use of advertising. Liberal candidate O'Connor emphasized radio and television advertising, believing it gave him credibility. With a budget about the same size as that of the NDP, the Liberals spent two-thirds of their funds on electronic advertising. Just producing a television commercial accounted for a large part of this budget. While the Conservatives spent only one-sixth of their budget on radio and television advertising, their total advertising budget of $33,300 was twice that of the NDP.

The New Democrat strategy reveals that creating the impression of a well-organized and successful campaign involves labour-intensive campaign techniques. Barkverd believes that it was the organizational strength of the campaign rather than the candidate that won them the riding: "A good candidate, a credible candidate, is helpful, but the critical factor was the aura of being well organized. In fact, one of the important jobs of a campaign manager is managing the candidate's ego and controlling them when they get 'antsy.' John was good to work with because he understood the practical demands of campaigning – finding workers, getting leaflets printed, and such things. But managers and candidates do not always see the campaign in quite the same terms."

The NDP was able to distinguish itself from its competitors just because it could accomplish this task, while the others could not. This was possible because of its access to workers and money. While the use of labour-intensive methods of campaigning was effective, it did take its toll on campaigners. Only Brewin's campaign made full use of the influential city media and the locally defined political agenda.

Because he was successful, Brewin is convinced that a subsidiary campaign such as his can win a high-profile riding like Victoria. But to some degree, his success was due to the campaign's access to substantial resources, which allowed it to mould the national party platform to local conditions. In some cases, this only meant saying much the same thing using an obviously locally produced advertisement, or by associating a policy with some local issue. But this requires expertise and resources, both of which Brewin had at his disposal.

Conclusion

All competitive candidates can be expected to have adequate resources, so it is the nature of the campaign team, intraparty relations, and riding contexts that shape the style and content of these campaigns. Robinson and Campbell were high-profile candidates with professional, component campaigns in city ridings. Both were central to the strategies of their campaigns. Freed from the mundane tasks of organizing the campaign, they spent most of their time on the hustings. Both received inordinate media attention, which underpinned the central role they played in their respective campaigns. In part, this was because both were in city ridings that were covered by major metropolitan media outlets. Yet despite outward similarities, the two differed in a number of ways.

Campbell's campaign made full use of the local autonomy available to campaigns in cadre-style parties. Robinson too pursued some of his own strategies, but within a framework dictated by the party. That he had this freedom, which is unusual in a mass party such as the NDP, is evidence of his special place within the New Democrat firmament (and perhaps within the wider Canadian community) as a candidate whose personal credentials are paramount to his political success. This encouraged him to think in independent terms, and required the party to allow him some freedom to do so.

Differences in the manner of the local contest thus altered the final shape of these campaigns. Both campaigns focused on the candidate, but Campbell was involved in a closely contested local race while Robinson was a clear front-runner who barely engaged his opponents. Robinson discovered early in the campaign that the other candidates posed no threat to his incumbency. While he maintained a strong local campaign, he was free to roam the country as an NDP spokesperson. He gave well-attended press conferences in several provinces, which reinforced his image as an important national politician in his home riding of Burnaby-Kingsway.

Campbell's campaign had a much sharper focus on her riding opponents. Unlike Robinson, she spent nearly all her time in the riding and concentrated on strong public performances in all-candidates debates. Her willingness to engage the free trade debate directly meant that her campaign did not waste its effort trying to steer around the issue that, with Centre's role as a component contest of the federal campaign, it was confronted with on a regular basis. Paradoxically, this helped the campaign focus on Campbell's abilities, which came to be its greatest asset.

The media coverage Campbell's debating style attracted was crucial to her image as a high-profile candidate. Candidates in city ridings such as Vancouver Centre most easily garner such media coverage. Moreover, this reporting and the associated political agenda provided her with an opportunity to make a name for herself as a party spokesperson. City voters appear to expect such performances from their local candidates, and may judge them on this basis. Campbell's win against the anti-Tory tide in British Columbia was a remarkable effort based on a capable campaign team willing to pursue its own local approach in opposition to national party strategists, and a candidate capable of playing the lead role in this electoral performance.

The country riding of Okanagan Centre presented Tory Al Horning with a different set of problems. The Tory government's Free Trade Agreement was not popular in the Okanagan, but fortunately for Horning, he was new to national politics and was not closely associated with the Mulroney government. This made it easier for him to steer an independent course, sometimes pointing to the need for special consideration for local industries under the free trade regime. Horning was also hampered by his lack of success at public forums – around which country campaigns are primarily constructed – which threatened his position as the front-running candidate. His well-organized, parochial campaign turned to the local media to spread his campaign message, allowing him to avoid public debates.

This strategy was possible because of the nature of this country riding and the local contest. Country ridings place a premium on candidates with the sorts of connections to the local community that Horning could demonstrate. Okanagan Centre has an influential and affordable media that the Tories used to control the self-contained local political agenda and inform voters of Horning's links with the community. The strength of the

Tory vote in the riding, and his control of the media agenda, allowed Horning to disengage from his opponents.

NDP candidate John Brewin in Victoria built a strong team with the help of experienced party campaigners. His campaign was a subsidiary of the national campaign and a good example of the organizational ethos of the NDP. Unlike the other candidates in city ridings, Brewin was not central to the campaign, which accepted party dictates concerning strategies. The campaign presented the image of a competent organization that was the natural successor to the Tories in the riding. The media coverage of the contest allowed Brewin to address a number of policy areas outside the main issues such as free trade on which he thought the NDP had a strategic advantage. The wide reporting of all-candidates debates encouraged candidates to take these other issues seriously. As a result, local campaigns in Victoria engaged with each other, though not to the degree found in Vancouver Centre.

Fortunately for Brewin, the previously uncompetitive Liberal association fielded a strong candidate in Michael O'Connor, whose Social Credit credentials helped split the anti-NDP vote, hurting the Tories. This peculiarly British Columbian logic helped ensure a New Democrat victory. The Liberals' impact on the local contest is an example of how a marginalized but not excluded third-place campaign can have a direct bearing on the final outcome.

9
Losing Campaigns

Given that most riding contests in Canada consist of between four and six campaigns, most are losers. Some are competitive and look much like those campaigns discussed in the previous chapter. But most losing campaigns are not competitive and struggle to build and finance a campaign team and generate local strategies. Amateurs run them, with inner circles made up of acquaintances or even relatives of the candidate. In a few instances, notably in the NDP, workers cleave to the uncompetitive campaign out of a sense of duty to the party. These campaigns have little or no relationship with their national headquarters, whose only interest may be in having its roster of candidates complete. As such, these campaigns rarely receive assistance from the national party.

There are two exceptions to this generalization. The NDP's attempts to ensure uniformity in local campaigning do involve it in relations with many of its less competitive campaigns that are more complex – depending on the resources it has available – than those of either the Liberals or Conservatives. And all parties make a special effort to help uncompetitive campaigns in ridings that they think will be strategically important to the wider federal election. Often this help is designed to make the local campaign appear credible despite the weakness of the local association. But even in these cases, uncompetitive campaigns are not integrated into the national campaign.

Less competitive campaigns are often linked to weak associations. Their limited size and resources mean that contacts in the local political community are limited, and the campaign may find it difficult to build a strong and reliable sense of the mood and character of the local riding and election contest. Such campaigns may be very reactive, pushed along by the actions of other campaigns or the ebb and flow of the federal election. As such, even if they are capable of developing some form of local strategy, forces beyond their control may subvert it. Three of the four losing campaigns presented in this chapter were uncompetitive, while one was marginally competitive.

The first story of a losing campaign is about a Tory incumbent who ran a component campaign, as do most incumbents. Unable to distance himself from the unpopular federal government, he suffered the fate of many BC Tories, losing his seat. The second story is of a Liberal stopgap candidate in a suburban Vancouver riding where a lack of media coverage prevented him from capitalizing on his notoriety as an ex-mayor of the region. He was forced to run a parallel campaign that mimicked national strategies but failed to reverse the pattern of defeat suffered by the Liberals in the province during the 1980s. The third story deals with a classic NDP subsidiary campaign of a party insider in a semirural riding on the outskirts of Vancouver. Although competitive enough to engage the incumbent Tory, she was never going to win one of the safest PC seats in the country. The final story is about another Liberal stopgap candidate contesting a city riding in Vancouver. In this case, the Liberals considered the riding high profile enough to feel obliged to help this campaign in order to be seen as a credible national party capable or running candidates across the country. Yet this candidate was never a serious contender for the riding, and his campaign strategies paralleled those of the national party.

Just as winning campaigns tend to see everything they have done as potentially important to their win – and therefore as strategically sound – the reverse is largely true for losing campaigns. It is often difficult to identify the real reasons for failure, and conclusions about what strategies and tactics lack merit must be seen in this light.

Bob Brisco: High-Profile Fall from Grace

The boundary changes that created Kootenay West-Revelstoke prior to the election made the seat much less safe for the incumbent Tory Bob Brisco. Brisco was renominated unopposed. Being an incumbent, he was a high-profile candidate. Unfortunately, his relationship with the local association was strained because of his long absences from the riding, and many party members who worked for him during the previous election refused to do so in the 1988 election. As a result, the subsequent campaign was weaker than in the previous election.

Despite this, Brisco managed to raise more funds than his opponents, and convinced a number of experienced campaigners to work on the campaign. The traditional strength of the Tories in the area gave him access to enough secondary workers and sympathizers to mount a credible campaign. As an incumbent, his campaign was a component of the national party campaign. Although Brisco tried to avoid national issues and focus on local concerns, he had become a strong supporter of free trade and the prime minister while in Ottawa. He could not avoid being linked with the

Tories' national platform, which he regularly defended. Although weakened, his campaign was engaged with the NDP in what was a contested constituency election.

Brisco's NDP opponent and party insider Lyle Kristiansen won a hotly contested, closed nomination over five other candidates. In winning, Kristiansen made good use of his profile both as a well-known local unionist in an association with a strong union component and as the former New Democrat MP for the area. The free trade issue not only enhanced the NDP's chances of winning the riding, but it helped strengthen the already robust association. It managed to raise more money than the campaign could legally spend in the riding, and had access to many experienced campaigners as well as secondary workers and sympathizers. Kristiansen's was a typically bureaucratic NDP campaign team made up of the local party faithful. It was a subsidiary campaign that adopted the strategies of the national party. Given the competitive electoral history of the riding, it was engaged with the Tories in a real contest.

The Liberal candidate was local doctor and councillor Garry Jenkins. Jenkins had organized the local Grit association, signing up many of its members, and was the only candidate for the nomination. He was a stop-gap candidate in a weak association and had to rely on his family and a few party stalwarts to run his campaign. The provincial party even sent him a campaign manager when the association could not fill the position. His funding base was very limited, and he raised about half as much money as his opponents. He had no chance of winning the seat. His was a parallel campaign that used federal party strategies and standard campaign literature despite the candidate's support of free trade in opposition to party policy. This ambiguity on the major issue of the election marginalized his campaign from the contest between the NDP and Tories.

The local contest was the fourth time Kristiansen and Brisco had faced each other. Brisco had won the seat in 1979, Kristiansen in 1980, and Brisco again in 1984. As the contest progressed, the NDP appeared to be increasingly dominant, though regular all-candidates debates and public meetings ensured that the campaigns engaged with each other. Brisco could not match his 1984 effort, and his vote share dropped 10 percentage points. This was fortuitous for Kristiansen. Although he won the seat by 10 percent, his vote share hardly changed from the previous election. Liberal Jenkins picked up 8 percent of the vote and may have accounted for much of the lost Tory vote.

The Candidate and Campaign Team

Brisco was widely considered by supporters and opponents to have done a good job for the riding. But his efforts on behalf of the riding and a heart attack that hospitalized him had kept Brisco in Ottawa, and as a result, away from the Kootenays for most of the life of the Parliament. In addition, he had gone through a divorce and remarried during the term, which had not endeared him to some association members. The stress of changes in his personal life and the lack of a warm welcome in his home riding encouraged him to stay in Ottawa. Consequently, his contact with his support base in his home riding was limited, and he had difficulty maintaining relations with his inner circle of workers from 1984. Even his constituency office could not help him maintain close links with local Tories.

Brisco returned home in September to organize his campaign less than two months before election day. Despite local annoyance, and perhaps because the Tories' chances in the riding were diminished, he was unchallenged for the nomination. The limited democracy of this closed, uncontested nomination robbed the association of any impetus that may have come from the recruitment drives and excitement of a contested nomination. It became immediately apparent that the association was lethargic, and Brisco had trouble convincing experienced campaigners to join his team. He was particularly dismayed to discover that no one was willing to be his campaign manager. As Tim Barry, chair of the strategy committee, notes, "Brisco was a good MP, but not a good politician. Having alienated his support base, his efforts to build a campaign team were ineffective – he did not recruit a campaign manager until September. For an incumbent's campaign, it was often in disarray. This emphasized the fact that he might lose, and further hurt our effectiveness. The campaign was too little, too late."

As an incumbent, Brisco expected to run a professional campaign that dealt with local and nonlocal issues. When no one volunteered as campaign manager, he and his local constituency office searched for a local Tory with management skills to run the campaign. In the end, they convinced Jack Chernoff, a manager at the Cominco smelter in Trail, to be campaign manager. In contrast to 1984, Brisco had to pay Chernoff, who was partially compensated for the loss of income he suffered from taking six weeks off work. As well, the campaign covered his day-to-day expenses. The campaign manager was relatively inexperienced, leaving Brisco and his spouse to do much of the organizational work.

Despite a late start, Chernoff and Brisco constructed a viable if inexperienced campaign team. They were able to find campaigners willing to chair eight key committees, which made for an inner circle of about a dozen. Along with Chernoff, the most important member of the inner circle was Tim Barry, chair of the strategy committee, the research committee, and a major contributor to the media committee. Barry had some experience in public relations and campaigning. Relations between the team and Brisco were relatively distant and formal in comparison to the 1984 effort.

Brisco laments that it was a team that could not run the type of campaign needed to beat the NDP: "There was less of a strategy than in 1984 and an absence of the drive to defeat the NDP. Of the campaign workers from 1984, there were many who did not join the campaign – we lost mainly key players." Moreover, the inner circle and candidate came to the campaign with very different views of what the local strategic focus should be. Brisco was a strong supporter of Mulroney and was keen to run a campaign linked to free trade and the national party strategy. Like a good incumbent from the governing party, he wished to run a campaign that celebrated the government's successes. Both Chernoff and Barry worked hard to impress on Brisco just how unpopular Mulroney and the Free Trade Agreement were in British Columbia, and the Kootenays in particular. In the end, Brisco agreed to try to distance himself from the national party but continued to defend free trade when challenged. This strategic difference unsettled the local team, widening the gap between it and the candidate.

The campaign set up three campaign offices to help cover the large riding. The main office was in Castlegar, staffed by about 15, an office in Nelson with 10 workers, and a Trail office with about 6 volunteers. While this was seen as necessary in a geographically large riding, running several offices exacerbated the campaign's organizational problems. It was forced to rotate second-tier workers, as many were not committed to the campaign and unwilling to work long hours. So although the campaign used about 130 such volunteers, they were not very effective. Tim Barry notes that "Outside the inner group, most workers were not committed. Even some of the inner circle lacked commitment, and there were few experienced campaigners among them. There were not nearly enough people, about 35 or 40 who could be relied on. For a riding this size, and an incumbent's campaign, that is not enough." This complicated the job of organizing the 500 or so sympathizers throughout the riding who play a critical canvassing role in geographically large ridings such as Kootenay West-Revelstoke.

Barry suggests two reasons why the campaign struggled to find workers. First, "With married couples both working, the pool of housewives has been lost. The syphoning off of workers to interest groups, very noticeable in 1988, means that campaigns struggle to find people." And second, Brisco's failure to maintain good relations with local party members who are critical in country ridings where the web of social relations is often more intimate than in cities or suburbs: "Bob started too late and with little method when he came to select campaign workers. He did not show much sensitivity to the feelings of local people, and as a result found them reluctant to join the campaign. He did not try to maintain the social connections that would have encouraged people to treat him more sympathetically."

Just as telling was the attitude of Brisco's official agent, Bill van Yzerloo, who filled the job in his capacity as an accountant rather than as a committed campaigner. In contrast to the highly personal nature of relations between members of campaign teams in other country ridings, relations in the Brisco team were more functional. Organizers were paid, volunteers tended to emphasize commitment to the party rather than to the candidate, and some clearly felt it was prudent or potentially valuable to work for the government party.

Perhaps the only bright spot for Brisco was his ability to raise funds, which promised the possibility of strategic innovation. His $61,232 was nearly $20,000 more than the successful NDP campaign. Most of this came from the local business community, which was strongly committed to the Tory platform given that the alternative, the NDP, was not perceived to be pro-business. Despite producing their own campaign literature and radio and newspaper advertisements based on locally conceived strategy, the campaign failed to take full advantage of its resources, seeming to be caught up in a national view of election issues. In part this reflects the inexperience of local strategists but also points to the difficulties faced by incumbents who attempt to distance themselves from the federal party, particularly if it is the government.

Intraparty Relations

Facing the NDP's effective anti-free trade, anti-Mulroney campaign, the Tories decided to run on Brisco's personal performance and local issues. His time as a member had been very lucrative for the riding, and campaign literature contained lists of money and projects that could be attributed to his efforts. These amounted to several hundred million dollars of federal money brought into the riding. However, an incumbent's campaign has a symbiotic relationship with its national counterpart that results from links developed with the party hierarchy while the MP is in Ottawa. Because of this, Brisco had a different perspective on the campaign than local strategists. As a strong supporter of the leader and free trade, Brisco felt a principled need to defend them in public. He was easily drawn into debating free trade and other government policies, highlighting his links to the party rather than his capacity to bring in federal funding. This resulted in a campaign that was a component of the national Conservative effort.

Brisco's campaign was not helped by national party advertising in the riding that referred to national issues, including free trade, and carried a tag-on mentioning him as the local Tory candidate. These advertisements reminded voters that Brisco was a member of the governing party sponsoring free trade. According to figures supplied by Kootenay Broadcasting System (KBS), the national party purchased about twice as much airtime in the riding than did the local campaign. The national Progressive Conservative campaign spent $5,149 on radio advertising during November, compared with $2,629 spent by the local campaign.

The local campaign led by communications coordinator Barry tried to change the party's approach in the riding: "We asked but could not find out what time or how much advertising was being run ... where it would be run or what it would contain. This was also true for national party advertising on BCTV, CBC, and the major Vancouver and national news-papers that are seen in the Kootenays. Not only was it damaging to our campaign, but we couldn't coordinate our own advertising with that of the national party."

The national party was unwilling to listen to local complaints about the impact of its advertising, or adjust it to suit local conditions. Its unwilling-ness to provide details of the content and timing of national advertise-ments meant the local campaign could not time its radio advertising to avoid placing it next to national advertisements. Contradictory local and national strategies were thought by local campaigners to have badly dam-aged their efforts to steer clear of the free trade issue. It seems the party expected to lose the riding and was willing to fund only a single, centrally directed campaign in British Columbia.

The relative strength of the national Tory campaign, and its willingness to override local politics, is clear from comparisons with the other parties. The 1:2 ratio in favour of the national Tory campaign was reversed in the case of both the NDP and Liberal campaigns, with the local campaign out-spending its national counterpart by a ratio of 1.5:1. The national New Democrat campaign spent $1,872 compared with expenditure of $2,549 by the local campaign, while the figures for the Liberal Party were $1,057 and $1,425 respectively. Local strategists felt that they were fighting the local NDP and Liberals and their own national party campaign. Chernoff notes that the local campaign was so distant from the regional or national campaigns that it was "like working in a vacuum." Barry observes that "The national party has its own 'secret' strategy which it allows only a few BC strategists to know. We had no idea about the overall direction of the campaign. It pretty much abandoned us. On one level this was okay, as we were trying to run our own campaign anyway, but the lack of contact meant we couldn't even stop them hurting us."

Mulroney's visit did not help the Tories in their efforts to avoid free trade. Brisco's view is that the visit was "peripheral to the campaign, but [that] Mulroney had been both generous and helpful." Indicative of differ-ences in the strategic view of Brisco and his campaigners, Chernoff notes that "He [Mulroney] brought lots of national media attention, which normally we would have used to our advantage. But because we were down-playing his role and free trade, we could not afford to let the campaign focus on his visit. The visit most probably hurt our campaign rather than helped it."

Brisco felt that provincial strategists were more sympathetic to the ordeals of local campaigners in the West, where the Tories were fighting the NDP and not the Liberals as were their colleagues in the East. He claimed the Tories had brought together a group of western issues, making it relevant in the West, but other campaign workers did not share his view. Time and again local strategists complained that the literature and advice they were receiving was aimed at the Liberals, yet the Liberals were not competitive in Kootenay West-Revelstoke nor in most other BC ridings. Little effort was made to modify the national anti-Liberal campaign into an anti-New Democrat campaign to suit the politics of British Columbia.

Although Brisco's campaign had access to many of the resources needed to run a strong, independent local campaign – and in some ways did so – it was in fact tied to the national campaign. This is another indication of the symbiotic relationship that exists between component campaigns and their national counterpart. Brisco could not fully divorce himself from the national party; part of him did not want to, and his functional links to the party made it difficult. An inexperienced campaign team did not help matters. In fact, efforts to make this break were noted in the media and by other campaigns, and undercut the strategy.

The Local Contest
Kootenay West-Revelstoke is a stable riding with a low population turnover and a high level of home ownership, which reinforces the strength and intimacy of local communities. The local economy is based on traditional industries such as forestry, mining, and smelting. Each town in the riding has one or two local newspapers that are capable of dealing with local issues, and hence its own well-focused political agenda. Constituency elections in Kootenay West-Revelstoke have been bipolar in recent years. The seat has alternated between the Tories and NDP, but free trade (which bound the local union population closely to the NDP), the unpopularity of Mulroney, and the addition of Revelstoke to the riding had all shifted the balance against the Conservatives and towards the NDP and Kristiansen.

The Tories' decision to emphasize Brisco's record as MP and local issues in the hope of avoiding free trade had merit. A personal style of politics is expected and plays well to local audiences in country ridings, as does concentrating on local issues. There were a number of local issues, such as the renegotiation of the Columbia River Treaty, a promise of action on a small boat harbour for New Denver, and the development of an Aboriginal archaeological site in the Slocan Valley for tourism. The Columbia River is a central social and economic resource for the region, and the treaty regulates the local use of the river on both sides of the Canada-US border. Brisco proposed a plan to extract money from the companies that use it to generate hydroelectricity and use the revenue for local development.

This local strategy required a sophisticated campaign organization. Issues relevant to all the local regions and towns had to be identified, and literature, advertising, and speeches modified for different parts of the riding. This put added strain on the Tories' limited campaign organization and inexperienced workers. Despite the Tories' efforts, these issues never took hold in the popular imagination, nor were they given priority by other campaigns or the media. Local journalists did not find the Tory campaign effort compelling. Local PC volunteers claimed that the Tory campaign was not up to the demands of such a strategy, and this is why it failed.

Unfortunately for Brisco's strategy of focusing on local issues, free trade came to dominate the riding contest. The structure of the local economy makes it vulnerable to American imports (particularly the Cominco smelter in Trail), and the partisan arguments of the national campaign were considered relevant to local conditions. Even some local issues came to be seen in this light. The British Columbian Power Commission was conducting hearings into Cominco's sale of its controlling share in West Kootenay Power to an American firm. Brisco supported the sale and was labelled as pro-American (anti-Canadian). The sale intensified concern about free trade, and Brisco's support played badly in the region.

This localization of the free trade debate was also encouraged by television beamed in from outside the riding. It was the main issue throughout the country. Interpretations of the national debates by the nonlocal media were believed to have affected the number of volunteers and worker morale on local campaigns. Positive interpretations of Turner's performance were thought to have moved some anti-free trade support from the NDP to the Liberals. As well, opinion polls reported in the media that suggested a Tory rout in British Columbia did not help the PC's local effort, despite the fact that none of these polls had a statistically significant local component. The prime minister's visit to the riding did not help Brisco's campaign. In an ageing riding like the Kootenays, the Mulroney government's attempt to de-index old age pensions during its first term had been unpopular, and never forgotten. The visit highlighted his leadership and the free trade debate.

Unlike Al Horning in Okanagan Centre, Brisco had to make use of all-candidates debates if he was to reach voters. The media in the riding are too fragmented and not influential enough to provide the basis for an alternative means of communicating with voters. As communications coordinator, Barry created a briefing book with one-line answers and comments on a range of issues to be used at debates and media conferences.

His efforts to raise local issues at all-candidates debates were, however, swamped by his opponents' continued emphasis on free trade. These attacks were carried in the local media across the riding, undermining Brisco's attempt to run on local issues and his personal credentials.

The all-candidates debate in Revelstoke encapsulates the difficulties that confronted Brisco. The Tories' organizational weakness was most pronounced in Revelstoke. Whereas the NDP organization from the old riding of Kootenay West had been able to link up with NDP supporters in Revelstoke, Conservative association members had little knowledge of the politics of the town. Given the disarray of the Tory organization leading up to and during the campaign, it was not in a position to develop a local support base. With few Tory supporters in the audience, it was simple for Brisco's opponents to keep the debate firmly focused on free trade, overwhelming his attempts to speak to local issues. Several all-candidates debates on local radio and two on local cable television were equally unhelpful to Brisco's campaign, as they too concentrated on free trade.

The inability to get supporters out to the meeting in Revelstoke affected Brisco deeply, and he came to see it as a harbinger of his defeat. This was doubly galling given the personal effort it took to travel the 500 kilometres from his base in the south of the riding, along treacherous mountain roads in poor weather, to speak in a hostile environment. To add insult to injury, attempts to advertise local issues in Revelstoke were hampered by the fact that the local newspaper used a distinctive typeset system that was not compatible with that used by all the other newspapers in the riding.

Like Horning, Brisco could afford to advertise in the local media. There are about ten weekly or daily papers in the constituency. The main local papers are the *Trail Times,* the *Nelson News,* and the *Castlegar News.* The first two are dailies and the last a biweekly. Each of the dailies has a circulation of about 6,000, while the *Castlegar News* sells about 5,000 copies per issue. At the time of the election, the Stirling News Service of Vancouver owned the *Trail Times* and the *Nelson News,* while the *Castlegar News* was an independent. All relied on the Canadian Press wire service with its head office in Toronto. Shaw Cable is the local, independent cable network in the southern part of the constituency encompassing Trail, Castlegar, and Nelson.

Although it lacks a television station, Kootenay West-Revelstoke has a number of radio stations. KBS is the biggest and runs radio stations covering the southern half of the riding, its broadcast area being nearly contiguous with the constituency's boundaries. There are two smaller radio stations elsewhere in the constituency. With seven reporters including a news director, KBS is the largest news service in the constituency. It runs three AM and one FM station under its parent company, Four Seasons Radio, with wire services provided by the Satellite News Network, which has its headquarters in Toronto. Local news is fed back to this service.

The Tories' large advertising budget reflects a campaign that relied on nonlabour-intensive methods of campaigning. The Tories' advertising expenditure represented 43 percent of campaign spending. It was the biggest spending campaign. The NDP spent 36 percent of its budget on advertising, and the Liberals 35 percent.[1] This means the Tory campaign spent 25 percent more of its total campaign budget on advertising than the NDP and 40 percent more than the Liberals. But as Barry notes, the Tories found it difficult to influence the local agenda: "We spent lots of money on advertising but had little idea about whether it was making an impact. We were very uncertain of the value of advertising in local media as the local media has limited credibility with voters. With four towns to cover, about 500 kilometres apart, with different needs and separate media outlets, it would have taken more money and a better coordinated campaign to swing the vote back to us." The need for more spending is a natural response to the failure of the campaign to make much headway against its opponents. In contrast to Horning's campaign, the media in the Kootenays did not have much influence on voters, and Brisco was unsuccessful in drawing political debate away from free trade and towards local issues.

While newspaper advertising is less expensive than radio, the decline in the status of local daily newspapers has encouraged campaigners to use radio. Radio advertising targeted certain high listening times, such as the drive to and from work. The greater use of radio in comparison with other ridings was the result of a number of factors. It was more affordable than in suburban or city ridings, and the local radio audience area matched the boundaries of the constituency quite closely. In addition, it was heard in remote, hard-to-canvass areas beyond the circulation zones of town papers.

Controversy over the placement of candidates' campaign signs on major roads highlights their importance to country campaigns. There were a number of disputes about whether the signs were legally allowed in some of the places used by the NDP, whose signs dominated the major highways linking the towns in the southern end of the riding. The Tories were unable to match this labour-intensive campaign technique, and this gave an added edge to complaints about the legality of some signs. The same is true for the distribution of literature. Relatively low-density country towns and environs require large numbers of volunteers to hand out pamphlets. A labour volunteer shortage meant the Conservatives were forced to rely more on Canada Post than were the New Democrats. Although personal contact is critical in country communities, the Tories struggled to reach voters either by phone or by foot canvass in this vast country riding. In another instance, the Tories' attempt to swamp the editorial pages with supportive letters – a common tactic in country towns – failed because the NDP was better organized and sent more to the papers. This emphasizes how important volunteers (an essentially cost-free component of a campaign) are to the successful implementation of campaign strategies.

The level of engagement between the various teams changed over the course of the campaign. The powerful Local 480 of the Steelworkers of America at the Cominco smelter ran a strong anti-free trade campaign that tied in with the NDP provincial strategy effort. To this, the local NDP added support of environmentalists concerned about Canada's obligations under the agreement to share resources, including water, with the United States. Campaigner Gerald Rotering notes, "We emphasized that this was union territory and that free trade was not in the interests of loggers or smelter workers. In addition, it would make it easier for America to interfere with Canadian natural resources, a big concern for environmentalists. This unified these groups which are sometimes at odds behind our campaign."

Brisco's efforts to use his resources and the media in each town to focus on local issues failed, and as the campaign progressed, he felt obliged to respond to critics of free trade. This pitted him directly against the NDP. Unfortunately for the Liberals, Jenkins was uncomfortable opposing free trade, conceding that "The Liberal Party had historically supported free trade, as I did myself." This entrenched the NDP as the anti-free trade party, and excluded the Liberals from the central debate, leaving his NDP and PC opponents engaged in a vigorous two-way contest. As the election progressed, it became clear that the NDP had the strongest campaign team and that Brisco's campaign could not match them in terms of volunteers. The Tories' failure to dominate the local agenda created a sense of fatalism that pervaded the campaign. Engagements between the two campaigns became less intense and carried less interest for the local media.

Understanding the public mood is a critical component of a good campaign and underpins the development of appropriate local strategies, as well as the role and presentation of the candidate. Assessing and influencing this mood in areas where there is little direct polling and limited investigative media require personal contact. In large ridings such as Kootenay West-Revelstoke, this requires plenty of campaign volunteers. As well, in communities where social contacts are more intimate, and informal networks of information quite powerful, the ability to attract respected community members to a campaign and to produce large numbers of supporters at town hall events is important to a candidate's credibility. All these were lacking in the Tory campaign, which was out of touch with the local communities and could not assert Brisco's claim to the seat.

While the localization of the free trade debate undercut the Tories' strategy of focusing on local issues, a well-run campaign may have saved the seat for Brisco, or at least have put him much closer to the NDP. However, its lack of experienced workers and numbers of volunteers prevented this.

Unable to shift the terms of the debate towards local issues, Brisco's component campaign suffered from its links to the national Tory platform.

Don Ross: Stopgap Candidate with Family and Friends

Ex-mayor of Surrey Don Ross believed that the creation of the new suburban riding of Surrey North gave him an opportunity to use his public profile to reshape the political landscape and win the seat for the Liberals. He had run and lost as a Liberal at the provincial level but knew nothing of the local federal association, and considered himself an outsider. Although well known locally, he was a stopgap candidate in a weak local association. Although formally contested, the nomination was very lopsided because of Ross's profile. It was much like the open, uncontested nominations of most stopgap candidates.

With a weak association, Ross put together a very limited campaign team. He relied heavily on his family to fill the core positions of the inner circle. A lack of all three types of workers banished his campaign to the margins. His profile helped him to raise twice the funds of his Conservative opponent, but this was still $13,000 less than the NDP. With few workers, and a reliance on expensive campaigning, this was just enough money to keep the campaign viable. Although Ross wanted to promote local issues, his was a parallel campaign caught up in the strategies of the national party. This Liberal campaign was marginalized from the real contest between the NDP and Tories, but its improved poll performance ensured it was not excluded from the race.

Ross's NDP opponent was former alderman and NDP insider Jack Karpoff. He won a closed but hotly contested nomination over three other candidates with strong support from among female members of the local association. With a strong local association and solid funding, he managed to build a good campaign team that had a typical bureaucratic NDP form. With experienced campaigners from the municipal, provincial, and federal levels of the party, the inner circle was very competent. It easily outclassed its opponents in canvassing the riding and fulfilling the other demands of campaigning. The campaign made some effort to address local issues but was largely a subsidiary of the federal effort, with little focus on the candidate. In fact, organizers noted that of the three major candidates, only Ross maintained a public profile throughout the campaign. Nevertheless, Karpoff engaged the Tories, even if mainly over national issues.

Tory Cliff Blair proved to be Karpoff's main competition. He had won an open, contested nomination over five other candidates. Although he had been a member of the party for a number of years, his strong views on abortion set him apart from many of the other nomination candidates. A local realtor and prominent in local pro-life groups, Blair was a local notable. Many members of this new Tory association left after their preferred candidate failed to win the nomination, limiting the size of Blair's campaign team and his capacity to raise funds. He also had to compete for funds with Ross, who was much better known and was effective at attracting donations from the local community, particularly businesses. Despite this, Blair had enough committed workers to run a solid, parochial campaign in which the strategies were decided locally. Blair was a strong supporter of free trade, and the campaign chose to focus on the agreement. Provincial party strategists worried about this approach, arguing the campaign would benefit from less enthusiastic support of the policy.

It is testament to the power of perceptions that the Tories would do poorly in British Columbia that Karpoff's campaign succeeded in convincing PC strategists that Blair had little chance of winning Surrey North. Just prior to election day, local and national strategists realized that they were engaged in a contested constituency election and as such had some chance of winning. A late infusion of funds by the party was insufficient to turn the tide, and Blair lost the riding by just 4 percentage points.

Surrey North is a good example of a suburban riding. There is little sense of a local political agenda. This is the result of a lack of truly local issues and of media capable of sustaining local political discourse. It may also reflect the fact that many local voters work outside the riding, in Vancouver, and that the area is new and rapidly expanding. Suburban homeowning families have general interests in the state of the economy and social issues affecting families. There has been a large influx of East Asian immigrants in recent years, which has added some diversity to a population that is predominantly of British extraction. It is not a wealthy riding, ranging from modest to middle income in the main, with about one-fifth of all households classified as low income, and education levels that are on average the lowest in the province (Eagles et al. 1991, 61).

With few means of communicating with voters, local campaigns made sure that street signs and pamphlets were distributed throughout the riding, and that as much of the riding as possible was canvassed by foot or phone. These are labour-intensive campaign methods that only the NDP had sufficient workers to fully implement. The Tory campaign had enough workers to mount a credible campaign, but struggled to find enough money to produce signs, local literature, and to run a phone bank, while the Liberals did very little.

The contest was amorphous. Local journalists and campaigners noted that the two leading candidates were relatively unknown at the end of the campaign. This highlights the fact that in many suburban ridings, the candidates are first and foremost representatives of their parties, and their personalities are of secondary importance. By default, the election revolved around the platforms and issues raised by the national parties. This atmosphere was reinforced by the dominance of the subsidiary NDP campaign. The NDP won 37 percent of the vote to the Tories' 32.8 percent. While the NDP vote had not changed since 1984, the Tories dropped 13.7 points. Most of this went to the Liberals, whose vote share increased from 14.4 to 24.9 percentage points. Local strategists from all parties attributed this 73 percent increase in the Liberal vote share to Ross's high profile. This suggests that it is the inability of most suburban candidates to single themselves out rather than voters' unwillingness to be influenced by public profiles that limits the impact of personalities on these contests.

The Candidate and Campaign Team
Ross was a stopgap candidate in a riding in which the Liberals were happy to have a name on the ballot. His local profile was an unexpected bonus. The nomination exhibited many of the characteristics of the latent democracy found in uncompetitive, cadre-style associations. Of the two candidates who contested the nomination, neither put much effort into winning. The nomination produced very little recruitment to the association, and as a result did not generate much enthusiasm or bring in membership dues. The lack of potential campaign workers became painfully clear to Ross after he won the nomination.

The local association had few resources and could provide only a handful of campaign volunteers, none with much experience. In the hope that it would help him run a professional campaign in line with his public image as ex-mayor of Surrey, Ross accepted the offer of assistance from Brian Hayes, a professional promoter, and installed him as campaign manager. Hayes left the campaign after just three weeks, forcing Ross to rely on his family to do most of the work, and creating a sense of fatalism that permeated the campaign. "It was a very negative experience. Hayes's lack of commitment was astonishing and soul-destroying. I am not about to go through the same experience again," says Ross.

After some heated disagreements between members of the association and the Ross family, the campaign ground to a halt, with a number of volunteers quitting. This left Ross relying even more heavily on his family to run the campaign. His son Brad stepped into the breach as campaign manager, to "maintain [his] father's dignity." Although he had assisted his father in municipal campaigns, he had no experience in coordinating a political campaign. He was, in his own words, just a figurehead; his father had to run the campaign.

The campaign was uncompetitive and lacked the organizational backing needed to attract and build a strong team. Ross, his wife, his two sons, and a couple of other local Liberals made up what was an intimate inner circle. The family made the strategic decisions and assigned the workload among the few volunteers. Ross was thankful for the support of some friends, who

helped out as secondary workers: "They worked for me out of personal loyalty. Not just from Surrey, but from all over the Lower Mainland, Burnaby,
Vancouver, Coquitlam, and Langley."

There were about twenty secondary workers willing to provide occa-
sional help, but only a handful of volunteers were reliable. Even less
committed were another fifteen sympathizers who often had to be
harangued by phone before they would come into the campaign office.
The size of the team was a disappointment for Ross, who was used to having
150 people work on his mayoral campaigns. Although the commitment of
the few volunteers was great, mixed as it was with a lack of experience, it
was counterproductive. Campaigners could not understand why the
Liberal Party would not give such a strong candidate money, or why party
members would not work for him. This anger distracted volunteers from
the task of running the campaign. More experienced campaigners might
have expected this response from the party.

To overcome a lack of volunteers schooled in the art of local campaigning at federal elections, Ross placed a high priority on fund-raising, seeing
it as a means of overcoming these deficiencies. When he approached the
local association for help, he was shocked to find that they could provide
only a $1,900 loan and a $2,837 contribution.[2] His request for help from
the national party was unsuccessful; it gave nothing to the local campaign.
This upset him, as he had understood that the party would be willing to
finance the campaign of a "suitably high-profile candidate such as myself."
It also set the tone for the rest of the campaign. Ross ignored national party
directives and addressed issues he felt were important. He felt he owed allegiance to no one.

Initial fund-raising efforts led by the first campaign manager, Hayes,
were relatively unsuccessful. Brad Ross blamed this on Hayes's lack of effort
and a style that alienated many potential donors. With the departure of
Hayes, Don Ross took control of the fund-raising effort. This is not
unusual, particularly in cadre-style parties such as the Liberals (Carty
1991a, 205-9 and Table 8.6). The candidate is often the target of funds
donated to cadre-style associations, and Ross made good use of his public
profile to generate funds. His son estimated that 70 to 80 percent of this
money came as a result of his father's personal connections with Surrey
North residents and business people, built up over his time in municipal
politics. But the campaign's reliance on Ross to make contact with potential donors was a little more pronounced than in most cadre-style
associations.[3] Even though Ross did much better than most other Liberal
candidates in British Columbia in raising funds, he was disappointed with
the support he received from the business community.

Ross had much more success in obtaining funds from other local voters.
He organized a number of speaking engagements where audiences made

donations, but the majority of his funds came as a result of requests for money while canvassing, and in response to appeals made in campaign brochures. He received solid support from members of the local Indo-Canadian community, and benefited from his close ties to the local Socred establishment, including MLA Rita Johnston. Although disappointed with the $31,193 he raised, it was twice as much as his Conservative opponent managed to collect despite the Tories being better placed to win the seat. Although access to money and a higher profile candidate allowed the Liberals to add 10 percentage points to their 1984 vote, this was 8 points behind the second-place Tories.

Successful fund-raising was the full extent of the local campaign's organizational achievements. While this held the promise of strategic independence, the lack of experienced local volunteers restricted its capacity to make use of this opportunity. The campaign suffered from volunteers having to learn their jobs as they went along, and lacked enough volunteers to adequately canvass the riding. While it had a clear focus on the candidate, with a secondary focus on issues, it was the existing profile of the candidate rather than the efforts of the campaign that had an impact on the local contest.

Intraparty Relations

The lack of financial support from the national party matched its indifference to the fortunes or direction of the local campaign. It did not provide volunteers or strategic advice. It was willing to settle for just having a Liberal candidate on the ballot in Surrey North. Because of its lack of resources, and despite Ross's efforts to focus on his personality and local issues, Ross's was a parallel campaign that could not be distinguished from the national campaign carried into the riding by the nonlocal media.

The local organization had little access to expert assistance from the party. After his campaign manager left, Ross was required to organize the media campaign, including writing and placing advertisements. As a newcomer to this aspect of campaigning, he contacted the provincial head office for help. "I was disillusioned to find that party headquarters did not have the wherewithal to help candidates in my position," comments Ross. In the end, Ross and his wife wrote the copy for his advertisements. Advertising and literature focused on his experience and knowledge of the riding, emphasizing regional issues he felt were important, including forest management and fishing.

Ross had expected more from the party because of claims by local Liberals during the nomination that a good candidate would receive assistance. However, the local association was frail, and the organizational and electoral weakness of the Liberal Party in British Columbia probably precluded it from providing substantial logistical support to a campaign that did not have much chance of winning. The difficulty of raising funds and extracting other assistance from the party aggravated the already dyspeptic view of the national party held by local campaigners. Ross believes that many local donations – particularly corporate donations – that should have gone to the local campaign were funnelled directly to the national campaign. This is because there is a perception that the most efficient way of helping the party, or of being seen to help the party, has been to direct donations to the national campaign. Ross sees this as symptomatic of the traditional Liberal weakness in British Columbia.

The inability of the Liberal Party to offer any substantial help, and of the local association to offer any real volunteer support, also poisoned the relationship between the campaign and the local party. Of Virginia Bardluck, the association president, Brad Ross notes: "She was overpowering and obnoxious, and quite incapable of helping to run a campaign. I was angry at her, and the atmosphere in the campaign office was very 'flat.'"

As a result of his disenchantment, Ross had little contact with the Liberal Party in the lead up to or during the election. He did not attend the school for candidates, as his nomination was too late, and he was largely unaware of strategies or tactics adopted by the wider party. As the campaign was nearly entirely cut off from the party, its strategies were very much the result of local decisions. Ross's attitude to the party platform was freewheeling, and his personal style of fund-raising allowed him a good deal of leeway to create strategy and respond to local circumstances. Comments Ross, "I am a poor example of a candidate sticking to the party line. I tried to adhere to the general principles of the party philosophy, but I called my own shots. The party is weak out here in the West and we are pretty much on our own – there is room within the party for different philosophies. The party is relieved to have a decent candidate, and headquarters provided little direction, or interference. I raised my own money, which strengthened my independence." This was made easier by the fact that much of the Liberal Party literature, and many of the party's advisors, focused on the Tories, forcing the local campaign to design strategies suitable for attacking the NDP. Ross found that "The Liberal campaign was not even well suited to British Columbia, as we had to fight the NDP as well as the Tories out here, yet the campaign did not really address the NDP. It was designed for Quebec and Ontario." Despite the obvious need for a locally focused strategy, the weakness of the local campaign and lack of assistance from its national counterpart left it unable to adequately redirect this strategy.

The only contact between the local campaign and the national campaign was when the National Strategy Committee made available the timetable for the leader's tour. Turner swung through the riding, but made little direct impression. On the other hand, Turner's performance in the national debates, the central theme of campaign reporting for the couple of weeks following the event, had a noticeable impact on the enthusiasm of workers, who became willing to work harder and more often on the campaign. Similarly, as the polls improved for the party around this time, it was easier to get volunteers into the campaign office.

The Local Contest

Surrey North is a fairly typical suburban riding, though it was established as a result of growth in Vancouver suburbs during the late 1980s and early 1990s that was the fastest in the country. It is populated primarily by younger, homeowning families who are supported by breadwinners who work mainly outside the riding. Because of this, their political interests are not strongly tied to the riding. Thus, most are not connected to the market-gardening or shipping industries that make up the local economy. Although increasingly culturally diverse, the concerns of raising a family dominate. Local campaigns have little if any access to indigenous media, often lack a distinct identity or set of riding issues, and as a result are easily swamped by neighbouring campaigns in large cities. Frequent changes to suburban boundaries due to the growth in the metropolitan population complicate the development of a community of interest among local voters.

Assessing the competitive position of the campaigns in this new riding was difficult. Although an area that had elected Tories in the past, the riding was made up of polls that had favoured the NDP as well as some of the weaker Tory polls from the old ridings. Given the unpopularity of the Mulroney government, the NDP felt it had a chance of winning the seat. Ross, using much the same logic, hoped that he could win by offering disenchanted Tory voters a middle option, holding on to traditional Liberal supporters in the riding, and attracting New Democrats interested in a party with a chance of forming government.

The Liberals' moderately sized campaign fund was large enough to afford the basics of campaigning – campaign literature and signs, as well as advertising and a phone bank. The campaign signs and literature emphasized work in local government, knowledge of the riding, and Ross's good reputation, trying to link this to a vote for the party. However, being understaffed, the campaign found it difficult to canvass the riding and put up signs. With a small association, it was also hard to find people willing to allow a sign to be erected on their property. Brad Ross noted that the lack of signs around the riding, in comparison with major parties, made it clear that the Liberals were the third party in the contest. His father did as much canvassing both by foot and by phone as possible, leaving the bulk of the office work to his family. Like Brisco in the Kootenays, a substantial amount of this work fell to his wife. Not only did she run the office in Whalley, she phoned volunteers daily to try to get them into the office to work. The Ross family – both parents and two sons – designed campaign strategies around the dinner table in the evenings. Organizing the campaign and canvassing the riding took its toll on the family, and the campaign suffered accordingly.

Ross tried hard to schedule as many all-candidates meetings as possible. With little media covering the riding, public events such as all-candidates debates were a rare opportunity to foster his public image, as Ross believed that he was the best public speaker of the three major party candidates. The first all-candidates debate of the campaign was held in Surrey North a week after the national debate in which Turner had done well. Ross was the star performer, exhibiting great skill as a debater and linking his public service as mayor of Surrey to his current campaign. Unfortunately, a number of factors conspired to limit Ross's ability to exploit this advantage.

Immediately following this success, Ross attempted to arrange further debates, but failed to convince other candidates to participate. As the perceived front-runner, New Democrat candidate Jim Karpoff wanted to avoid engaging with his opponents for fear public defeat might diminish his campaign in some way. The NDP openly admitted that Karpoff attended the first debate only because it was a minimum condition for being seen as a credible candidate in the contest. He knew that Ross was a better public speaker and that these events provided the Liberal candidate with an opportunity to raise his profile, and perhaps undercut the NDP's position as the main opponent of free trade. Tory Cliff Blair was less hostile to the suggestion but knew he was no match for Ross.

The lack of any subsequent all-candidates debates denied Ross his best platform for making use of his public profile. Unfortunately, as with most suburban campaigns, there were no influential media interested enough in the local contest to take up Ross's complaints that the other candidates feared public debate and democracy. As a result, no real pressure to continue the debates was brought to bear on the NDP or PC candidates. Whereas in the Okanagan, well-organized local media organizations followed up on the Tory candidate's fear of public debates, this never became an issue in Surrey North. It appears that suburban campaigns condemn candidates to relative obscurity. As a result, the strategy of focusing on the candidate – even one as competent as Ross – can be of only limited value.

Like many campaigns that lack workers, the Liberals relied heavily on advertising and literature, and Ross made use of his contacts with community newspapers, built up over his time as mayor, to gain whatever media coverage there was. These activities were rated as the most important by campaigners. However, the printing of literature was expensive, and the campaign did not have enough workers to deliver election pamphlets, having instead to pay for this service. The advertising campaign absorbed a massive 63 percent of campaign spending, revealing the campaign's reliance on this method of communication over more labour-intensive canvassing. In comparison, the unsuccessful Tory campaign spent 57 percent of its total campaign expenditures (only half that of the Liberal campaign) on advertising, while the successful New Democrat campaign spent a mere 21 percent of its funds on advertising.

The Liberal campaign spent money in local community newspapers such as *Surrey Delta Now* and the *Surrey Leader*. It advertised in two Indo-Canadian publications, *Canada Darpan Weekly* and the *Indo-Canadian Times,* in order to reach the local Indo-Canadian community. It also spent a small sum on radio advertising, using CISL, a station based in the nearby suburb of Richmond but broadcasting to all of Vancouver. Unfortunately, money spent on advertising was poorly directed. The major city media are too expensive for a local campaign and their broadcast or distribution region is much greater than a single riding. Meanwhile, the small local media are affordable, but not very influential. Even the local community newspapers are delivered to parts of at least two other ridings besides Surrey North, and newspapers aimed at ethnic groups are even more widely distributed.

At the time of the election, the *Now* newspaper had only a satellite office in Surrey North, with the main work for the newspaper being done at the office in Burnaby. The paper was trying to cover three riding contests. The other community newspaper, the *Leader,* was considered by candidates to be the only reliable source of coverage for local politics. While the media made a real effort to cover the campaign, they were limited by the need to cover local municipal elections as well. The municipal vote was just two days before the national vote. Frank Bucholtz at the *Leader* noted that the paper gave more coverage to the municipal election because it considered this to be its territory. The municipal election had between thirty and forty candidates who needed to be covered. In addition, the paper reported three federal ridings – Surrey North, Surrey-White Rock, and Delta. As a result, the coverage given any particular candidate was limited.

From a media perspective, the Surrey North federal race was exceptional only in that for the first time anyone could remember, all three leaders of the national parties visited the riding. This was taken as an indication that all parties saw it as a potential swing riding. The main element of the *Leader's* coverage of the candidates was a questionnaire asking their positions on the major issues. This was published in the week before the election. There were no face-to-face interviews. Rather, communication was by fax or phone, including press releases. Bucholtz outlines the *Leader's* coverage in this way: "The NDP in particular tried hard to interest us in stories. We covered the all-candidates debate and the cable television interviews of the candidates. The paper tried to keep an approximate balance in the partisan nature of letters in the editorial page."

Reporters from *Now* did one interview with each candidate and wrote some stories as a result of campaign press releases. *Now* also ran weekly poll results provided by a national polling company, and shared stories and resources with other *Now* newspapers in the lower mainland. The municipal election was seen as a higher priority, taking about 70 percent of the space and resources put over to election coverage. *Now* editor Jeff Beamish estimates that the coverage of the national election required less than half the working time of one journalist. The local cable station ran an interview with each of the candidates. Some of the Ross's comments were picked up on the most-listened-to radio station in Vancouver, CKNW. He also appeared on a cable political forum, where he was interviewed by long-time political commentator Jack Webster. Ross and his opponents in the riding were surprised at the number of people they met who had seen these shows.

Ross benefited from his reputation as mayor and his established contacts with the media. He believes this helped him run a close third behind the Tory candidate in an election in which most Liberal candidates in British Columbia finished a distant third. The local newspapers treated his campaign seriously, more so than many other Liberal campaigns in the province. Karpoff emphasized his service as a local municipal councillor. Conservative candidate Blair was less well known. Blair's own polling supported this conclusion. Sadly for Ross, the local contest did not revolve around the candidates; rather, it focused on party platforms. The partisan ambience of the contest was accentuated by the free trade debate, which, in British Columbia, was polarized between the Tories and the NDP. This left the Liberals in a very difficult position that was conducive to alternative strategies that attempted to focus on other issues, including Ross's capabilities.

All three major party candidates had reason to believe they would be fully engaged in the local contest. That campaigns engaged indirectly in clichés drawn from the party platform rather than at all-candidates debates is typical of the style of suburban campaigns. As for Ross, despite his difficulties, he managed to attract one-quarter of the total vote, and was marginalized but not excluded from the race. This constituted a two-thirds improvement in the Liberals' notional 1984 vote share. According to his opponents, local journalists, and his own campaign volunteers, this was due to his personal appeal. Given that the Tories polled fewer votes than Elections Canada calculations suggested it notionally would have in 1984, and the NDP did not improve on its 1984 performance, the Liberals were important to the final outcome.[4]

The Surrey North Liberal campaign failed to implement its own strategic vision. The contest was hostile to its two most obvious strategies for controlling the local agenda. It could not make use of its main advantage – Ross's profile – because of its failure to persuade other candidates to attend public debates. And the lack of local media and a well-developed local political agenda prevented it from using this to embarrass its opponents, and limited the routes available to it to counter the dominance of the federal campaign and free trade debate. The national debate could not even be localized, as in some ridings, because of the lack of a mechanism for articulating local interests. Its collapse into a parallel campaign that mimicked the national party was a poor outcome for local Liberals, as it forced it into the free trade debate in a province where both sides of this issue were already taken.

Lynn Fairall: The Faithful Party Insider

Although it was not likely to win, only the NDP could challenge the long-serving and well-entrenched Conservative incumbent Bob Wenman in the mainly country riding of Fraser Valley West. Lynn Fairall, a union shop steward and federal government worker, won a closed but contested NDP nomination. Although she had recently moved into the riding, she was a long-time party insider, having been involved in various NDP associations. In classic NDP bureaucratic fashion, the local association executive had hired office space and set up the basics of a campaign team well before the nomination meeting.

Despite the lack of federal or provincial success in the area, the NDP had a small but capable local association. About 80 members were involved in the nomination and campaign process. This is evidence of the impact of organizational solidarity and commitment characteristic of the NDP. The local party had enough workers and experienced organizers to cover the basic demands of the campaign period. While Fairall did campaign on the Tories' sales tax proposals and environmental issues, by and large, her campaign stuck to the federal strategy of promoting Ed Broadbent and discussing free trade. As such, it was a subsidiary campaign. Wenman's big lead in the riding meant that Fairall's campaign was excluded from an uncontested constituency election.

Conservative incumbent and high-profile candidate Wenman had a strong hold on the riding going into the election. It was considered to be one of the safest Tory seats in Canada. The only hiccup occurred within his own association, when a member challenged him for the nomination, accusing the MP of failing to champion conservative social issues. Wenman easily won the nomination, but some association members switched their allegiance to the Christian Heritage Party, whose leader was running in the riding. Such challenges are rare in Canadian electoral politics. With Wenman's vast resources and contacts to the federal party, he ran the sort of component campaign expected of an incumbent. As a front-runner, he managed to avoid engaging with his opponents.

Liberal Tony Wattie won an open, weakly contested Liberal nomination over one other candidate. There was little enthusiasm for the nomination, which resembled the uncontested nominations found in many uncompetitive associations. A lawyer, Wattie had been president of both the Fraser Valley West and the Fraser Valley East Liberal associations, and was willing to run as a stopgap candidate. The local association was very weak, and his campaign was run by a handful of party stalwarts and friends, with the job of campaign manager being shared between two volunteers. There were another twenty or so secondary workers and sympathizers. Although he performed well in public, Wattie was not considered a serious contender for the riding. He campaigned only part time and continued practising law. His was a parallel campaign that failed to generate a distinct image for itself. Although the Liberals vote improved over 1984, Wattie attributed this to Turner's performance in the national leaders' debates. Like Fairall, he was excluded from the constituency election.

The boundaries of Fraser Valley West were moved eastward in the electoral redistribution just prior to the election to take account of the spread of Greater Vancouver eastward into once rural parts of the Fraser Valley. It includes several distinct communities, including Langley, Aldergrove, Matsqui, and Clearbrook, into which manufacturing and service industries are moving. It still encompasses commercial farms, but they are being converted to smaller hobby farms. The riding remains largely rural, with one-third of its polls being urban. The average income is below the provincial average, and unemployment is higher than in Vancouver. The population is predominantly European, with the majority of British origin, but with sizeable Dutch and German minorities. Local candidates had access to newspapers, radio stations, and the local cable service in these communities without having to compete with city or suburban campaigns. This allowed them to direct messages at a local audience. Some campaign teams had offices in at least two of these communities, and all had to deal with the difficulties of reaching voters spread across some distance.

There was not really a local contest in Fraser Valley West. Voters in this riding appear to have found it difficult to imagine an alternative to Wenman, and he avoided engaging the other candidates. As a result, there was little sense of local political agenda, despite the presence of media willing to report the contest. Still, failure to engage other candidates may have caused the shifting of votes away from Wenman, who lost votes to parties on his left and right. The Reform and Christian Heritage Parties together captured over 8 percent of the vote. They appealed to the conservative, church-going population of this semirural riding. The Liberals managed to double their vote to nearly 20 percent. Fairall added 1.4 percentage points to the New Democrats' previous result by capturing 24.1 percent of the votes cast. In the end, Wenman's vote share dropped by over 16 percentage points. The strength of his hold on the riding can be seen in the fact that this left him with a still comfortable 20 percentage point margin over Fairall.

The Candidate and Campaign Team
For an association that had no chance of winning, the organizational strength of the NDP in Fraser Valley West was impressive. Local members move between the local municipal, provincial, and federal associations as each level faces an election. Local organizers estimated that the federal association had about 800 members.

A preelection committee of fifteen began work nearly a year prior to the election. It organized initial fund-raising events, oversaw the candidate search, and rented campaign office space by the time of the nomination in June, well before the election was announced. Prior to the nomination, the preelection committee kept candidates informed about community events, encouraging them to attend. This included renting a table on behalf of the association at a weekly flea market. This greater role for the local association executive in organizing campaigns and choosing strategies is more common in the NDP than in either the Liberal or Conservative Parties (Carty 1991a, Table 7.1 and Figure 7.2).

A friend who was a member of the search committee approached Fairall and asked her to run for nomination. She won on the first ballot, ahead of two insider candidates in what was a classic party-democracy-style nomination. To run for the nomination, she took a leave of absence without pay from her federal public service job. Her union ties, and the support of the large contingent of women members in the association, won her the nomination over Charles Bradford, a long-time association member. The inexperienced Fairall put together a campaign team in consultation with the association executive. They made good use of members with campaign experience, and in particular local unionists and women interested in supporting a female candidate.

The association immediately formed a number of campaign committees to deal with election planning, communications and media relations, foot canvassing, phone canvassing, literature, and fund-raising. The relationship among the inner circle, many of whom were executive members, was bureaucratic. All were committed party members who saw Fairall as the front person of a true team effort. The inner circle of workers numbered about a dozen, with a larger group of about 50 willing to do some phoning. Outside this was a large circle of about 200 people willing to put up signs and the like. Unions contributed $3,000 to her campaign, and women dominated the campaign's inner circle. Fairall recalls the team: "There was a great feeling working with the volunteers, some of whom took two weeks' holiday from their jobs to work on the campaign. We were like a family – in fact, the hardest worker was my husband."

Despite relying on a network of female association members, Fairall's main rival for the nomination, Charles Bradford, was appointed campaign manager. Given that there was some animosity between candidates during the nomination, this outcome is evidence of the ethos of solidarity found in NDP associations. As Fairall notes, "We all know each other, and after the nomination, there was a sense that the best person for the job should do that job. There was some tension between the winners and losers, but we were able to manage it by careful selection of people for different jobs." Despite this, Bradford was out of place in the campaign. He was given control of the campaign office covering Fort Langley and Aldergrove, which became the secondary campaign office. The other office, covering Clearbrook and Matsqui, was managed by a friend of Fairall's, Lyn Bomford. This became the main campaign office, and Bomford the actual campaign manager. This was her third campaign as an office manager for the NDP, but her first in the Fraser Valley as, like Fairall, she had arrived in the riding only in July of the election year. Bomford sees the need to accommodate personalities as a necessary part of any campaign: "This was just a more acute example of one of the jobs of campaign organizers – finding the right job and the right place for the different personalities that work on a campaign. The mix of personalities is important in keeping people happy and effective as campaigners."

The association began collecting funds at the nomination, where party members were encouraged to donate to the campaign. Once the election was announced, the party organized a picnic and raffle to help raise money. Because of the close relationship among associations at different levels of the party, the federal campaign had access to lists of voters and records of contributors, volunteers, and supporters developed by these other organizations. This helped the campaign to canvass and raise funds. Fairall also benefited from the NDP's policy of equalizing funds across local associations in order to help those with limited finances (see Stanbury 1991; Morley 1991). But the $26,191 her campaign raised was only $1,000 more than that raised by the local Liberal association, and actually $3,000 less than what the local Christian Heritage Party campaign raised. All these totals pale in comparison with the $60,618 that Wenman raised.

Strategic decision making for the campaign rested with the provincial and national levels of the party. Like all NDP campaigns in British Columbia, Fairall and local campaign organizers spoke with party strategists several times a week in an attempt to ensure the local strategy was in keeping with that of the wider party. The party also organized a number of events to which candidates were invited, at which the focus was the party platform and leader. Fairall ranked the leader, the party, and the party platform as more important than her own impact on voters, as did office manager Bomford. Fairall saw her role as maintaining the cohesion and morale of the team, while the strategic focus remained the campaign mapped out by the federal party: "The candidate brings purpose to the workers, provides inspiration, and is a motivational force." This indicates the organizational mindset of New Democrats, who believe that a federal campaign is only as good as its local campaigns; but only when embedded in a well-run federal campaign can local campaigns be successful.

Intraparty Relations
The integration between local and nonlocal elements of the NDP was evident well before the election. Fairall attended the party's candidate school at the University of British Columbia. This was designed to familiarize candidates with modern communication technologies, develop candidates' public speaking and capacity to deal with reporters and hecklers, and encourage them to maintain a good personal appearance. As well, candidates were given seventeen major policy statements and instructed to follow the party line: "We were told to leave free trade alone and go with taxation issues. To let the national campaign make the running on issues, and not to engage in any policy freelancing. We were urged to respect the expertise and polling of the party."

The skills covered at the school were taught in a manner that reinforced this conservative attitude to candidates' freedom to speak off-the-cuff. As Fairall notes, "Candidates were warned that the media and their opponents would try to sidetrack them, to get them to speak off-the-cuff – to speak emotionally – by upsetting them. This should be avoided because the type of campaign it would be meant local candidates comments will be important, so [the candidates] should be cautious." Fairall was surprised by the extent to which the party attempted to stifle local initiative. She thought that local candidates should be trusted to make comments in areas that were germane to their own riding or area of special interest. For example, her own union work had involved her in courses and seminars on free trade, and she felt capable of dealing with it in her own way.

The organizational and strategic integration of local and national branches of the party was evident in the attitudes and actions of local campaigners, who believed solidarity to be an important part of the NDP ethos. They were committed to running a good subsidiary campaign that adopted national party strategies. Even if unsuccessful, they believed this would be good for the wider fortunes of the party. This party-centred view of electioneering is evident in Fairall's observations that "When all federal candidates appear to give the same message, it gives the impression of an effective organization. To do this we needed to run an effective local campaign. The role of the candidate is to be the public face of the party, to announce party policy in the local area, and connect the party to the local situation." Similarly, Bomford notes that "the candidate is less important than the party."

The local campaign at first adopted strategies in line with those set by the national party. This was built on the appeal of Ed Broadbent, and on the promise of "fair, open, and honest government," with emphasis on fairness of taxation. But as the election progressed, some NDP strategists, and the BC provincial NDP in particular, came to believe that the party would benefit from pushing its anti-free trade position. Most New Democrat campaigners interviewed for this study made mention of tension between the provincial and national offices of the party over this matter. The strength of the provincial NDP, and the appropriateness of the policy in a province where the party can fend off the Liberals and make itself the leading opponent of the Conservatives, meant that local campaigns adopted the provincial view of strategy.

The federal campaign did not make a particular effort to become involved in the Fraser Valley West campaign. Most contact was with the provincial wing, which kept the campaign apprised of Broadbent's policy announcements and provided detailed supporting literature. Provincial campaign coordinator Ron Johnson was in constant contact, pointing out the special priorities of the BC campaign and giving the latest regional polling figures. There were regular weekly meetings of candidates and campaign managers at the party's head office in Burnaby. The provincial women candidates gave two press conferences, and all the BC NDP candidates attended two dinners organized by the party.

The local campaign in Fraser Valley West was both organizationally and strategically integrated with its nonlocal counterparts. This integration was with both the national campaign and with the national campaign as interpreted by the powerful provincial party. This led to tensions as strategies adopted at the two levels diverged over the course of the campaign. But despite this, and its very limited chances of success, the local campaign was sustained by its members' commitment to the principle that the party should run strong, centrally controlled campaigns in every riding across the country. The widespread acceptance of this integration among campaigners is remarkable. The campaign was part of a national effort, and campaigners part of a national team.

The Local Contest

The Fraser Valley is renowned for its social conservatism, which has underpinned its long support of the Tories. Given this, the area has not been good to the NDP. With a committed core of workers, 75 percent of whom had experience working on NDP campaigns, but limited other resources, the local organization decided the best way of carrying the New Democrat banner was to concentrate on the basics of campaigning and attract any undecided voters by face-to-face contact with the candidate. As well, it hoped to take every opportunity to attack the record of incumbent Bob Wenman at public forums.

Office space was chosen from a list developed in previous federal and provincial elections, and rented before the nomination. As soon as the nomination was over, campaign signs were produced using provincial party funds and erected at places used previously. A phone bank was set up to contact potential donors and campaign workers. Lists of donors from previous elections were used to send requests for funds, and voter support was identified and classified on the basis of information collected at recent federal, provincial, and municipal elections. The campaign produced and started distributing leaflets as part of its door-to-door canvassing campaign. The use of locally produced campaign literature was extensive, but the campaign also relied on national party hand-outs. Because of lack of funds, it sent provincial and national campaign literature to voters who made specific policy enquiries.

The continuity between elections evidenced in the way the local New Democrat campaign got under way is a feature of many BC NDP campaigns. Local campaigners consider recording useful information for future campaigns an important part of their campaign effort and essential to the eventual success of the party. This tends to set these campaigns apart from many campaigns in cadre-style associations, which, with the exception of ridings where there is an incumbent, either rely on the informal networks of experienced campaigners or work in a more episodic fashion from one campaign to the next.

Fairall worked hard meet as many voters as possible. She canvassed by foot about four hours a day; worked around the office, often making calls to voters; and spent evenings researching and keeping up with the national and provincial campaigns. Like the other candidates, she made a point of visiting community centres and important local institutions, such as the Sikh temple, in order to woo cultural and social groups. The campaign used high-profile candidates from other ridings such as Johanna den Hertog in mainstreeting and press conference appearances with Fairall.

Canvassing is labour intensive and relatively specialized work. A semi-rural and therefore large riding such as Fraser Valley West, dotted with farms and small communities, is difficult to canvass by foot. As Bomford notes, this poses the greatest challenge to parties, particularly in large ridings: "Only committed workers are willing to canvass. And you want people who are capable and presentable. You need to develop a kit that contains the necessary literature, maps of where to canvass, a suggested script, and suitable responses to voters' questions. And you might want to train them to do this. Even just dropping literature requires the first two of these."

To overcome the difficulties of covering the riding by foot, the campaign relied heavily on phone canvassing. Each office had half a dozen phones, used by canvassers to identify voter preferences. This allowed the campaign to focus on undecided voters. With a competent campaign organization, the candidate was free to foot canvass in crucial areas, and contact undecided voters, or voters with specific questions, by phone. Phone banks were used to answer voter queries about party policy and the location of polling booths.

In terms of issues, the local campaign followed the party line. In the early part of the campaign, it used literature sent out by the party, and the timed release of policies by Broadbent gave the campaign focus. While some national issues presented themselves – a greater emphasis on the Tories' tax proposals and environmental record – there were few obvious local issues for the campaign to adopt. Fairall did try to modify the campaign by focusing on issues of particular concern to women, and attended a press conference dealing with this issue organized by the provincial party. But as the campaign progressed, provincial strategists felt that the focus on Broadbent was the wrong approach, and they decided instead to concentrate on free trade more than the national party did. Fairall worked to emphasize the local impact of the agreement. This was a decision of the provincial party that local BC campaigns were willing to adopt. But NDP campaigners are loath to focus on local issues unless they are of extraordinary importance, and generally follow the dictates of the party, in this instance, the strong provincial branch.

Unfortunately for Fairall, Wenman's electoral position was unassailable, and he stifled the local contest by refusing to attend all-candidates debates to which minor parties were invited, afraid of giving his opponents an opportunity to gain at his expense. He expected awkward questions from voters unhappy with free trade, and also from Christian Heritage Party regarding his position and the Tories' record on abortion. As well, the NDP's literature made it clear they would question him about his overseas travel, which had restricted him to just eight speeches in the life of the previous Parliament. The other candidates insisted minor parties be included in all debates. Wenman created a furore when he sent high-profile anti-abortion Conservative parliamentarian Beno Friesen to a debate at a local theological college at which Friesen had been an instructor. Wenman felt obliged to attend the next meeting to save face.

Wenman did not entirely dominate the local campaign or agenda, but he could avoid the contest by staying away from other candidates and communicating with voters via the media. As Bomford notes, Fairall did not have the public profile nor access to enough canvassers or advertising funds to force issues onto the agenda: "There were no burning local issues, although as a woman and unionist, Lynn was interested in abortion and the impact of the Free Trade Agreement on jobs and wages. In addition, as a small farm owner, she was aware of the implications of free trade for the intensive agriculture sector, such as egg producers in the riding."

And even if the campaign had managed to advertise more widely, the influence of the local media was uncertain, as it competes in part with major Vancouver outlets, and was considered sympathetic to the Tories. Wenman dominated the media, spending about 55 percent of his large campaign budget on advertising. This was much more than most other competitive campaigns, and 30 percent more than local Tories spent in 1984. The Liberals spent the same proportion of a much smaller budget, while the NDP spent just 35 percent of its budget on advertising. Although clearly a front-runner, Wenman's position in the riding was deteriorating, and local Tories admitted his campaign was lacklustre in comparison with 1984's.

The riding has a number of newspapers centred on each of the local communities. These include the *Abbotsford Times,* the *Abbotsford News,* the *Abbotsford Now,* the *Aldergrove Star,* the *Langley Advance,* and the *Langley Times.* Campaigners felt that they were too understaffed to provide detailed coverage of the campaign, though they are larger and better organized than suburban community papers, and play a more central role in delivering news in this semirural area. The existence of local communities in this riding separated from the Vancouver suburbs is the basis of this distinct media presence, which itself encourages the development of a local agenda. Local papers gave basic coverage of the candidates' positions, all-candidates debates in their community, and the main issues on which the election was being fought. Fairall's campaign tried to get a press release out to these papers once a week, and all campaigns spent most of their advertising budgets in the print media. The NDP also advertised in the *Indo-Canadian Times* and the *Ranjeet News,* both of which are aimed at the Indo-Canadian community. Fairall considered advertising important for maintaining credibility and aimed to have the maximum amount of advertising in the week prior to the election. The local papers offered low rates to local campaigns.

Two radio stations and a cable television station service the area but not the Vancouver suburbs. This helps put advertising rates on radio within reach of local campaigns in the Fraser Valley, and motivates the local cable station to run all-candidates debates. As in the Kootenays and the Okanagan, radio can reach voters across a wide area that is difficult to canvass in person. While the NDP spent proportionately less than the other campaigns on advertising, it alone used radio advertising. It spent $800 on one advertisement, which was repeated over the last two weeks of the campaign on Star FM 104, which covers Abbotsford and Chilliwack, and is run by Fraser Valley Broadcasting. The national campaign also used Star. Unlike the Tories in Okanagan Centre, the local NDP campaign was not concerned about the impact of national advertising on the riding contest, as the party's organizational approach ensured the message was much the same at both levels.

Another local station, CFER 850, hosted an all-candidates debate and had each candidate in for an open-line show. The local cable station also hosted a debate, with each candidate giving a five-minute speech, after which viewers phoned in with questions. Campaign workers were surprised at the number of voters that mentioned that they had seen the debate, which was aired a number of times. Fairall thought it had more impact than any other of the all-candidates debates. As well, the day after Fairall was nominated in June, Vancouver radio stations CKNW and JR-Country had called to interview her, but showed no interest after that. The large city media, the Vancouver Sun and the Province, covered the riding sporadically, as did Vancouver television and radio. But these media outlets were seen as relatively uninterested in, and having little effect on, the local campaign.

With the one exception of the all-candidates debate, Fairall and the other candidates could not force Wenman to engage in the local contest. His easy win despite the loss of about one-third of his 1984 votes is evidence of a riding that really had only one competitive campaign in the uncontested riding. The main impact of the federal campaign was negative, with a feeling among New Democrats that focusing on Broadbent may not have been the best campaign strategy for the local riding, and an annoyance among Tories that they could not escape free trade. Neither the media nor the voters believed either the NDP or Liberals could win. Because of this lack of credibility, these campaigns were unable to generate the momentum needed to challenge the status quo. The lack of any defining local issues also made it difficult to gain some strategic advantage over the Tories.

Fairall and her team were confronted with a semirural and conservative riding in which many NDP policy positions are difficult to promulgate. As a subsidiary of the nonlocal campaign, the Fraser Valley West NDP team was not well suited to formulating and adopting strategies to exploit local conditions. That it fulfilled all the basic requirements of a riding campaign despite a hostile local environment is evidence of the commitment of members to the party and its centrally orchestrated strategies. Even on election day, campaigners worked hard to find every possible NDP voter and got him or her to a polling booth. Fairall and others spent all day on the phone contacting supporters and urging them to vote. Other workers provided transportation and relevant information to voters. The political spectrum in the riding does not easily entertain a contest because of the dominance of the conservative politics in the riding. The only exception might be between two socially conservative candidates.

Tex Enemark: Smoke and Mirrors

Liberal candidate in Vancouver Centre Tex Enemark is a special case: a stopgap candidate who was given substantial financial support by the party to achieve goals other than a win in Centre. The profile of the local riding contest and the need to be seen as competitive in British Columbia encouraged the party to help this campaign. But although in third place in the riding, the Liberals were weak in British Columbia, and the local association had few members. As a result, Enemark struggled to find volunteers and relied on a few friends to help him run the campaign.

The collapse of Enemark's efforts to generate a local strategy created a parallel campaign that followed the national party's lead. Whereas the NDP and Tory campaigns of den Hertog and Campbell were engaged in a close contest, Enemark was never a serious contender and was marginalized from the contest. In an attempt to keep up with the well-staffed component campaigns of his high-profile rivals, Enemark spent heavily on advertising. This strategy failed, and the campaign had remarkably little impact on the local contest. The Liberal vote share went down 2 percentage points to just below 23 percent, while Campbell beat den Hertog by just 0.4 of 1 percent. The Liberals' poor showing indicates the critical role that volunteers play in local campaigns.

The Candidate and Campaign Team

The nomination in the small Liberal association in Vancouver Centre was open but only nominally contested. Enemark easily beat an environmental activist in what was a noncontest. Campaign manager Allan Gould suggested that the association had withered in the period since 1983, before which it had ridden on the back of a strong national party. Following the nomination, the weak local association was unable to provide the nucleus of a campaign organization and donated just $678.96 worth of goods and services to the campaign.

Enemark's first task was to build an inner circle of campaign workers from outside the association, including a campaign manager and official agent. He had high hopes for his campaign, and contacted friends, many of them in management and public relations occupations, to help. Some had been members of the party, and many were broadly sympathetic to its objectives, but few of them were current members. They were a motley mix of professionals – lawyers, accountants, and managers – with little campaign experience, held together by their friendship for Enemark and a memory of the past glory of the Liberal Party. While the dozen workers who made up the inner circle had professional careers, they were not experienced campaigners, and were too few to be effective.

Enemark soon realized he would have to do much of the organizational work of the campaign. As Gould notes, "Tex approached me and asked me to work on the campaign. I agreed to out of friendship for Tex, not because of some commitment to the party. I think this was true for most of us campaigners. He played the central role in organizing the campaign." To make matters worse, few of the volunteers appear to have been committed to getting Enemark elected, but rather thought of themselves as doing him a favour by being present.

The redeeming feature of the inner circle personnel was that, while unschooled in campaigning, their professional skills could be put to use organizing a campaign. These included managing an office, writing advertisements, and dealing with the media. But the weakness of the association made it difficult to find people to do the mundane chores such as canvassing by foot and running the phone bank. In addition, many Liberals from Vancouver chose to work on John Turner's campaign in the neighbouring riding of Quadra, which depleted the Liberal ranks in Centre. In the words of the president of the Vancouver Centre association, "Turner's campaign suffered from an embarrassment of riches."

Enemark's campaign had access to about twenty-five secondary workers, whose commitment varied. There were about another 100 sympathizers, some from surrounding Liberal campaigns, including Turner's, at times called in to cover emergency situations when Enemark could not find workers. These numbers pale against the help available to the PC and NDP campaigns in Centre. Moreover, the struggle to find help shocked members of the inner circle, including Gould, who remembered the halcyon days of Liberal organizations during the Trudeau era: "We went into the campaign expecting 1,000 people to show up and help us. We simply did not have enough workers to run a good campaign let alone keep up with the other major parties. It was a smoke and mirrors campaign." As well, the lack of commitment from all but a handful of inner circle workers undermined the morale of the campaign team.

Despite its weakness in the number and experience of volunteers, the campaign had access to substantial campaign funding. This was both a function of Enemark's contacts in the riding and in the Liberal Party, and party strategists' willingness to spend money in a high-profile riding to make the Liberal campaign seem competitive. Enemark was able to raise $54,053, two-and-a-half thousand dollars more than the spending limit in the riding.

Decision making on campaign strategy was local, dominated by Enemark. Most other campaigners were too inexperienced and/or uninterested to offer alternative strategic advice. It is not surprising that this strategy focused strongly on the candidate. Not only was this a product of Enemark's control of the campaign, but it also reflects the lack of a strong Liberal organization in British Columbia, and the party's inability to project any coherent strategic plan into the province from Ottawa. Local BC Liberal campaigns were very much left to their own devices.

Intraparty Relations

The main support offered Enemark's campaign by the federal party was money. It provided $23,945, or 44 percent, of Enemark's campaign funds, more than four times the absolute average amount the party gave to all campaigns in British Columbia.[5] This strategy appears to have been based on the party's desire to be seen to run a credible campaign in a riding with a high media profile where both the NDP and Tories were running strong campaigns. A solid campaign in Centre helped the party maintain a good image and gave it a chance of winning the riding at some future time. The Canadian electorate is relatively volatile, and maintaining a presence in ridings across the country that are in the short term unwinnable is a rational strategy for any party that wishes to remain truly national, and in so doing retain the hope of forming the government (Blake 1991). In addition, Enemark called on favours from among his personal acquaintances in the party hierarchy. The juxtaposition of local and provincial organizational weakness and extraordinary financial support from the national party in the hope of generating the appearance of competitiveness captures the essence of the Liberal campaign.

Despite the assistance offered the local campaign by the national party, there were tensions between the two. In contrast to the national campaign, the local campaign decided to ignore free trade as much as possible. Enemark (and many of his campaigners) did not agree with Turner's opposition to the deal, and in the polarized NDP-versus-PC environment of federal elections in British Columbia, he could not see how he might win on the issue. In place of free trade, the campaign focused on Enemark's personal qualities. As many campaigners knew him well and he dominated strategy making, this is not surprising. Enemark believed he was the campaign's greatest asset: "My experience in Ottawa, my demonstrated competence as a bureaucrat and businessman, and my knowledge of the political process including the workings of the Liberal party made me well suited for a candidate-centred campaign. British Columbia has not provided many first-class people to Ottawa, and I believed I would be such an MP. In fact, Vancouver Centre had the three best candidates in the province."

Relations with the national party were regular, but of little importance. The party did not think Enemark had a great chance of success and was not deeply involved in the campaign, but wanted to keep its options open in case the election swung its way. Local campaigners thought that the national campaign offered very little useful assistance and derided much of the literature available as poorly produced and irrelevant to the polarized politics of British Columbia.

The major impact of the national campaign on the local effort was indirect. According to association president Norman Morrison, Turner's strong performance in the leaders' debates saw Enemark's campaign taken more seriously. The morale of the team improved, and new volunteers were attracted to the campaign. Unfortunately, the debates led to some difficulties, as the local campaign was subjected to greater scrutiny. In particular, as Enemark had been touted as a possible cabinet minister, the media and voters became interested in his views on a range of subjects, including free trade. This forced the local strategists to engage in free trade debates that they believed they could not win. This did not please Gould: "We were happy to let other people do the running on free trade. Once it became a big issue after the debate, we were forced to hand out lots of anti-free trade literature and defend the party's position, with which we did not agree. The more free trade became an issue, which helped the party in other parts of the country, the better the NDP did in British Columbia and the more we suffered. [Furthermore,] the national campaign's '40 points' program became controversial because it was not clear how it would be funded."

As the election progressed, it became clear that few local volunteers supported the party's anti-free trade position, and some even quit the campaign over the issue. Enemark complained that Quebec and Ontario politics dominated the Liberals' strategic thinking, leaving little room for a British Columbian view of how to deal with issues such as free trade.

Despite the local campaign's efforts to generate its own strategy, the force of the free trade debate was irresistible. This made the national party platform more important and left the local campaign increasingly marginalized in the provincial political milieu. Even its alternative strategy of focusing on the candidate faced problems, as Enemark found his unwillingness to speak on free trade was at odds with his desire to be seen as an important candidate involved in national debates. From its early position as apparent challenger to the New Democrats and Tories, it fell to a distant third.

While there was little integration between the two levels of the party, this was not because of the capacity of the local campaign to develop and implement a distinctive electoral strategy. Rather, the local campaign was forced, reluctantly, to simply mimic its national counterpart. The lack of independence of this parallel campaign set it apart from the component campaigns of its opponents in the riding.

The Local Contest

The failure of the Liberal campaign to engage its NDP and Tory opponents was manifest in a number of ways. Enemark did not support Turner's opposition to free trade and was excluded from the polarized free trade debate between the New Democrats and Tories. This limited the strategic options available to the campaign and complicated Enemark's role, as he could not make full use of public debates. Strategists rejected the cosmopolitan definition of the riding community adopted by the Tories and NDP, seeing it as straightforwardly middle class and developing a very different campaign message. Finally, a lack of volunteers prevented the Liberals from competing with other campaigns in canvassing the riding, forcing it to rely on direct mail and advertising to communicate its message.

At odds with Turner's anti-free trade position, and with little national guidance as to alternative strategies, local Liberal strategists focused their campaign on Enemark. Lacking the workers to canvass the riding directly, they turned to alternate means of communicating with voters. This included a glossy brochure, professionally produced and distributed by direct mail, followed by drop pamphlets and signs emphasizing Enemark's personal qualities. In addition, the campaign adopted other tactics that did not require many campaign workers but which maximized Enemark's public exposure. "Bermashave" stunts, such as standing on street corners with balloons and placards during rush hour, were popular, as was mainstreeting.

But it was to the media that the campaign directed most of its resources. The media used local candidates in Centre as sounding boards on a range of election issues. The Liberals tried hard to maximize Enemark's media coverage. They ran advertising in local community newspapers and on local radio, faxed daily press releases, and organized press conferences. This campaign strategy demanded professional and expensive expertise. Although the total spending of the three major campaigns was about the same, a massive 67 percent ($32,438) of Liberal spending was on advertising.[6] Ray Torresan, of Ray Torresan and Associates, provided advice on and produced the main campaign brochure. And professional public relations manager Jim Gilmour, who had done work for the British Columbia Medical Association, worked closely with Enemark to orchestrate the advertising campaign.

Unfortunately, Enemark's main opponents had much higher profiles and played much bigger roles in their parties' national campaigns in a province where the Tories and NDP were the major players. Moreover, Enemark was not sought out as a party spokesperson as were den Hertog and Campbell, as this role fell to party leader John Turner in Quadra. So although this strategic choice made sense in terms of the Liberal campaign itself, it meant taking on the NDP and Tories on their terms. Every interaction or comparison of local campaigns served to highlight the difficulties facing the Grit campaign. It is not surprising that as a member of a losing campaign that emphasized its candidate, Enemark finds problems with the media: "The lack of media attention to candidates reinforces their irrelevance to elections. The focus is on the national campaigns, even when there are no real issues being debated. This leads to stupid, often inconsequential, news stories." Enemark also bemoans voters' failure to give adequate weight to the candidate, but feels that candidates remained central to local campaign organization: "The candidate is becoming less and less important over time in terms of voting. Where they are most important is in raising money, attracting volunteers, and setting strategy." Gould's comments regarding the Liberals' failure endorse Enemark's perception of the organizational role of a candidate. They also point to the fact that Enemark's perceptions of the riding may not have been current. Gould comments that

> Tex was too connected to the old Liberal establishment, which meant his view of how a campaign was run – what to expect in terms of financial and volunteer help, what strategies to pursue – was not relevant to the nature of the contest in Vancouver Centre. He thought he could win just on his name and connections ... he put together an inappropriate campaign. For example, the classy brochure we did focusing on Tex may have worked in a traditional campaign but did not [in this election] in Vancouver Centre. We failed to address free trade and did not get the organizational support we needed from the party.

The candidate's organizational abilities help determine the quality of the campaign, and hence its capacity for identifying and implementing sound election strategies. Enemark may not have been well suited to this role.

Unlike the Liberals, the NDP and Tory campaigns designed campaign messages to appeal to the group-based politics they believed dominated this socially heterogeneous riding. They made explicit attempts to court gays, lesbians, environmentalists, pro-choice groups, and so on. Enemark considered this to be a false view and aimed his message at a stereotypically middle-class audience concerned with "bread and butter" issues rather than the politics of special interests: "The view of Vancouver as a microcosm of Canada is media-inspired. Vancouver Centre is very much like other middle-class ridings; it responds to the same issues and is impressed by candidates with relevant qualifications for being in government. It's about name recognition – it's like selling soap."

Enemark is correct in believing that Centre is not a microcosm of Canada in that it does not mirror the demographic profile of Canadian society. But it is heterogeneous, and as a result, local voters have diverse interests. As well, the media and local voters expect candidates in high-profile ridings like Centre to address a wide range of issues, some of which may seem peripheral to the local contest. And national campaigns regularly intrude into these contests to take advantage of the media coverage available in city ridings, complicating the local political agenda. In rejecting this view of the riding, Enemark missed the fact that the local agenda resonates to issues of interest to voters in many parts of the country, and the word "microcosm" captures this representative quality.

Enemark's difficulty with what he believed to be the increasingly group-based nature of politics in Canada – epitomized in Centre – was reflected in his consternation with questionnaires sent to him by various interest groups. He saw these groups as too powerful and inconsistent with democracy. He believed that answering the questionnaires was dangerous, as responding could be seen as endorsing this type of politics, and the answers could be used against him. Furthermore, they required too much volunteer time in an overstretched campaign, so he ignored them. Some Liberal volunteers suggested that his decade-long absence from active politics at a time when it and the demography of Vancouver were changing rapidly may have accounted for what they believed was a misguided view of Centre.

The inability of the Liberals to compete with the NDP and Tory campaigns was evident at public events, such as all-candidates debates. It was clear to the media and campaign workers from all parties that the Liberals failed to attract as many supporters as the other campaigns to these occasions. The image of a campaign that was out of its league was heightened when Enemark vacillated over his position on free trade. Unwilling to defend Turner's position and unable to make his own support for the agreement known, he could not engage with the other campaigns on this most crucial of issues. The parry and thrust of this debate gave a focus to the New Democrat and Tory campaigns but left Enemark floundering. The Liberal campaign was no match for its opponents who had access to hundreds if not thousands of secondary workers and sympathizers. It had no way of keeping up with the extensive foot and phone canvassing of the Conservatives and New Democrats. It could purchase street signs but had a limited number of people willing to erect them. Although it had access to professional help, this was not the sort of campaign-hardened assistance that is of the greatest use to a local organization.

The lack of workers did not just reflect a weak local association. The nearby Turner campaign in Vancouver Quadra attracted many Liberal volunteers who might otherwise have worked in Centre. A national leader has a strong pull on the party faithful, particularly in British Columbia, where the party expected to have little success, and its volunteer base was limited. Gould noted that except for the office manager, all Enemark's inner circle came from outside Vancouver Centre. With the public sensitized to the weakness of the Liberals in the West, this perception of the campaign was soon widespread. Most insidious of all, these failings were felt acutely by Liberal workers and damaged morale.

Despite Enemark's difficulties with the media, the close contest between at least two and perhaps three credible candidates attracted strong interest. Journalists in British Columbia agreed that it received at least as much coverage as any riding in the province. One of the few times Enemark's campaign was taken seriously was when the national affairs magazine

Maclean's and the *Toronto Star* ran articles about a possible Liberal cabinet that included him. This heightened profile encouraged the provincial media to pay him more attention. The *Vancouver Sun* and the *Province* interviewed him, as well as Vancouver television stations CBC, BCTV, and CKVU, and radio stations CKNW and CBC.

The impact of the federal election campaign on the local contest and the Enemark campaign was profound. The growing dominance of the issue of free trade as the campaign progressed encouraged the local Liberals in their desire to focus their strategies on Enemark, worsening an already dangerous situation. Media fixation with national poll results, which began to run against the Liberals, further damaged perceptions of Enemark's chances. As the party faded in the polls, particularly in the West, worker morale and numbers declined in what became a vicious circle. Fewer workers made it harder for the Liberal campaign to implement its strategies and appear competitive, and the lack of Liberal canvassers was reflected in voters' responses to polling questions. As the local campaign collapsed, it became increasingly a cipher for the national effort. The more it paralleled the federal campaign, the less relevant it became to the local contest. It was mainly the closeness of the race that ensured the Liberals were to some degree taken account of in the media and by their opponents, leaving them marginalized but not excluded from the local contest.

Conclusion

Local conditions and partisan organizational style both play a part in shaping a campaign's chances of success. Many uncompetitive, weak associations struggle to find adequate resources. First, they find it difficult to attract credible candidates – the lynchpin of a campaign and critical to its capacity to attract further resources and eventually votes. Some of these campaigns have money but few volunteers, whereas others have volunteers but little money. In most cases, however, it is a struggle to find enough of these two resources with which to mount an effective campaign.

The local political agenda, which reflects the underlying economic and sociodemographic character of the riding, may not fit well with the strategies of the wider party. The national party may refuse to help a local campaign that it believes has little chance of success. And the particular constellation of media resources that have some influence in a constituency may limit the strategies available to a second- or third-place campaign as it attempts to shape local opinion to its advantage.

Given all these difficulties, it may seem remarkable that four or more campaigns are mounted in many Canadian constituencies. Besides the desire of some people to be involved in the electoral process regardless of their candidate's chances of winning (something institutionalized in many NDP associations), a number of other factors underpin this pattern of involvement and point to the value of understanding the role of these campaigns in electoral outcomes. The volatility of the Canadian electorate, with relatively wide swings in support for different parties, holds out the possibility of success to challengers. So too does the relatively small margin by which many seats are held. Together, these factors ensure that few incumbents are safe from challenge. Narrow margins of victory suggest that, in most cases, not only do second-place parties have a chance of winning, but third- and even fourth-place parties can have a bearing on electoral outcomes by soaking up support for one or other of the leading parties.

In Fraser Valley West, the Christian Heritage Party had little chance of success. However, it knew that it could take votes away from Tory incumbent Bob Wenman. In so doing it hoped to both convince him of the need to move closer to its policy position and show the wider party the dangers of ignoring the moral issues it thought were most important. In Kootenay West-Revelstoke, where the NDP and PC candidates had each held the seat at different times with very small margins, the NDP candidate, Lyle Kristiansen, who was worried about the loss of votes to the Green Party, tried to convince its candidate not to run. A good Liberal Party performance in Vancouver Centre contributed to a close result between the Tories and the NDP and may have been instrumental in the New Democrats success in Surrey North. Relatively few campaigns are entirely excluded from the local contest. Second-place campaigns are usually critical to the outcome, and, in many cases, so too are the more marginalized third- and fourth-place campaigns.

The next chapter restates the main elements of the framework for analyzing local campaigns developed here, looks at some of the insights that result from this bottom-up approach to Canadian politics, and suggests directions for further study.

10
Parties, Candidates, and Constituency Campaigns in Canadian Elections

Local campaigns reflect the associations that spawn them, and the constituency elections in which they compete. The ways in which local conditions (riding style) and partisan organizational methods (party ethos) interact within an association are critical to our understanding of local campaigns. Associations are not ciphers for local political interests or the organizational norms of the wider party. Rather, each one combines the two idiosyncratically. Associations and campaigns in the same party vary across different ridings in response to local conditions, while in any one riding, local party organizations retain distinctive partisan styles. This explains how Canadian parties have retained distinctive organizational styles while at the same time allowing the "main variation in electioneering techniques in Canada to be ... less between the parties ... than among various constituencies" (Meisel 1962, 84).

Focusing on the role of local associations throws Canadian parties into sharp relief against those of other Westminster-style parliamentary systems. In particular, it helps explain why successful national parties in Canada have not developed mass-party forms of organization common in these other systems, yet retain elements of party discipline and organization not found in the more loosely organized parties of the United States.

Even in the most mass-like Canadian party, the NDP, central control has proved elusive. Robinson stands out as an important example of how the party, which is most inclined to reproduce its campaign in every riding in the country, cannot easily dictate strategy to a candidate who has a national profile and a strong local following. Given the volatility of the Canadian electorate, the party knows that it cannot take its support for granted, not even in a strongly NDP area such as Burnaby-Kingsway. It must make use of whatever electoral advantages it has at its disposal if it is to be successful. Moreover, local control of the nomination, the strength of the local association, and Robinson's local following make it unlikely that his renomination could be blocked. The party could invoke the leader's veto, but this is fraught with danger. Removing such candidates is much easier in parties where, as in most mass parties, central or regional committees control the nomination process. Similarly, trying to control Robinson's locally run and financed campaign would be very difficult, as there are few sanctions available to the central party. Nor could the party easily impose its will on campaign strategists drawn from the local association that strongly supports Robinson.

Central control of associations and campaigns makes even less sense in the Liberal and Conservative Parties. Electoral volatility means that there are always parts of the country where national parties struggle to win seats. Maintaining a constant presence or even attempting to ensure that whatever party activity there is, is centrally controlled is likely to be expensive and futile in these areas. It is arguably cheaper and easier for parties if their associations are all but moribund between elections. If enough people are interested (one assumes this is linked to the likelihood of success), local associations develop at election time, and being locally controlled, are best placed to make sense of local conditions in this diverse country.

The NDP has suffered from its attempts to maintain a centrally sponsored presence in parts of the country where it does not do well. The older, cadre-style parties have arguably benefited from avoiding this approach. So loose are their associations that half of the Grit and Tory candidates in this study joined the party for the first time to contest the nomination. That associations and members come and go so easily limits the capacity for and wisdom of central control. Liberal associations in Victoria and Vancouver Centre were small and of little interest to the central party, except to the degree the local media could be used to further the party's wider ambitions. Yet in 1993, the party won both ridings with strong local campaigns. Predicting this cycle in order to avoid wasting scarce resources would be difficult.

Of the newer parties, the Bloc Québécois has made little effort to sustain permanent local branches, but the Reform Party has. Nevertheless, recent evidence suggests Reform is finding it difficult to deal with the stresses of this arrangement (Flanagan 1995), and the party assembly in 1995 saw disagreements about the direction of the party and about the influence of Ottawa-based advisors in the party. Association presidents from several Alberta associations suggested that they would desert the party if it continued to employ strategists from central Canada with links to the Tories and other establishment parties. Moreover, they also suggested that the assembly brought into question the value of maintaining associations between elections and the policy development structures of the party. Some felt that the efforts of association members in developing policy to take to the assembly were overturned by key party figures bent on getting their way.

Western populism and central Canada establishment sit uncomfortably in any political organization. Gaining power in Ottawa may require Reform to dispense with some western shibboleths, which might threaten its core support in the West. The search for success seems to offer Reform three routes: direct confrontation between central and western visions of the country in the hope of gaining support in Ontario; sleight of hand to reduce apparent tensions; or disengagement by the party hierarchy from the rest of the party to allow it greater flexibility, a traditional Canadian response epitomized in the disaggregated structures of the Liberals and Tories.

This points to another great advantage of the loose cadre-style that, until recently in the case of the Tories, served the Liberals and Conservatives so well for so long. Just as cadre-style parties do not maintain permanent local organizations and links with their provincial counterparts, neither do they have permanent or powerful extraparliamentary policy making bodies. This is useful, as it allows the parliamentary wing of the party, and in particular the leader, to formulate policy. This allows leaders to respond to the diversity and volatility of Canadian politics. They are not tied to a particular policy, nor are they sensitive to national issues such as the Quebec question regularly debated by the party in open forums. Given the emotions attached to such issues, and their at least perceived intractability, avoiding such debates and the need to come to a policy position or "solution" allows greater flexibility and avoids potentially divisive debate. The NDP's attempts to promote continual policy debate have often been exhausting, and rarely fruitful in providing profound solutions to some of Canada's political problems.

The persistence of provincial political cultures and distinctive party systems complicates the task facing national parties. Variation in election dynamics from one province to another is endemic to Canadian elections and can be found in both riding and regional studies of the 1962 federal election (Meisel 1964).

Liberal campaigners in British Columbia constantly complained that the national campaign strategy was not appropriate given provincial conditions. In Vancouver Centre, Enemark's campaign felt obliged to distribute the Liberals' anti-free trade literature despite the candidate's support for the agreement and the campaign's belief that the NDP had captured the anti-free trade vote in British Columbia. National strategies and campaign literature offered BC Liberals neither alternative positions nor serious arguments for wresting the anti-free trade high ground from the NDP. Rather, it was directed at the PCs, who faced near annihilation in British Columbia, and hardly needed opposing.[1] Despite the Liberals' poor showing in most BC ridings, they were not irrelevant to electoral outcomes. They managed to improve on their performances in a number of ridings, and in so doing may have helped the NDP defeat the Tories. Michael O'Connor in

Victoria and Don Ross in Surrey North both increased the Liberal vote share by 50 percent, a much better outcome than for the average Liberal campaign in British Columbia. Although not good enough to win, in both cases this was less than the margin between the NDP and Tories.

The national NDP was caught in a three-way contest with the Tories and Liberals. It opposed free trade and wanted to convince voters that it, rather than the Liberal Party, was the real opponent of the agreement. It considered that in this sort of contest, an emphasis on Ed Broadbent's leadership and opposition to free trade was a sound strategy. New Democrats in British Columbia were involved in a two-way contest with the Tories, whose support had weakened in the West. Provincial New Democrats felt that a strong confrontational stand on free trade was the best strategy. Early on in the campaign, local strategists toed the national party line before switching to the issue of free trade.

Ron Stipp, den Hertog's campaign manager, felt particularly aggrieved that the national party had decided to focus on Broadbent. Because of den Hertog's close relationship to the national party, she tended to favour this approach. Unfortunately, while she was doing this, Kim Campbell was gaining credibility in Vancouver Centre by addressing the free trade issue. It was only late in the campaign that, with the help of the powerful provincial party, the Vancouver Centre NDP campaign came to focus its attention on free trade. This meant a quick change in the emphasis of campaign literature and canvassing. Given that den Hertog lost, it may have been too little, too late.

The variety of provincial political cultures and party systems with which national parties must cohabit adds to the advantages of maintaining organizationally loose parties. The Liberal and Conservative Parties each have few formal links between their national and provincial wings. Once again, the NDP is the exception, but some of this is pretence fighting hard against the realities of Canadian politics. As for the Reform Party, it has explicitly refused to allow the development of provincial wings. By avoiding the need to manage these relationships, both organizationally and in terms of trying to maintain a cohesive policy outlook, these parties are released from a heavy burden and able to be more flexible and responsive. What they forego is the capacity to internalize policy debate and generate strong party platforms.

The bifurcation of Canadian parties into a national wing and local wings underpins the power of local party organizations. Unlike in US parties, this power does not reside with local candidates or members of Parliament but with the associations that control the nomination and campaign process. Associations stand somewhat apart from candidates and the party. They are the local interpreters of party tradition, and the transmitters of riding conditions to the nation. They, not candidates or parties, control local politics. Even a powerful incumbent such as Robinson cannot do just as he pleases. He is bound by the principles of the mass-party New Democrats as understood by local members. Most NDP association members are as loyal to the party and its principles as to any candidate. Given this, Robinson cannot afford to stray from the party platform if he is to maintain support among local members who control his renomination chances, and who help run his campaign. The challenge to Tory incumbent Wenman was not orchestrated by the party, nor a party-wide faction, as might occur in other parties in Westminster-style systems. Rather, it came from within the association, including members of the local executive. In contrast to the United States, support for an incumbent is more than personal; it is embedded in associations.

Campbell's win in Vancouver Centre can be seen as a personal triumph, but she and her supporters moved into an existing local party structure. The campaign manager and other members of the inner circle were experienced local party members. Moreover, the association chose Campbell for the nomination as much as she chose it. It did so in part by arguing that ridings such as Centre favour high-profile candidates, are volatile, and can be won with a good campaign. That the association had remained coherent and self-directed following the retirement of Pat Carney is evidence that it had a life of its own, separate from the incumbent.

Candidates are subject to both the advantages and disadvantages of party membership in that policy platforms and campaign techniques sometimes are well suited to local conditions and sometimes complicate the task of local campaigners. Carrying the party banner can be a heavy burden. The effort of Brisco's campaign to distance him from the party's policy on free trade ran into two substantial barriers. As a loyal party member, Brisco was uncomfortable with denying a party policy, particularly one he felt to be correct. Second, free trade resonated too strongly with the local community to be ignored. Brisco's opponents worked to draw him into debating the issue at every chance, and he felt obliged to respond.

Katz and Mair (1994a) suggest that parties can best be understood by considering how they operate in three arenas: the constituency, the head office, and the legislature. At the constituency level, cadre-style Liberal and Conservative associations have a cyclical existence but are important and powerful as a result of their control over the nomination process. As such, they allow parties to remain responsive to changes in local political conditions over time. Even the NDP, which attempts to retain persistent party organizations between elections, struggles to do so. This gives Canadian parties a decidedly representative hue (Lawson 1988). At the national level, these parties have head offices and parliamentary organizations that persist between elections and that are designed to deal with the disciplining logic of the House of Commons. That is, they are designed not so much to be representative but to aggregate and integrate public opinion so that they may present a unified, coherent policy agenda in the Commons. This is more consistent with the dynamics of mass parties, or what Lawson calls participatory parties. This party structure has been described as "a short, truncated pyramid" (Kornberg et al. 1979).

While allowing for responsiveness at the margins and coherence at the centre, this structure leaves a vacuum at the intermediary level. That is, there are few permanent bodies that offer party members a role in policy development and that can limit or direct the policies adopted by the parliamentary wing. As well, there are few linkages between the national and provincial party of the same name. This vacuum may be essential if party elites are to integrate the diverse opinions and forces present at the margins, as it allows them to avoid direct confrontation between incompatible objectives and policies. It also allows the party to avoid public policy debate on the well-known but intractable problems of Canadian politics. That is, this hollow centre allows Canadian parties to negotiate the representativeness of local associations with the majoritarian cohesiveness of the party in the legislature, and even the head office. Given this, it is useful to add a fourth aspect of party structure to those suggested by Katz and Mair (1994b), namely, the nature of intermediary structures designed to develop policies and link various levels of a party in a federation. The strength of these structures in comparison with the party in the legislature and head office, and the party in the constituency, provides an indication of the locus of power and policy making within a party and their role in the political order.

The Nature of Canadian Politics
The style and content of local campaigns in Canada is intimately connected with the nature of the local associations that control the nomination of candidates for federal elections. They represent the peculiar interaction of a partisan ethic and a local riding style that records the efforts of Canadian political parties to operate within a polity that has a surfeit of geography and is marked by ethnolinguistic diversity. This is true also of local campaigns and constituency contests. Like associations, they reflect the interaction of the distinct local political communities defined by riding boundaries and the imperatives of partisan politics.

What does this imply for our understanding of Canadian politics? First, it suggests that it is impossible to fully comprehend the nature of Canadian parties from a national or even provincial level. Similarly, if local campaigns are shaped so strongly by local influences, our view of federal elections as primarily national events is misguided and our ability to understand them is seriously limited. As seminal components of the political system, a better understanding of associations and the local politics that shape them should also be able to tell us something about why parties, and Canadian politics more generally, are structured as they are.

The power to select candidates places constituency associations at the centre of political parties, and of the democratic process. Just because of this, the riding-based picture of politics presented here is more than a collection of interesting local stories; it provides a means of connecting the nature of the Canadian political system with the society that underlies it. The patterns that mark politics at this local level, and in particular the balance struck between partisan and riding forces within associations, suggest something about the nature of Canadian politics.

Sartori (1976, xi) notes that parties connect the rigid political institutions of the state and the wider, always mobile, society. Constituency associations constitute the very membrane that separates parties from the society. The permeability of this membrane and the way in which these local institutions construct politics are crucial for the role of parties as intermediaries between state and society. Moreover, the collapse of earlier modes of organization that relied on regional bosses, and the disengagement of provincial parties from their national counterparts (Carty 1988a), has meant that associations now play a critical role in a party's relationship with the wider society.

The integrative and representational role of local associations seems particularly crucial in Canada. This is a polity that has defied the unifying assumptions of most social science and shows no sign of becoming any more socially or politically integrated than it was in 1867. In fact, it may well be less so today. Yet neither has it been torn asunder by the often competing discourses and claims that constitute its diverse politics.

The local variability that underpins this diversity requires a political system that is responsive to local variation. With political parties, this implies association autonomy, in order that they are given maximum room to respond to local conditions. That is, the capacity of associations to play their representational and integrative roles depends very much on the balance between local and national concerns within a political party.

Two pressures that encourage centralization of power and control within parties are the drive to organizational coherence found in integrated mass parties, and the professionalization of the hierarchies of modern parties. This latter development can affect both mass- and cadre-style parties as they search for electoral success. This has been seen in the development of powerful central offices, which in Canada's leader-centred parties has meant strong leaders' offices.

It is notable that unlike in most other Westminster-style systems, Canada's most successful parties have retained a cadre style. It is possible that this reflects the fact that in maintaining the flexibility necessary to win Canadian elections, they have not been able to adopt a mass form.

Canadian national parties vary enormously in strength across Canada. They may hold nearly all the seats in one province, and nearly none in the next. This may also be true in the same province across time, from one election to the next. Dramatic changes in electoral performances favour the cyclical existence and loose organizational form of cadre-style parties that do not attempt to maintain elaborate local organizations between elections.

For example, there is little doubt that the spectacular growth of the previously only modestly competitive Liberal Party association in Eglinton (a Toronto riding) prior to the 1962 election (Smith 1964, 71-2), where some party activists admitted to having voted Conservative in 1958, would have been reproduced in Vancouver Centre in 1993. Such openness and organizational flexibility is uncommon in NDP associations. This reflects also the underlying volatility of Canadian ridings, which are more contested than either their British or American cousins (Heintzman 1991, 98). This electoral variability favours parties that can come and go over time.

This argument suggests that the electoral failure of the New Democratic Party in Canada reflects the essential tension between mass parties and local autonomy. The diversity of Canadian electorates is anathema to centralized organizational forms and the imposition of consistency across ridings. The party does not nurture the type of association that is capable of transmitting local impulses to its leadership. As such, the party is unable to respond adequately to the underlying variability of Canadian politics. Moreover, the party expends a good deal of effort in maintaining consistency across ridings and continuity between elections. Changes in the nature of Canadian society may take longer to flow through a more organizationally coherent and hence less permeable mass party such as the NDP than a more loosely organized cadre-style party.

Although the loose organizational style of Canadian cadre-style parties has been advantageous up to now, it brings its own difficulties. It has juxtaposed the personalized machine needed to build and sustain a coalition of support for the leader's policies with open, participatory, extraparliamentary organizational elements (Carty 1988a, 24). The importance of party leaders in these cadre-style parties, promoted by the centralization of the media and its growing focus on the leaders, has meant there is a small coterie of organizers in the leaders' offices who run these parties (Fletcher 1987, 363-7).

The relatively small coterie of party organizers in the leader's office, cut off from the grass roots of the party, has been susceptible to the trend towards professionalization of party elites found in many liberal democracies (Panebianco 1988). This process, most well developed in the Progressive Conservative Party prior to its defeat in 1993, has the capacity to alienate the centre from the grassroots of a party. Just as a mass party may prevent its associations from fulfilling integrative and representational roles, a professionalized party may be unaware of local impulses.

National dominance, or inattention to local concerns, diminishes the influence of local associations in the life of a party. In damaging a party's capacity to respond to local impulses, this reduces its ability to fulfil representational and integrative roles. In a country as geographically and socially diverse as Canada, this is dangerous for the party, and for politics more widely. It is even more so at a time when intervention by interest groups in association affairs is increasing and challenges the parties' dominance of electoral politics (Carty 1991a, 230).

When we speak of the health of Canadian parties, it is necessary to be clear what, in the Canadian context, qualifies as healthy. It seems that strong, centralized parties are likely to be ill suited to Canadian politics. Responsiveness is likely to be a more useful attribute. In this case, flexible, decentralized parties are likely to do well. This seems reasonable in a highly diverse polity. If responsiveness is the test of health, Canadian parties are a mixed bag: some parties are obviously healthy, and others less so, but not all are found wanting.

This suggests also that beyond the health of the political parties themselves, it is important to enquire more widely as to the state of Canadian democracy. If local association democracy, the involvement of various groups in politics via political parties, the responsiveness of the political system to local impulses through the party system and elections, variation in style and content of constituency campaigns by both party and region, and so on, are accepted as signs of well-being, then Canadian democracy is robust. That Canadian politics does not suit or cannot support some parties – or particular forms of parties – is beside the point. This being said, because Canadian political parties play such a central role in translating mass opinion into elite policy making, they define possibilities for and limitations of Canadian politics more than parties in polities where other institutions offer efficacious access to the state.

Canada in Comparative Perspective

The level of autonomy enjoyed by constituency associations in Canada is most probably unmatched in any other Westminster-style parliamentary system (see Butler and Kavanagh 1992, 211-46). The selection of candidates is a local process, as is much of the work of campaigning itself. In this way, the character of the local riding community works through associations to shape local campaigns. Local campaigns are not dominated by their national branches, and they exhibit a riding style. In many parties in other Westminster-style parliamentary systems, associations are mainly just organizational units of the party. Constituencies may be necessary to give order to elections, but they do not organize political life much beyond this. Constituency elections seem to mimic much more the wider contest between political parties.

Despite the lack of direct interference in local affairs by the party hierarchy, associations in Canada are deeply embedded in partisan structures and history. These shape the ways in which they go about the task of selecting candidates, building campaign teams, and prosecuting a local campaign. Unlike their counterparts in the United States, the personalized machines of candidates do not dominate local party organizations. Certainly the incumbent has not replaced the party as in the United States (Heintzman 1991, 119). Candidates are important, but party rules and norms, as well as local party stalwarts, have substantial influences over the conduct of nominations and campaigns. As such, local campaigns still embody a partisan ethos that reflects the character of the wider party.

The balance between riding and partisan forces with Canadian constituency associations, and local campaigns, points to their unique role in political life. Activists in the United States work for a particular candidate or member of Congress. Volunteers often identify with the candidate at a personal level or relate to his or her particular set of interests. In Britain or Australia, political activism is frequently focused above the level of the constituency, in the often permanent secretariats that parties use to discuss policy and make collective decisions.

In contrast to both these cases, candidates and incumbents in Canada come and go too readily to develop as the focus of political activism. On the other hand, there is relatively little in the way of permanent institutions at any level of most Canadian parties, membership of which activists can make their goal. Rather, associations, with their often cyclical existence, define the organizational life of parties and set the terms on which party activists gain access to parties and the political system more generally.

This balancing act is also evident within local campaigns. The personality of the candidate and his or her choice of issues do not habitually dominate local campaigns. Neither do the policies and platforms of the parties dominate them. Rather, local campaign organizations each have the opportunity to strike their own balance, within the constraints determined by the particular constituency election in which they are engaged. The balance of local as opposed to regional or national issues, the role of the candidate, and the place of national party platforms are all negotiable. Thus, Kim Campbell's win in Vancouver Centre was in part due to her personality and ability to gather around her professional help. Yet many of her workers were long-time party stalwarts and strategists who were there as much for the party as for Kim Campbell. Svend Robinson's electoral success is based in part on his personal appeal and his work in the local riding but also on the national issues and broad policy positions he and his party are associated with.

Local campaigns, and the local forces that shape them, may become even more important in the next few years. There appears to be an important trend in mass media towards audience fragmentation, and a growth in the number of local broadcasters, such as cable stations. If this tendency away from media concentration gains strength, it may reverse the process of political centralization that began with the advent of mass communication earlier this century (Spencer and Bolan 1991, 30-3). This could breathe new life into local politics, and our understanding of its role in the wider polity.

Local campaigns play a vital role in determining the final form of federal elections and politics in Canada. In his concluding remarks on the 1962 election, Alford links the fact that the bases of support for parties in Canada are localized with the fact that more than in any other country, Canadian parties are temporary associations brought together solely because of "the necessities of the strategy of power" (1964, 232). As well, he points to the possibility that region, religion, and the rural-urban divide hold out more hope of explaining voting behaviour in Canada (1964, 233) than more commonly adopted explanatory variables such as class. Such conclusions fit well with the thrust of this work, which suggests that Canadian elections and politics can be fully understood only through a matrix that takes account of local and regional phenomena often overlooked in favour of broader, national forces.

Notes

Chapter 1: Introduction

1 Local campaigns easily outspend the national campaigns of political parties. During the 1988 federal election, for example, the election expenses of all local campaigns totalled $31,341,494, while the head offices of the national parties spent a total of $22,425,849 on the election (Canada, Elections Canada 1988a).

2 For an example of the former, see Lee (1989), and of the latter, Johnston et al. (1992). A number of the studies produced for the Royal Commission on Electoral Reform and Party Financing (1991) have also been directed at filling this lacuna (Fletcher and Bell 1991; Carty 1991a, 1991b; Erickson 1991; Fletcher 1991a, 1991b).

3 The ridings that are the focus of this book are in British Columbia. In British Columbia in 1988, the Tories won twelve seats, the NDP nineteen, and the Liberals one. In 1993, the Tories won no seats, the NDP two, the Liberals six, and Reform twenty-four. In 1997, the Tories won no seats, the NDP three, the Liberals six, and Reform twenty-five.

4 Competitiveness refers to an association's chances of winning the next election. The assessment of competitiveness is based on historical electoral performance and a judgment about how changes in local circumstances and the general competitive relationship between the parties will influence the local election. It is not unusual for local party officials to make exaggerated claims about association competitiveness in order to attract candidates, sometimes citing "internal party polling" as the basis of their belief.

5 Perlin (1964) and Davis (1964) provide accounts of the impact of local issues and candidates on riding contests.

Chapter 2: Research Methodology and Choice of Ridings

1 Agnew attributes this to the developmental assumptions of much of liberal social science, and the absolutizing of commodification in Marxist political economy. These approaches tend to view social phenomena at a national level and are linked to a national integration thesis that is common in the social sciences, and that denies the explanatory power of local context (1987, 79, 141). This is a generalization to which there are many exceptions. For example, Siegfried (1913), Key (1949), Beck (1974), and Huckfeldt and Sprague (1992).

Chapter 3: Candidate Nomination

1 Only 35 percent of all nominations nationwide were contested in 1988. Of these, about 57 percent had only two candidates. The vast majority were won on the first ballot (Carty and Erickson 1991, 120).

2 The special attraction of urban ridings for high-profile candidates has long been noted (Smith 1964, 68; Land 1965, 2).

3 Although such challenges attract disproportionate media attention, they are rare (Carty and Erickson 1991, 134). In 1997, two Bloc Québécois, one Liberal, and one Reform Party

candidate were denied renomination by the constituency associations. In three of these cases, the replacement candidate was successful.

4 In regions where the party is weak, associations will have a more cyclical existence and will therefore make fewer long-term demands of members.

5 Insurgent candidates are defined as those who have had little or no previous contact with the party and/or local association, and who often have a narrow set of policy interests.

6 The lack of links between the NDP and ethnic groups has been noted by Schwartz (1964, 267-8).

7 Table 3.17 in Carty and Erickson (1991) does not include associations with incumbents. This deflates the proportion of competitive associations in the table that report having no candidate search. In addition, because these are figures for 1988, the number of Conservative incumbents in this category was very high, reflecting the party's 1984 performance. As the authors themselves note (109, 133), this confounds the effect of incumbency on candidate searches with that of Tory partisanship.

8 In 1988, Brian Mulroney went against the wishes of the local association (and apparently his own preference) in refusing to sign Sinclair Stevens's papers in order to appease Quebec MPs annoyed at losing some of their number in this manner. Liberal leader Jean Chrétien appointed a dozen candidates in 1993, and six in 1997, which in effect vetoed local association candidates.

Chapter 4: Nominations and Democracy

1 As a "flash party" (Converse and Depeux 1966; Carty 1991a, 30-9), Reform was more permeable than any of the three major parties.

2 For a seminal discussion of the relationship between ethnicity and politics in Canada, see Schwartz (1964).

3 He had some success at this. From a membership of 39 a year before the election, the association grew to over 350 by the time of the nomination and paid off a $4,000 debt from the 1984 election.

4 Such candidates are likely to have strong social contacts with influential members of the party. Scarrow labels such advantages "natural" selectors (1964, 53-4).

5 Ward makes this point about the 1962 NDP campaign in Vancouver Burrard (1964, 193-4).

Chapter 5: Campaign Teams

1 Data collected by Carty (1991a, 168) suggests that the average number of workers in campaign teams in 1988 was 94. However, this figure may underrepresent the number of sympathizers in campaign teams, as sympathizers are difficult to count given their sporadic involvement.

2 Tory Bob Wenman in Fraser Valley West had a straightforward view of the life cycle of a campaign volunteer. A volunteer in his or her first campaign is enthusiastic but inexperienced and thus not very effective. By the second campaign, the volunteer is experienced and hard working, the backbone of a campaign. By the third campaign, the volunteer is a little jaded but effective because of his or her experience. At this point, it is important that experienced workers pass on their knowledge to new campaigners, because they are unlikely to be back for a fourth campaign.

3 Occasionally, if the campaign manager cannot or will not meet all the demands of his or her position, the campaign chair will take over important management functions. But in most campaigns, the chair is a member of the advisory group shown in Figure 5.2.

4 In 1988, 66.7 percent of Liberal and 60.2 percent of Tory official agents were lawyers or accountants, while only 19.4 percent of NDP agents were from one of these professions (Carty 1991b, Table 3.1).

5 But note that paid campaign managers are much more common in British Columbia, where the party is strong, than elsewhere in the country (Carty 1991a, Figure 7.3).

6 The Liberals spent $32,438 on advertising, nearly twice as much as the NDP ($17,553) and one-third more than the Tories ($24,602), the two campaigns with a chance of winning the riding (Canada, Elections Canada 1988a).

7 A good example of this can be seen in Land's (1965) descriptions of the high-profile campaigns in Eglinton in the 1962 federal election.
8 This tendency is more evident in Liberal and Conservative campaigns, as New Democrats expect even high-profile candidates to adopt the team approach preferred by the party.

Chapter 6: Toeing the Party Line
1 This chapter distinguishes between local and nonlocal or national campaigns. The terms "national" and "nonlocal" are used interchangeably to describe a party's national campaign. The term nonlocal includes instances where the provincial wing of the party plays an important role in prosecuting the national campaign; such usage will be noted. The term "federal election campaign" describes the entire system of campaigns at all levels and by all parties, as well as media reporting on the election.
2 Of course, it is always possible for the national campaign to intervene directly in the local contest rather than via the local campaign. This extraparty intervention is discussed in the next chapter.
3 Campaigns such as those in Centre receive more media coverage than most. According to CBC news reporter Wayne Williams, the propinquity of Vancouver Centre to the headquarters of major Vancouver media outlets and the quality of the candidates in the riding encouraged journalists to ask them to commentate on election issues and events. Such news coverage provides parties with a conduit for their message and attracts party strategists. In addition, party offices, with their strategists and resources, are likely to be located near the major centres in which high-profile campaigns disproportionately occur, and are likely to have close links with the local campaigns, giving the latter access to the latest information from the party.

Chapter 7: The Constituency Contest
1 The significance of the urban-rural divide has been noted in a number of studies of local riding contests in Canada (Meisel 1964; Regenstreil 1964, 237).
2 In favouring transience over population growth and density as an explanatory factor, Kasarda and Janowitz are suggesting that "the systemic model of community organization based on length of residence is a more appropriate model than the linear development model (based on population size and density) for the study of community participation in mass society" (1974, 338).
3 In part, this wider socialization model is attractive because it avoids what Kasarda and Janowitz see as the tautological nature of linear population-based models (1974, 338-9). Blake (1978, n. 6) provides examples of studies that have explored systemic effects.
4 This is unusual. In city and suburban ridings, individual campaigns struggle to fund such advertising, except in small community newspapers.
5 The impact on riding politics of economic divisions between prosperous cities and declining country areas has long been noted in Canada (see, for example, Lemieux 1964, 50-1).
6 Political parties have tried to protect their right of access to these voters in Section 82.1 of the *Canada Elections Act,* which reads: "A candidate and the candidate's representative may enter any apartment building or other multiple residence during reasonable hours for the purpose of conducting the campaign" (Canada, *Canada Elections Act* 1993).
7 The exception to this may be a new party such as Reform, which burst onto the scene in such as way as to draw attention to itself.

Chapter 8: Winning Campaigns
1 The media that covered the contest in some detail were the local community newspapers, the *WestEnder* and the *Courier;* the main Vancouver television stations, including CBC, BCTV, and CKVU; several radio stations, including both French and English CBC as well as CKNW; and the daily Vancouver newspapers, the *Vancouver Sun* and the *Province.* The local Rogers Cable station hosted an all-candidates debate. Vancouver Centre also attracted attention from the *Globe and Mail,* the *Toronto Star,* national editions of several news programs, and Dutch, West German, British, and American television.

2 D. Keith Heintzman argues that the ability of incumbents to reach campaign expenditure limits helps them win. These limits also prevent other candidates from using extra campaign spending to overcome the advantage of incumbency (1991, 143-4).

3 In fact, dwellings in the riding are about evenly split between single-detached houses and all others, which is proportionally much greater than the provincial average. The riding also has a very high level of rented accommodation, at about 41 percent (Canada, Statistics Canada 1987, 135-6).

Chapter 9: Losing Campaigns

1 In addition to the amounts spent by the national parties, local spending on radio advertising accounted for 25 percent of the Tory advertising budget and 26 percent and 42 percent respectively in the NDP and Liberal campaigns.

2 This was in fact more than most BC Liberal associations provided their candidate.

3 This is much less true for the mass-style NDP, with its more collective mentality (Carty 1991a, 205-9 and Table 8.6; see also Padget 1991, 346-7, and Tables 8.17 and 8.18).

4 Elections Canada calculates nominal vote shares for new seats given the poll results from the previous election (Canada, Elections Canada 1988b).

5 The average donation to BC campaigns by the federal party was $4,436.

6 The comparable figures for the Conservatives and New Democrats were 54 percent (or $24,602) and 35 percent (or $17,553).

Chapter 10: Candidates, Parties, and Constituency Campaigns in Canadian Elections

1 Whereas the NDP and Tories appeal disproportionately to members of different social and economic groups, the Liberals attempt to appeal to voters across a wide range of class and social groupings (Alford 1964, 209). As such, they are uncomfortable with and ill suited to the polarized politics of British Columbia.

References

Agnew, John. 1987. *Place and Politics: The Geographical Mediation of State and Society.* Boston: Allen and Unwin

Alford, Robert L. 1964. The Social Bases of Political Cleavages in 1962. In *Papers on the 1962 Election,* ed. John Meisel. Toronto: University of Toronto Press

Ames, H.B. 1905. Electoral Management. *Canadian Magazine* 25

Axworthy, Thomas S. 1991. Capital-Intensive Politics: Money, Media and Mores in the United States and Canada. In *Issues in Party and Election Finance in Canada,* ed. F. Leslie Seidle. Vol. 5 of the research studies of the Royal Commission on Electoral Reform and Party Financing. Ottawa and Toronto: RCERPF/Dundurn

Barton, Allan H. 1968. Bringing Society Back In. *American Behavioral Scientist* 12: 1-9

Beck, Paul Allen. 1974. Environment and Party: The Impact of Political and Demographic County Characteristics on Party Behaviour. *American Political Science Review* 68, 3: 1229-44

Beer, Samuel H. 1974. *British Politics in the Collectivist Age.* New York: Alfred A. Knopf

Bell, David V.J., and Catherine M. Bolan. 1991. The Mass Media and Federal Election Campaigning at the Local Level: A Case Study of Two Ontario Constituencies. In *Reaching the Voter: Constituency Campaigning in Canada,* ed. David V.J. Bell and Frederick J. Fletcher. Vol. 20 of the research studies of the Royal Commission on Electoral Reform and Party Financing. Ottawa and Toronto: RCERPF/Dundurn

Bernier, Luc. 1991. Media Coverage of Local Campaigns: The 1988 Election in Outremont and Frontenac. In *Reaching the Voter: Constituency Campaigning in Canada,* ed. David V.J. Bell and Frederick J. Fletcher. Vol. 20 of the research studies of the Royal Commission on Electoral Reform and Party Financing. Ottawa and Toronto: RCERPF/Dundurn

Black, Edwin R. 1965. Federal Strains within a Canadian Party. *Dalhousie Review* 45, 3: 307-23

Blake, Donald E. 1976. LIP and Partisanship: An Analysis of the Local Initiatives Program. *Canadian Public Policy* 2: 17-32

–. 1978. Constituency Contexts and Canadian Elections: An Exploratory Study. *Canadian Journal of Political Science* 11: 279-305

–. 1985. *Two Political Worlds: Parties and Voting in British Columbia.* Vancouver: UBC Press

–. 1991. Party Competition and Electoral Volatility: Canada in Comparative Perspective. In *Representation, Integration and Political Parties in Canada,* ed. Herman Bakvis. Vol. 14 of the research studies of the Royal Commission on Electoral Reform and Party Financing. Ottawa and Toronto: RCERPF/Dundurn

Blake, Donald, R.K. Carty, and Lynda Erickson. 1991. *Grassroots Politicians: Party Activists in British Columbia.* Vancouver: UBC Press

Bowler, Shaun. 1990. Consistency and Inconsistency in Canadian Party Identification: Towards an Institutional Approach. *Electoral Studies* 9: 133-46

Brodie, J., and J. Jenson. 1988. *Crisis, Challenge and Change: Party and Class in Canada Revisited.* Ottawa: Carleton University Press

Brook, Tom. 1991. *Getting Elected in Canada: An Insider Demystifies the Canadian Election Process*. Stratford, ON: Mercury Press

Butler, D.E. 1951. *The British General Election of 1951*. London: Macmillan Press

–. 1955. *The British General Election of 1955*. London: Macmillan Press

–. 1967. *The British General Election of 1966*. London: Macmillan Press

Butler, D.E., and Dennis Kavanagh. 1974. *The British General Election of February 1974*. London: Macmillan Press

–. 1975. *The British General Election of October 1974*. London: Macmillan Press

–. 1980. *The British General Election of 1979*. London: Macmillan Press

–. 1984. *The British General Election of 1983*. London: Macmillan Press

–. 1988. *The British General Election of 1987*. London: Macmillan Press

–. 1992. *The British General Election of 1992*. London: Macmillan Press

Butler, D.E., and Anthony King. 1964. *The British General Election of 1964*. London: Macmillan Press

Butler, D.E., and Michael Pinto-Duschinsky. 1971. *The British General Election of 1970*. London: Macmillan Press

Butler, D.E., and Richard Rose. 1959. *The British General Election of 1959*. London: Macmillan Press

Canada. Canada Elections Act, R.S.C. 1985, c. E-2

–. Canada Elections Act, R.S.C. 1993, c. 19, s. 39

–. Election Expenses Act, S.C. 1973-74, c. 51

–. Elections Canada. 1988a. *Thirty-Fourth General Election: Report of the Chief Electoral Officer Respecting Election Expenses*. Ottawa: Minister of Supply and Services Canada

–. Elections Canada. 1988b. *Transposition of Votes: Representation Order 1987 Western Provinces and Territories*. Ottawa: Minister of Supply and Services Canada

–. Elections Canada. 1988c. *Guidelines and Procedures Respecting Election Expenses of Candidates*. Ottawa: Ministry of Supply and Services Canada

–. Elections Canada. 1989. *Report of the Chief Electoral Officer of Canada as per Subsection 195(1) of the Canada Elections Act*. Ottawa: Minister of Supply and Services Canada

–. Statistics Canada. 1987. *Federal Electoral Districts – 1987 Representation Order: Part 1 and 2*. Ottawa: Minister of Supply and Services Canada

Carty, R.K. 1988a. Three Canadian Party Systems: An Interpretation of the Development of National Politics. In *Party Democracy in Canada: The Politics of National Party Conventions*, ed. George Perlin. Scarborough: Prentice-Hall

–. 1988b. Campaigning in the Trenches: The Transformation of Constituency Politics. In *Party Democracy in Canada: The Politics of National Party Conventions*, ed. George Perlin. Scarborough: Prentice-Hall

–. 1991a. *Canadian Political Parties in the Constituencies*. Vol. 23 of the research studies of the Royal Commission on Electoral Reform and Party Financing. Ottawa and Toronto: RCERPF/Dundurn

–. 1991b. Official Agents in Canadian Elections: The Case of the 1988 General Election. In *Issues in Party and Election Finance in Canada*, ed. F. Leslie Seidle. Vol. 5 of the research studies of the Royal Commission on Electoral Reform and Party Financing. Ottawa and Toronto: RCERPF/Dundurn

–. 1992. *Canadian Political Party Systems: A Reader*. Peterborough: Broadview Press

Carty, R.K., and Lynda Erickson. 1991. Candidate Nomination in Canada's National Political Parties. In *Canadian Political Parties: Leaders, Candidates and Organization*, ed. Herman Bakvis. Vol. 13 of the research studies of the Royal Commission on Electoral Reform and Party Financing. Ottawa and Toronto: RCERPF/Dundurn

Carty, R.K., Lynda Erickson, and Donald Blake. 1992. *Leaders and Parties in Canadian Politics*. Toronto: Harcourt Brace Jovanovich Canada

Christian, William, and Colin Campbell. 1990. *Political Parties and Ideologies in Canada*, 3rd ed. Toronto: McGraw-Hill Ryerson

Converse, Philip E., and Georges Depeux. 1966. Politicization of the Electorate in France and the United States. In *Elections and the Political Order*, ed. A. Campbell, P. Converse, W. Miller, and D. Stokes. New York: Wiley

Courtney, John C. 1973. *The Selection of National Party Leaders in Canada*. Toronto: Macmillan

Cunningham, Robert. 1971. The Impact of the Local Candidate in Canadian Federal Elections. *Canadian Journal of Political Science* 4: 287-90

Davis, Morris. 1964. Did They Vote for Party or Candidate in Halifax? In *Papers on the 1962 Election*, ed. John Meisel. Toronto: University of Toronto Press

Denver, David, and Gordon Hands. 1997. *Modern Constituency Electioneering: Local Campaigning in the 1992 General Election*. London: Frank Cass

Dion, Léon. 1964. The Election in the Province of Quebec. In *Papers on the 1962 Election*, ed. John Meisel. Toronto: University of Toronto Press

Duverger, Maurice. 1954. *Political Parties: Their Organization and Activity in the Modern State*. London: Methuen

Dyck, Rand. 1989. Relations between Federal and Provincial Parties. In *Canadian Parties in Transition: Discourse, Organization, Representation*, ed. A.G. Gagnon and A.B. Tanguay. Toronto: Nelson Canada

–. 1991. Links between Federal and Provincial Parties and Party Systems. In *Representation, Integration and Political Parties in Canada*, ed. Herman Bakvis. Vol. 14 of the research studies of the Royal Commission on Electoral Reform and Party Financing. Ottawa and Toronto: RCERPF/Dundurn

Eagles, Munroe. 1990. Local Effects on the Political Behaviour of Canadians. In *Canadian Politics: An Introduction to the Discipline*, ed. Alain Gagnon and James P. Bickerton. Peterborough: Broadview Press

Eagles, M., J. Bickerton, A. Gagnon, and P. Smith. 1991. *The Almanac of Canadian Politics*. Peterborough: Broadview Press

Erickson, Lynda. 1991. Women and Candidacies for the House of Commons. In *Women in Canadian Politics: Towards Equity in Representation*, ed. Kathy Megyery. Vol. 6 of the research studies of the Royal Commission on Electoral Reform and Party Financing. Ottawa and Toronto: RCERPF/Dundurn

Fenno, Richard F. 1978. *Home Style: House Members in Their Districts*. Boston: Little Brown

–. 1990. *Watching Politicians: Essays on Participant Observation*. Berkeley, CA: IGS Press

–. 1996. *Senators on the Campaign Trail: The Politics of Representation*. Norman: University of Oklahoma Press

Ferejohn, John, and Brian Gaines. 1991. The Personal Vote in Canada. In *Representation, Integration and Political Parties in Canada*, ed. Herman Bakvis. Vol. 14 of the research studies of the Royal Commission on Electoral Reform and Party Financing. Ottawa and Toronto: RCERPF/Dundurn

Fischer, Claude S. 1982. *To Dwell among Friends*. Chicago: University of Chicago Press

Flanagan, Tom. 1995. *Waiting for the Wave: The Reform Party and Preston Manning*. Toronto: Stoddart Publishing Company

Fletcher, Frederick J. 1987. Mass Media and Parliamentary Elections in Canada. *Legislative Studies Quarterly* 12, 3: 341-72

–. 1991a. Mass Media and Elections in Canada. In *Media, Elections, and Democracy*, ed. Frederick J. Fletcher. Vol. 19 of the research studies of the Royal Commission on Electoral Reform and Party Financing. Ottawa and Toronto: RCERPF/Dundurn

–, ed. 1991b. *Reporting the Campaign: Election Coverage in Canada*. Vol. 22 of the research studies of the Royal Commission on Electoral Reform and Party Financing. Ottawa and Toronto: RCERPF/Dundurn

Fletcher, Frederick, and David V.J. Bell, eds. 1991. *Reaching the Voter: Constituency Campaigning in Canada*. Vol. 20 of the research studies of the Royal Commission on Electoral Reform and Party Financing. Ottawa and Toronto: RCERPF/Dundurn

Fraser, Graham. 1989. *Playing for Keeps: The Making of the Prime Minister, 1988*. Toronto: McClelland and Stewart

Frizzel, Alan, Jon H. Pammett, and Anthony Westell. 1989. *The Canadian General Election of 1988*. Ottawa: Carleton University Press

Graham, Ron. 1986. *One-Eyed Kings: Promise and Illusion in Canadian Politics*. Toronto: Collins

Heintzman, D. Keith. 1991. Electoral Competition, Campaign Expenditures and Incumbency Advantage. In *Issues in Party and Election Finance in Canada*, ed. F. Leslie Seidle. Vol. 5 of the research studies of the Royal Commission on Electoral Reform and Party Financing. Ottawa and Toronto: RCERPF/Dundurn

Hirschman, Albert. 1970. *Exit, Voice, and Loyalty: Responses to Decline in Firms, Organizations, and States*. Cambridge, MA: Harvard University Press

Huckfeldt, Robert, and John Sprague. 1992. Political Parties and Electoral Mobilization. *American Political Science Review* 86, 1: 70-86

Irvine, William P. 1982. Does the Candidate Make a Difference? The Macro-Politics and Micro-Politics of Getting Elected. *Canadian Journal of Political Science* 15: 755-82

Jacobs, Francis. 1989. *Western European Political Parties: A Comprehensive Guide*. Harlow, UK: Longman

Johnston, Richard. 1980. Federal and Provincial Voting: Contemporary Patterns and Historical Evolution. In *Small Worlds: Provinces and Parties in Canadian Political Life*, ed. David J. Elkins and Richard Simeon. Toronto: Methuen

–. 1996. The 1993 Canadian General Election: Realignment, Dealignment or Something Else. Paper presented at 1996 annual meeting of the Canadian Political Science Association

Johnston, Richard, André Blais, Henry Brady, and Jean Crete. 1992. *Letting the People Decide: History, Contingency and the Dynamics of Canadian Elections*. Montreal: McGill-Queen's University Press

Kasarda, John D., and Morris Janowitz. 1974. Community Attachment in Mass Society. *American Sociological Review* 39: 328-39

Katz, Richard S., and Peter Mair. 1994a. The Evolution of Party Organizations in Europe: Three Faces of Party Organization. In *Political Parties in a Changing Age*, ed. William Crotty, special issue of *American Review of Politics* 14: 593-617

–, eds. 1994b. *How Parties Organize: Change and Adaptation in Party Organizations in Western Democracies*. London: Sage Publications

Key, V.O. 1949. *Southern Politics in State and Nation*. New York: A.A. Knopf

Kirchheimer, Otto. 1966. The Transformation of Western European Party Systems. In *Political Parties and Political Development*, ed. Joseph LaPalombara and Myron Weiner. Princeton: Princeton University Press

Kornberg, Allan, Joel Smith, and Harold D. Clarke. 1979. *Citizen Politicians: Canada*. Durham, NC: Carolina Academic Press

Krashinsky, Michael, and William J. Milne. 1991. Some Evidence on the Effects of Incumbency in the 1988 Canadian Federal Election. In *Issues in Party and Election Finance in Canada*, ed. F. Leslie Seidle. Vol. 5 of the research studies of the Royal Commission on Electoral Reform and Party Financing. Ottawa and Toronto: RCERPF/Dundurn

Land, Brian. 1965. *Eglinton: The Election Study of a Federal Constituency*. Toronto: Peter Martin Associates

Laschinger, John, and Geoffrey Stevens. 1992. *Leaders and Lesser Mortals: Backroom Politics in Canada*. Toronto: Key Porter

Lawson, K. 1988. When Linkages Fail. In *When Parties Fail: Emerging Alternative Organizations*, ed. Kay Lawson and Peter Merkl. Princeton: Princeton University Press

Lawson, Kay, and Merkl, Peter, eds. 1988. *When Parties Fail: Emerging Alternative Organizations*. Princeton: Princeton University Press

Lee, Robert Mason. 1989. *One Hundred Monkeys: The Triumph of Popular Wisdom in Canadian Politics*. Toronto: MacFarlane Walter and Ross

Leithner, Christian. 1997. Electoral Nationalisation, the Focus of Representation and Party Cohesion: A Five-Nation Anglo-American Analysis. In *Australian Political Studies* 2: 509-37

Lemieux, Vincent. 1964. The Election in the Constituency of Lévis. In *Papers on the 1962 Election*, ed. John Meisel. Toronto: University of Toronto Press

Maclean Hunter. 1988. *Canadian Advertising Rates and Data* 61, 11. Toronto: Maclean Hunter

MacDermid, Robert. 1991. Media Usage and Political Behaviour. In *Media and Voters in Canadian Election Campaigns*, ed. Frederick J. Fletcher. Vol. 18 of the research studies of the Royal Commission on Electoral Reform and Party Financing. Ottawa and Toronto: RCERPF/Dundurn

Meisel, John. 1962. *The Canadian General Election of 1957*. Toronto: University of Toronto Press

–. 1963. The Stalled Omnibus: Canadian Parties in the 1960's. *Social Research* 30, 3

–. 1975. Howe, Hubris and '72: An Essay on Political Elitism. In *Working Papers on Canadian Politics*. 2nd enl. ed. Montreal and Kingston: McGill-Queen's University Press

–. 1979. The Decline of Party in Canada. In *Party Politics in Canada*, 4th ed., ed. Hugh G. Thorburn. Scarborough: Prentice-Hall

–. 1991. Dysfunctions of Canadian Parties: An Exploratory Mapping. In *Party Politics in Canada*, 6th ed., ed. Hugh G. Thorburn. Scarborough: Prentice-Hall

–, ed. 1964. *Papers on the 1962 Election*. Toronto: University of Toronto Press

Morley, J.T. 1984. *Secular Socialists: The CCF/NDP in Ontario: A Biography*. Montreal: McGill-Queen's University Press

Morley, J. Terence. 1988. Annihilation Avoided: The New Democratic Party in the 1984 Federal General Election. In *Canada at the Polls, 1984*, ed. Howard Penniman. Durham, NC: Duke University Press

Morley, Terry. 1991. Paying for the Politics of British Columbia. In *Provincial Party and Election Finance in Canada*, ed. F. Leslie Seidle. Vol. 3 of the research studies of the Royal Commission on Electoral Reform and Party Financing. Ottawa and Toronto: RCERPF/Dundurn

–. 1994. Federalism and the New Democratic Party. In *Parties and Federalism in Australia and Canada*, ed. Campbell Sharman. Canberra: Federalism Research Centre, Australian National University

Munro, John M. 1975. Highways in British Columbia: Economics and Politics. *Canadian Journal of Economics* 8: 192-204

Noel, S.J.R. 1987. Dividing the Spoils: The Old and New Rules of Patronage in Canadian Politics. *Journal of Canadian Studies* 22, 2: 72-95

Padget, Donald. 1991. Large Contributions to Candidates in the 1988 Federal Election and the Issue of Undue Influence. In *Issues in Party and Election Finance in Canada*, ed. F. Leslie Seidle. Vol. 5 of the research studies of the Royal Commission on Electoral Reform and Party Financing. Ottawa and Toronto: RCERPF/Dundurn

Panebianco, Angelo. 1988. *Political Parties: Organization and Power*. Cambridge: Cambridge University Press

Pelletier, Rejean. 1991. The Structures of Canadian Political Parties. In *Canadian Political Parties: Leaders, Candidates and Organization*, ed. Herman Bakvis. Vol. 13 of the research studies of the Royal Commission on Electoral Reform and Party Financing. Ottawa and Toronto: RCERPF/Dundurn

Perlin, George. 1964. St. John's West. In *Papers on the 1962 Election*, ed. John Meisel. Toronto: University of Toronto Press

–, ed. 1988. *Party Democracy in Canada: The Politics of National Conventions*. Scarborough: Prentice-Hall Canada

Peterson, T., and I. Avakumovic. 1964. A Return to the Status Quo: The Election in Winnipeg North Centre. In *Papers on the 1962 Election*, ed. John Meisel. Toronto: University of Toronto Press

Preyra, Leonard. 1991. Riding the Waves: Parties, the Media and the 1988 Federal Election in Nova Scotia. In *Reaching the Voter: Constituency Campaigning in Canada*, ed. Frederick J. Fletcher and David V.J. Bell. Vol. 20 of the research studies of the Royal Commission on Electoral Reform and Party Financing. Ottawa and Toronto: RCERPF/Dundurn

Regenstreil, Peter S. 1964. Group Perceptions and the Vote: Some Avenues of Opinion Formation in the 1962 Campaign. In *Papers on the 1962 Election*, ed. John Meisel. Toronto: University of Toronto Press

Sabato, Larry J. 1981. *The Rise of Political Consultants: New Ways of Winning Elections*. New York: Basic Books

Sartori, Giovanni. 1976. *Parties and Party Systems: A Framework for Analysis.* Cambridge: Cambridge University Press

Sayers, Anthony M. 1991. Local Issues Space in National Elections: Kootenay West-Revelstoke and Vancouver Centre. In *Reaching the Voter: Constituency Campaigning in Canada,* ed. Frederick J. Fletcher and David V.J. Bell. Vol. 20 of the research studies of the Royal Commission on Electoral Reform and Party Financing. Ottawa and Toronto: RCERPF/Dundurn

Scarrow, Howard A. 1964. Three Dimensions of a Local Political Party. In *Papers on the 1962 Election,* ed. John Meisel. Toronto: University of Toronto Press

Schwartz, Mildred A. 1964. Political Behaviour and Ethnic Origin. In *Papers on the 1962 Election,* ed. John Meisel. Toronto: University of Toronto Press

Selle, Per, and Lars Svasand. 1991. Membership in Party Organizations and the Problem of Decline of Parties. *Comparative Political Studies* 23: 459-77

Siegfried, André. [1906] 1966. *The Race Question in Canada.* Carleton Library Series, no. 29. Toronto: McClelland and Stewart

Siegfried, André. [1913] 1964. *Tableau Politique de la France de l'Oest sous la Troisième République.* Paris: Armand Colin

Simpson, Jeffrey. 1988. *Spoils of Power: The Politics of Patronage 1988.* Toronto: Collins

Smiley, D.V. 1987. *The Federal Condition in Canada.* Toronto: McGraw-Hill Ryerson

Smith, Anthony. 1981. Mass Communication. In *Democracy at the Polls: A Comparative Study of Competitive National Elections,* ed. David Butler, Howard R. Penniman, and Austin Ranney. Washington, DC: American Enterprise Institute for Public Policy Research

Smith, David. 1985. Party Government, Representation and National Integration in Canada. In *Party Government and Regional Representation in Canada,* ed. Peter Aucoin. Vol. 36 of the research studies of the Royal Commission on the Economic Union and Development Prospects for Canada. Toronto: University of Toronto Press

Smith, Denis. 1964. The Campaign in Eglinton. In *Papers on the 1962 Election,* ed. John Meisel. Toronto: University of Toronto Press

Spencer, David R., and Catherine M. Bolan. 1991. Election Broadcasting in Canada: A Brief History. In *Election Broadcasting in Canada,* ed. Frederick J. Fletcher. Vol. 21 of the research studies of the Royal Commission on Electoral Reform and Party Financing. Ottawa and Toronto: RCERPF/Dundurn

Stanbury, W.T. 1991. *Money in Politics: Financing Federal Parties and Candidates in Canada.* Vol. 1 of the research studies of the Royal Commission on Electoral Reform and Party Financing. Ottawa and Toronto: RCERPF/Dundurn

Stewart, Gordon. 1986. *The Origins of Canadian Politics: A Comparative Approach.* Vancouver: UBC Press

Stewart, Marianne C., and Harold D. Clarke. 1998. The Dynamics of Party Identification in Federal Systems: The Canadian Case. *American Journal of Political Science* 42, 1: 97-116

Tanguay, A. Brian, and Barry J. Kay. 1991. Political Activity of Local Interest Groups. In *Interest Groups and Elections in Canada,* ed. F. Leslie Seidle. Vol. 2 of the research studies of the Royal Commission on Electoral Reform and Party Financing. Ottawa and Toronto: RCERPF/Dundurn

Ward, Ian. 1991. The Changing Organizational Nature of Australia's Political Parties. *Journal of Commonwealth and Comparative Politics* 29, 2: 153-74

Ward, Norman. 1964. The Counter-Revolution in Saskatchewan. In *Papers on the 1962 Election,* ed. John Meisel. Toronto: University of Toronto Press

Wearing, Joseph. 1988. *Strained Relations: Canadian Parties and Voters.* Toronto: McClelland and Stewart

Whitaker, Reginald. 1977. *The Government Party: Organizing and Financing the Liberal Party of Canada 1930-58.* Toronto: University of Toronto Press

Wood, David M., and Philip Norton. 1992. Do Candidates Matter? Constituency Specific Vote Changes for Incumbent MP's 1983-1987. *Political Studies* 40, 2: 227-38

Woolstencroft, Peter. 1992. "Tories Kick Machine to Bits": Leadership Selection and the

Ontario Progressive Conservative Party. In *Leaders and Parties in Canadian Politics,* ed. R.K. Carty, Lynda Erickson, and Donald Blake. Toronto: Harcourt Brace Jovanovich Canada

Young, Walter D. 1964. The NDP: British Columbia's Labour Party. In *Papers on the 1962 Election,* ed. John Meisel. Toronto: University of Toronto Press

–. 1969. *Anatomy of a Party: The CCF 1932–1961,* Toronto: University of Toronto Press

–. 1983. Political Parties. In *The Reins of Power: Governing British Columbia,* ed. J. Terence Morley, Norman J. Ruff, Neil A. Swainson, R. Jeremy Wilson, and Walter D. Young. Vancouver: Douglas and McIntyre

Index

British Columbia Medical Association, 209

British Columbia Power Commission, 181

Broadbent, Ed: and debates, 129; and den Hertog, 45; and Free Trade Agreement, 164-5, 195, 217; as party leader, 61, 104, 114, 149, 200, 202; and Svend Robinson, 145-6; and tax issues, 97

Brown, Michael, 21

Bucholtz, Frank, 193

Burnaby-Kingsway riding: campaign teams in, 74, 80, 92, 99-100, 102, 136; description of, 15-9, 123-4, 214; nominations in, 33-4, 41, 44, 55, 60, 62, 64; winning campaign in, 142-51, 158, 171

Burnaby North High School, 143

Burnaby *NOW,* 150

Campaign: in Burnaby-Kingsway riding, 16, 55, 142-51, 170-1; and candidate, 39, 41; in Fraser Valley West riding, 16, 20, 195-204, 213; of incumbent, in symbiotic relationship, 178; in Kootenay West-Revelstoke riding, 14, 21-2, 174-85, 213; local-national relations, 90-1, 106-8; and nomination, 30, 33, 51-2; in Surrey North riding, 16, 58, 185-95, 213; in Vancouver Centre riding, 14, 24, 135-42, 169-71, 205-13; in Victoria riding, 16, 36-7, 161-70, 172

Campaign, local: bifurcation of parties in, 217; of high-profile candidates, 133-5, 139-42, 147-51, 170-1, 180-5, 188, 195, 201, 218; and national campaign, 66, 82-3, 85-6, 173; and intraparty relations, 156-7, 164-5, 178-80, 189-91, 199-200, 207-8; of party insiders, 133-4, 166-70, 200-4; of stopgap candidates, 133-4, 136, 162, 174, 185, 191-5, 196, 205, 208-12; in symbiotic relationship with national campaign, 89-108, 139, 145-6

Campaign activities, 67, 81

Campaign teams: characteristics of, 87-8; of high-profile candidates, 83-87; of local notables, 71-5, 162; of party insiders, 76-9; and resources, 71-2, 82, 93, 95-6, 100-2, 106-7; of stopgap candidates, 79-83, 143, 162; structure of, 66-71

Campaign workers: inner circle, 67, 69, 71, 81, 84, 87-8; secondary workers, 67-9; sympathizers, 67-8

Campaigns: and all-candidates' debates, 127-8; in city ridings, 115-7; in country ridings, 111-3; insurgent, 14, 34; and

media, 118-25; parallel, 83, 99-101, 134; parochial, 91-9, 134; subsidiary, 95-9, 134; in suburban ridings, 113-5; uncompetitive, 173-4, 212-3

Campbell, Kim: campaign finances of, 137-8; campaign strategies of, 140; campaign team of, 84-6, 116, 137-8; in candidates' debates, 103, 127, 140-1, 171; and feminism, 139; and Free Trade Agreement, 139-40, 217; as high-profile candidate, 24, 34, 135-6, 170, 209; intraparty relations of, 45, 138-9; local contest of, 139-43, 171, 205, 223; and media, 141-2, 171; nomination of, 33, 61

Canada Darpan Weekly, 193

Canada Elections Act, 69

Canada-US Free Trade Agreement. *See* Free Trade Agreement, Canada-US

Canadian electorates, 221

Canadian parties, 6-7, 11-2, 214, 219-24

Canadian politics, 3, 5, 12, 213, 216, 219-20, 222, 224

Canadian Press, 182

Candidate recruitment, in cadre-style associations, 74

Candidate school at University of British Columbia, 90, 92, 95, 146, 199

Candidate searches: contested, 28; in cadre-style associations, 41-3, 47, 53, 55-6; in competitive associations, 40, 43, 48; contested, 28; and electability, 39-46, 49-50; in impermeable associations, 59; in permeable associations, 40, 47-8, 53, 56; uncontested, 28

Candidates: archetypes of, 63; and association appeal, 29-34; and association permeability, 34-9; in Burnaby-Kingsway riding, 19, 142-51, 214; and campaign teams, 63-5, 66-88, 136-8, 143-5, 154-6, 163-4, 173, 175-8, 187-9, 197-9, 205-6, 223; and charisma, 80; in city ridings, 115-7, 123-5; in component campaigns, 101-5, 107; in constituency contest, 109-32; in country ridings, 111-3, 125; and election contest, 9, 17, 212-3; in Fraser Valley West riding, 19-20, 195-204; high-profile, 11, 41, 44-5, 48; insurgent, 36, 39, 43, 55, 142; in Kootenay West-Revelstoke riding, 20-2, 174-85; in latent democracy, 59-60; in limited democracy, 60-63; in local democracy, 52-6; local notable, 11; and media, 10-1, 118-25, 128-30, 140-1, 149-51, 159-60, 168-9, 182-3, 203, 211-2; and nominations, 4-9, 12, 17, 27-8,

46-9, 51, 63, 215; in Okanagan Centre
riding, 22-3, 151-61, 171-2; in parallel
campaigns, 99-101, 107; in parochial
campaigns, 91-5, 106-7; in party democ-
racy, 56-9; party insider, 11; stopgap, 11;
in subsidiary campaigns, 95-9, 107; in
suburban ridings, 113-5, 121-3, 125; in
Surrey North riding, 23, 185-95; in
Vancouver Centre riding, 24-5, 135-42,
171-2, 205-12; in Victoria riding, 25-6,
161-70, 172
Capital News, 159
Carney, Pat, 24, 60-1, 136, 138-40, 218
Castlegar, BC, 21, 177, 182
Castlegar News, 182
CBC, 123, 150, 159, 168, 179, 212
Central Business District (Vancouver), 24
Centre for Arms Control, 167
CFER 850, 204
CHEK-TV, 168-9
Chilliwack, BC, 203
Chinatown, 124
Chernoff, Jack, 176-77, 179
Chretien, Jean, 33, 45
Christ Church Cathedral, 140
Christian Heritage Party, 20, 23, 127, 195-
6, 195, 198, 202, 213
CILK, 159
CISL, 193
CKIQ, 159
CKNW, 150, 194, 204, 212
CKOV, 159
CKVU, 212
Clark, Joe, 156
Clearbrook, BC, 19-20, 196, 198
Columbia River Treaty, 180
Cominco smelter, 21, 58, 112, 176, 181,
184
Competitive associations, and resources,
6, 9, 28, 37, 40
Constituency. *See* Burnaby-Kingsway rid-
ing; Fraser Valley West riding; Kootenay
West-Revelstoke riding; Okanagan
Centre riding; Surrey North riding;
Vancouver Centre riding; Victoria riding
Constituency contest: by archetype, 12;
and changed riding boundaries, 152,
156; and contestedness, 125-7; and
interviews, 26; and local campaign, 109-
11, 125-7, 130-2, 222; and media, 126-7,
158, 190-10, 118-25; and resource flows,
134; by riding type, 11; and social networks, 111-3
Constituency elections, 3, 13-4, 212, 220-
1, 223-4
Cook, Chuck, 105

Coquitlam, BC, 188
CTV, 123, 150

Daily Courier, 159
Delta, BC, 23
Delta riding, 193
Democracy, 52; Anglo-American, 4;
Canadian, 222; liberal, 221; popular, 55;
Western, 12
Democracy, forms of: latent, 50-1, 59-60,
64-5, 79, 133, 187; limited, 50-1, 60-5,
83, 133, 136, 144, 176; local, 41, 50, 52-
3, 56, 63-4, 71-2, 133; party, 40, 50-1,
56, 63-4, 76, 133
Democratic politics, 63
Democratic process, 220
den Hertog, Johanna: campaign team of,
69, 86, 116, 144, 201, 217; as candidate,
24, 34, 135-6, 209; in candidates'
debates, 127; intraparty relations of, 45,
103; local contest of, 205; and media,
104, 125, 141; nomination of, 33, 61;
subsidiary campaign of, 98
Duncan, Glenn, 154-5, 15

EastEnder, 150
Economic development, as issue, 34, 112,
130
Election contest: national party intervention in, 9; role of media in, 10-11
Elections Canada, 14, 69, 194
Enemark, Tex: campaign finances of, 205-
7; campaign strategies of, 208-10, 216;
campaign team of, 81, 116, 205-6; in
candidates' debates, 127, 211; city riding of, 210-1; intraparty relations of, 37,
82; and media, 128-9; 209, 211-2; parallel campaign of, 99-100, 136, 205, 212;
as stopgap candidate, 24, 61, 136, 205
Environment, as issue, 20, 34, 57-8, 105,
117, 124, 144-5, 158, 167, 195, 202, 210
Esquimalt Naval Base, 26
Esquimalt-Saanich, 18

*Fairall, Lynn: campaign finances of, 197-
8; campaign strategies of, 200-1;
campaign team of, 77, 197-8; as candidate, 20; in candidates' debates, 204;
country riding of, 196; intraparty relations of, 78; and media, 203-4;
nomination of, 58, 195, 197; subsidiary
campaign of, 95, 97-8, 195, 198-200,
204
Federal campaign: and local campaigns,
3, 5, 11; and media reporting, 128-30
Feminism, as issue, 34, 57-8, 139

Set in Stone by Aitken+Blakeley

Printed and bound in Canada by Friesens

Copy editor: Judy Phillips

Proofreader: Randy Schmidt

Indexer: Patricia Furdek

Visit the UBC Press Web site at

www.ubcpress.ubc.ca

**for information and detailed descriptions
of other UBC Press books**

If you liked this book, look for these related titles:

Politics, Policy, and Government in British Columbia
Edited by Ken Carty

❧

Mr Smith Goes to Ottawa: Life in the House of Commons
David C. Docherty

❧

Manipulation and Consent: How Voters and Leaders Manage Complexity
David J. Elkins

Ask for UBC Press books in your bookstore or contact us at
Toll-free fax: 1-800-668-0821
Toll-free number: 1-UPRESS-WEST
E-mail: orders@ubcpress.ubc.ca